CIVIL PROCEDURE

IN A NUTSHELL®

TENTH EDITION

ARTHUR R. MILLER
University Professor and Chief Justice
Warren E. Burger Professor of
Constitutional Law and the Courts
New York University

ADAM N. STEINMAN
Professor of Law
Texas A&M University

WEST
ACADEMIC

860 Blue Gentian Road, Suite 350
Eagan, MN 55121
1-877-888-1330

Published in the United States of America

ISBN: 979-8-31770-201-4

PREFACE

This edition follows the same format and approach of those that preceded it. The primary revisions have been to update the work in light of important procedural developments that have occurred since the Ninth Edition was published in 2022.

As has been the case for nearly ninety years, many of the most significant procedural changes arise first, and sometimes exclusively, in the federal court system. With respect to the Federal Rules of Civil Procedure, this edition addresses the 2025 adoption of Rule 16.1, which governs practice under the multidistrict litigation statute. This edition also includes important recent Supreme Court decisions on civil procedure—including two significant ones on personal jurisdiction, *Mallory v. Norfolk Southern Railway Co.*, 600 U.S. 122 (2023), and *Fuld v. Palestine Liberation Organization*, 606 U.S. 1 (2025)—as well as decisions on topics including standing, jury trials, arbitration, and Rule 60(b) motions for relief from judgment.

The overall objective of this Nutshell remains an important, but limited, one—to present a view of the forest instead of the trees in the procedure landscape. There is no way in the confines of these few pages for more in depth coverage. Readers who find a need for more can consult our Hornbook on this same topic, J. Friedenthal, M. Kane, A. Miller & A. Steinman, *Civil Procedure* (6th ed.2021).

We remain deeply grateful to the late Mary Kay Kane, our friend, co-author, and professional colleague, who authored earlier editions of this Nutshell. She was a true giant in the field of civil procedure and in the legal academy. We are honored to carry on her work in this new edition.

ARTHUR R. MILLER
ADAM N. STEINMAN

October 2025

OUTLINE

TABLE OF CASES

References are to Pages

TABLE OF STATUTES

References are to Pages

TABLE OF RULES

References are to Pages

CIVIL PROCEDURE
IN A NUTSHELL®

TENTH EDITION

CHAPTER 1
INTRODUCTION

§ 1.1. General Background

The basic law school civil procedure course is designed to teach how lawyers choose a proper court and how they frame and present their cases throughout the proceedings until a judgment has been reached and all available appeals have been pursued. The effect of judgments on future litigation also may be explored. Thus, the primary focus in this book is on the methods and tools available to lawyers as litigators. This study requires an inquiry into judicially developed doctrines, as well as an examination of various rules and statutes governing the operation and process of the civil courts. At times it will raise questions that are theoretical or constitutional; at other times issues of careful or strict rule interpretation will be paramount.

Throughout, it is important to keep in mind the purpose underlying the development of civil procedure rules and doctrine—to provide a just, efficient, and economical means by which parties can resolve their disputes. This purpose may not always be met. Indeed, some of the existing procedures have been used by attorneys to thwart this goal. Nonetheless, the desire to achieve justice, efficiency, and economy in our civil dispute resolution process underlies the way courts apply and interpret the governing rules.

In studying the procedures by which legal rights are vindicated, it also is important to note that the Anglo-American judicial system is based on the adversary model. By and large, the judge sits solely to rule on disputed questions, as presented by the parties, and to apply sanctions when they are properly requested by a party. The lawyers shape the contours of the action. Issues not raised, objections not made, or points not challenged are, with very few exceptions, waived. The case moves forward only in response to the demands of the parties. Although judges in recent times have tended to take a somewhat more active role in guiding and managing the litigation before them, it still remains true that the ultimate responsibility for each case rests with the litigants and their attorneys.

Finally, it should be noted that there is a very important aspect to framing litigation that typically is not taught in the basic civil procedure course and will not be discussed in this book: how to select a particular remedy as the one most likely to succeed or best suited to the needs of the client. That inquiry concerns matters such as whether injunctive relief or damages may be sought or whether some form of restitutionary relief might be most appropriate. Historically, the question of what type of relief was involved also dictated the court in which suit should be filed. This was because separate courts were established—e.g., law, equity, ecclesiastical—to dispense certain types of relief or to hear certain types of disputes. Modern court systems are not so designed. Typically, any civil court is authorized to dispense whatever remedy is appropriate. Thus, the problem of framing a remedy, although an essential step in preparing the case, is not necessarily relevant in the selection of a court and is left to a course in remedies.

§ 1–2. Current Structure of Court Systems

In the United States, each of the fifty states, as well as the District of Columbia, has its own fully developed independent system of courts. There is also a separate federal court system. The federal courts are not superior to the state courts; they are an independent, coordinate system authorized by the United States Constitution, Art. III, § 2, to handle matters of particular federal interest. The presence of parallel federal and court systems often raises questions concerning the relationship of the state and federal systems, presenting important issues of federalism. See §§ 9–2—9–5, below. The United States Supreme Court, composed of nine justices, sits as the final and controlling voice over all these systems. Even its authority is not absolute, however. State courts retain the final say over interpretations of state law.

Although a few states, such as Maine and Montana, have a two-tiered system, most states, as well as the federal courts, are based on a three-tiered model. That means that a litigant will have the opportunity to present his case in a trial court, and then there are two levels of appeal at which the losing trial litigant ultimately may succeed. For example, in the federal system the trial court is the United States District Court, of which there is at least one in every state and in the District of Columbia, Puerto Rico, the Virgin Islands, Guam, and the Northern Mariana Islands. Many larger states are divided into two, three, or even four judicial districts, depending on population, geography and caseload. There are 94 districts in the United States and each district court has at least one district judge, or more commonly three or more. After an adverse judgment in the district court, a litigant may appeal to the United States Court of Appeals for the circuit in which the district court is located. There are eleven numbered intermediate appellate courts in the federal system, each including anywhere from three to ten states and territories. Additionally, there is a Court of Appeals for the District of Columbia Circuit, hearing appeals from the federal district court there, and one for the Federal Circuit, taking appeals from various specialized federal tribunals, such as the Court of Federal Claims, and from all courts on certain specialized matters, such as patents. Each court of appeals has six or more judges (the Ninth Circuit has 29) who sit in panels of three to review district court decisions, as well as some decisions of administrative agencies. A losing litigant in the court of appeals may, in some cases, be able to obtain review by the United States Supreme Court. Cases in the state courts similarly may proceed through a trial court, a state appellate court, and then the state supreme court. If a federal constitutional question or certain other federal matters are involved, the decision of the state supreme court may be reviewed by the United States Supreme Court. Since 1988, review by the Supreme Court in civil cases is up to that Court's discretion; virtually all civil appeals as of right to the highest court have been abolished.

Three-tiered systems vary on the role that the highest court plays. The approaches taken reflect differing philosophies on the circumstances under which review by the highest court is available. For example, in California only criminal cases in which capital punishment has been imposed are appealable as of right to the state supreme court. Similarly, in the federal courts, except in a few very limited circumstances, appeals to the United States Supreme Court are discretionary, by writ of certiorari. The Supreme Court decides for itself what are the most important questions that deserve its attention and will refuse to review decisions raising issues that it feels are not as crucial. In this way it supervises the administration of law by the lower courts on an ad hoc basis. At the other end of the spectrum, such as in New York, appeals to the state's highest court are as of right in a great many cases. This approach emphasizes the function of New York's highest court to assure that cases are correctly decided. Recognizing the wide disparity among judicial systems on this question, it is necessary for lawyers to check carefully the statutes of the system in which suit is filed to determine the specific rules regarding review by those appellate courts.

CHAPTER 2

CHOOSING THE PROPER COURT

A. SUBJECT MATTER JURISDICTION

1. IN GENERAL

§ 2–1. Principles Governing

The first question that must be addressed when deciding where to file suit is which courts have the requisite power or competence to decide the type of controversy involved. This requirement typically is stated in terms of whether the court has subject-matter jurisdiction. Questions of subject-matter jurisdiction are determined by referring to federal and state statutes, which authorize jurisdiction over particular types of cases.

For state courts the statutes establishing the different courts in the state typically will set each court's subject-matter jurisdiction boundaries. State subject-matter jurisdiction limits exist primarily as a means of regulating the flow of judicial business before the state courts. In some instances jurisdiction will be distributed according to the type of proceeding involved, as in the case of probate proceedings or criminal matters. Amount restrictions also may serve to delineate court boundaries. For example, matters involving less than $10,000 may be assigned to Municipal Court, while matters involving more than that amount will be heard by the Superior Court. Few problems arise in applying these limitations. The question is not whether the plaintiff can bring an action in state court, but which of the existing state trial courts is authorized to hear the case.

The approach changes when federal subject-matter jurisdiction is involved. All federal district courts are trial courts of equal jurisdictional power with respect to subject-matter jurisdiction; there is no division among the district courts as to what cases can be tried in which tribunal. A federal district court may entertain an action based on almost any area of the law. The one exception to this principle is the existence of specialized federal courts to handle certain matters, such as the Tax Court, the Court of Federal Claims, and the Bankruptcy Court. However, even in those cases the plaintiff is sometimes allowed the option of filing suit in the specialized federal court or in federal district court.

The problem in defining federal court subject-matter jurisdiction arises because Article III, § 2 of the U.S. Constitution limits federal jurisdiction solely to those matters specifically listed in that clause. All other controversies are left to the state courts to decide. Further, Article III delegates to Congress the task of deciding what lower federal courts to establish. Congress, in enacting enabling legislation for the judicial power clause, is under no obligation to give the federal courts all the jurisdiction authorized under the Constitution; in some instances it has refrained from doing so. As a result, a plaintiff who wants to file an action in federal court must first determine whether any federal court can entertain the controversy at all. A defendant may also be able to invoke federal subject-matter jurisdiction by removing an action filed against it in state court to federal court.

There may be a number of reasons why a party may prefer a federal court over a state court. The applicable procedural rules may be viewed as more favorable in federal court than state court. The federal court may be more conveniently located than the nearest state court. Federal judges often are perceived as having more expertise than their state counterparts, at least with respect to certain issues. Further, federal judges may be subject to fewer outside pressures because they are not elected but are appointed for life. Federal and state courts also may draw potential jurors from different geographic areas. Whatever the reason, federal subject-matter jurisdiction is strictly limited.

When federal subject-matter jurisdiction does exist, it usually is *concurrent* with state courts, meaning that litigants can choose whether to sue in federal or state court. In a few instances, however, jurisdiction statutes will give federal courts *exclusive* jurisdiction over a particular type of controversy. For example, the federal courts have exclusive jurisdiction over actions based on patents and copyrights (28 U.S.C.A. § 1338), and over all proceedings in bankruptcy (28 U.S.C.A. § 1334); no action on those matters can be brought in the state courts. Conversely, probate and divorce actions are within the exclusive jurisdiction of the state courts and, in most instances, only properly brought before certain specialized state courts established to handle those cases. Interestingly, the exclusive jurisdiction of state probate and family courts is not of statutory origin. It is an historic division of authority that the state and federal courts have continued to recognize, although they are not required to do so as a matter of statutory or constitutional law.

Before turning to an examination of federal subject-matter jurisdiction, a distinction must be drawn between *original* and *appellate* jurisdiction. Courts having original jurisdiction are courts of first instance; that is where litigants go to obtain a trial of the case. Courts having appellate jurisdiction function as reviewing courts; the case may be brought to them only on appeal from an order or judgment in a lower court. Thus, any inquiry into subject-matter jurisdiction must consider not only whether the court has been given the power to hear a certain controversy, but also whether it is a trial or an appellate tribunal.

A brief introduction to the main types of federal subject-matter jurisdiction and its restraints follows. Readers interested in a more detailed review should refer to J. Friedenthal, M. Kane, A. Miller & A. Steinman, *Civil Procedure* §§ 2.1–2.14 (6th ed.2021), or C. Wright & M. Kane, *Federal Courts* 93–233 (8th ed.2016).

2. FEDERAL JURISDICTION

§ 2–2. Federal-Question Jurisdiction

Article III, § 2 of the Constitution permits federal court jurisdiction whenever a case "arises under" federal law. Many federal statutes create the right to sue for the violation of the rights or duties enumerated therein (e.g., federal antitrust or securities laws), and at the same time explicitly grant jurisdiction to the federal courts to hear those matters. In this way *special federal-question jurisdiction* is established. Congress also has provided in 28 U.S.C.A. § 1331, that the federal courts may take jurisdiction over any civil action arising under the Constitution, laws, or treaties of the United States. The chief problem in invoking this *general federal-question jurisdiction* has been in determining how to apply the "arising under" requirement in the statute. Stated most simply, a right or immunity created by federal law must be a basic element of the plaintiff's cause of action, not merely a collateral issue or introduced by way of defense. Gully v. First Nat. Bank in Meridian, 299 U.S. 109 (1936).

The notion that a case does not "arise under" federal law if the defendant, rather than the plaintiff, introduces the federal issue was established by the United States Supreme Court in Louisville & Nashville R. Co. v. Mottley, 211 U.S. 149 (1908). No language in the Constitution mandates that interpretation. Indeed, the Court has interpreted the constitutional language much more liberally, holding that as long as a federal question is an "original ingredient" in the case, even if it does not present an issue to be litigated, Article III of the Constitution may be satisfied. Osborn v. Bank of the United States, 22 U.S. 738 (1824). Nonetheless, the Court has firmly embraced the "well-pleaded complaint" rule on numerous occasions as the appropriate interpretation of congressional intent in using the "arising under" language in Section 1331.

Federal court jurisdiction can be invoked under Section 1331 only when the statement of the plaintiff's claim, properly pleaded, shows that it is based on federal law. Emphasis is placed on what are the proper and necessary elements of a claim for relief. Jurisdiction is not proper if the plaintiff improperly anticipates a defense or if jurisdiction is based on the defendant's counterclaim. Although the well-pleaded complaint rule has been criticized because it makes jurisdiction turn on technical pleading rules when rigid pleading no longer is part of federal procedure, see § 3–4, below, it remains the governing principle in federal-question cases under Section 1331. Further, it has been extended to declaratory-judgment actions, requiring an inquiry in those suits as to how the action would have been pleaded but for the availability of declaratory relief. As a practical matter this means that federal-question jurisdiction will exist only if the coercive or damage action that would have been brought if the declaratory-judgment remedy did not exist would have satisfied the well-pleaded complaint rule. Skelly Oil Co. v. Phillips Petroleum Co., 339 U.S. 667 (1950).

§ 2–3. Diversity-of-Citizenship Jurisdiction

Article III, § 2 of the Constitution provides for jurisdiction over cases between citizens of different states, as well as cases between citizens of U.S. states and foreign citizens. In the principal statute authorizing diversity jurisdiction, 28 U.S.C.A. § 1332(a), Congress restricted jurisdiction to disputes involving more than $75,000, see § 2–4, below, however. No federal jurisdiction is provided for actions between two foreign citizens or when one of the parties is a United States citizen but has no state citizenship. State courts are the only available fora in those cases. A further restriction on the invocation of federal diversity jurisdiction is the interpretation of the statute given by the Supreme Court in Strawbridge v. Curtiss, 7 U.S. 267 (1806). The Court ruled that there must be *complete diversity* to satisfy Section 1332(a); in multi-party suits no plaintiff can share the same state citizenship with any defendant.

State citizenship is determined on the basis of a party's domicile, as opposed to mere residence. A person's domicile is where the person has a permanent home or principal establishment. Domicile requires the physical presence of a residence within the state plus the intention to make that residence one's present home. It is not required that the party whose domicile is in issue intend to reside there permanently. Persons such as members of the armed services, prisoners, and students can establish a domicile even though they may be only involuntarily or temporarily residing in a state. The key is whether they intend to maintain their principal establishment there for the time being. Once established, a domicile continues unless and until a new one is acquired.

The application of diversity requirements to actions involving business entities provides some problems. In the case of corporations, the diversity statute provides for citizenship both where the corporation is incorporated and where it maintains its principal place of business. 28 U.S.C.A. § 1332(c)(1). These requirements apply to all corporations, whether their place of incorporation or their principal place of business is located inside or outside the United States. In many instances, this provision reduces the availability of diversity jurisdiction because a corporation is deemed a citizen of two states. A major difficulty in applying the statutory criteria was in deciding what constitutes a principal place of business. The Supreme Court resolved the question in 2010, when it adopted the "nerve center" approach, effectively looking to the location of the corporate headquarters. Hertz Corp. v. Friend, 559 U.S. 77 (2010). With unincorporated associations, such as labor unions, there are no special statutory guidelines, so the diversity statute has been interpreted to require an inquiry into the citizenship of all the members of the association. If any of the members are domiciled in the same state as the opponent, there is no complete diversity. Carden v. Arkoma Assocs., 494 U.S. 185 (1990).

Whether diversity of citizenship exists is determined as of the time the action is commenced. The citizenship of the parties at the time the cause of action arose or during the later course of the proceedings is not determinative. Grupo Dataflux v. Atlas Global Group, L.P., 541 U.S. 567 (2004). Thus, the plaintiff can change domiciles just before filing suit in order to create diversity. In some cases, plaintiffs sought to create diversity artificially by appointing an out-of-state representative or assigning the claim to a party diverse from the defendant. These tactics may violate the federal anti-collusive jurisdiction statute, 28 U.S.C.A. § 1359, and assignments to create diversity have been struck down by the Supreme Court. See Kramer v. Caribbean Mills, Inc., 394 U.S. 823 (1969). However, many lower courts were reluctant to consider the motives behind the appointment of a representative in order to determine if Section 1359 had been violated. Congress addressed the problem in 1988 when it amended the diversity statute to provide that the citizenship of legal representatives of estates or of infants or incompetents shall be deemed the same as the state of the decedent or the infant or incompetent being represented. 28 U.S.C.A. § 1332(c)(2). Consequently, there no longer is any incentive to appoint an out-of-state representative in order to fit within the diversity statute.

The historic premise for diversity was that it allowed entry into the federal courts to protect out-of-state residents from any potential prejudice that might exist in the local fora. But many courts and commentators have questioned whether the historic rationale still presents a valid concern. With the caseload of the federal courts constantly increasing as new federal laws and claims are created, it is not surprising that several proposals have been made in the Congress to eliminate or seriously curtail diversity jurisdiction. To date, none have been successful, although the pressure for some restrictions continues. In 2005, Congress enacted legislation that expanded diversity jurisdiction to reach certain high-value class actions even when complete diversity does not exist, as long as at least one plaintiff class member is a citizen of a different state than at least one defendant. 28 U.S.C.A. § 1332(d)(2).

§ 2–4. Amount in Controversy

As a means of limiting access to the federal courts, Congress has included amount-in-controversy requirements in some of the jurisdictional statutes since the earliest days. Until 1980, when the requirement was eliminated entirely for federal-question cases, actions brought under general federal-question jurisdiction or diversity jurisdiction required that the matter in controversy exceed $10,000, exclusive of interest and costs. Further, the $10,000 amount has been upwardly adjusted over the years. Most recently, in 1996, the amount was raised to $75,000. This requirement acts to assure that only the more significant diversity cases (in terms of size) reach the federal courts, and in this way it controls the federal court caseload. It also protects small litigants from what may be the increased costs of federal court litigation.

Perhaps because amount-in-controversy requirements are merely judicial housekeeping measures and not constitutional barriers, the test for ascertaining whether they have been met is quite liberal. If the sum claimed by the plaintiff is made in good faith and it is not clear to a legal certainty that more than $75,000 will not be recovered, the requirement is met. The burden is placed on the party resisting federal jurisdiction to show that the minimum amount is not involved. In suits seeking injunctive relief, the amount in controversy typically is established by looking at the cost to the plaintiff if relief is denied, in other words the value of the right sought to be protected against the defendant's interference. However, some courts have held that the requirement is satisfied if either the value to the plaintiff or the cost for the defendant to comply with the proposed injunction exceeds the $75,000 threshold.

If it becomes apparent during the course of the trial or at the entry of the judgment that less than the requisite amount is involved, the case need not be dismissed for lack of subject-matter jurisdiction at that time. Rather, the statute provides that the court may assess costs against the plaintiff. 28 U.S.C.A. § 1332(b). In practice this measure is used infrequently and typically will be applied only when the plaintiff has acted in clear bad faith.

The largest difficulties in applying the amount-in-controversy requirement have arisen in cases involving multiple parties and multiple claims. The problem is whether multiple claims may be *aggregated* to satisfy the requirement that the amount in controversy exceed $75,000. The general rules governing aggregation of claims are the following. In a simple two-party action between A and B, A may join all the claims—related and unrelated—she has against B and aggregation will be allowed. When aggregation of A's claims is involved there is at least the possibility that, if they are all sustained, more than the jurisdictional minimum will be recovered. The court will not allow the aggregation of A's claims with any counterclaims made by B in order to meet the applicable amount-in-controversy requirement, however. To allow aggregation in that situation would permit the parties to consent to subject-matter jurisdiction indirectly and that is impermissible. Further, if both claims are valid, the claim and counterclaim will offset one another and there will be no possibility that more than $75,000 will be recovered.

Another scenario is multiple party litigation in which two plaintiffs (A & B) sue C, or in which one plaintiff (A) sues two defendants (C & D). If no single claim meets the requisite amount, courts generally have upheld jurisdiction only when both plaintiffs, A & B, or both defendants, C & D, have a "joint and common interest" in the subject matter of the action, rather than "several interests" or interests that are "separate and distinct." This test also has been applied to class actions: each class member must possess a claim above the jurisdictional minimum, unless the members possess a joint and common interest in the action. Zahn v. International Paper Co., 414 U.S. 291 (1973); Snyder v. Harris, 394 U.S. 332 (1969).

What constitutes a joint and common interest can present a difficult question in certain cases. Suffice it to say that the requirement will be satisfied only in a small class of cases in which the law essentially has ruled that various interests are to be treated as one. For example, a husband and wife are deemed to hold a joint interest in their home in community property states. Partners similarly possess a joint interest in the partnership assets. The fact that the parties are united in interest in terms of desiring the same relief or resisting the same claims does not give them a joint and common interest, however. A parent seeking damages for injuries to his minor child and reimbursement for the medical expenses that were incurred on behalf of the child cannot aggregate those claims so as to be able to obtain federal court jurisdiction. The personal-injury claim belongs to the child and the medical-expenses claim represents damage to the parent; the parent-child relationship in itself does not create a joint and common interest in the action. More generally, tort claims by multiple plaintiffs may not be aggregated to meet the amount-in-controversy requirement—even if they are suing the same defendant and their claims arise from the same event, transaction, or business practice.

As discussed in § 2–5, below, the 1990 supplemental jurisdiction statute has allowed jurisdiction over some plaintiffs or class members with low-value claims if they form part of the same "case or controversy" with those whose claims do meet the required amount in controversy. Also, in 2005, Congress enacted a specialized form of diversity jurisdiction that requires a higher amount-in-controversy threshold (in excess of $5 million) but allows aggregation of all class members' claims to reach that amount. 28 U.S.C.A. § 1332(d)(2), (6).

§ 2–5. Supplemental Jurisdiction

In 1990, Congress enacted a statute authorizing what was termed "supplemental jurisdiction" over all related claims that are part of the same case or controversy as claims in the action that are within the court's original jurisdiction. 28 U.S.C.A. § 1367(a). The statute represents a codification of two forms of nonstatutory subject-matter jurisdiction developed earlier by the courts—ancillary and pendent jurisdiction. Thus, a brief look at those two forms of jurisdiction provides necessary background to understanding the current scope of supplemental jurisdiction.

Ancillary and pendent jurisdiction were developed by the courts for use in multiple-claim actions to permit entire disputes to be tried in the federal courts, thereby avoiding multiple lawsuits. Both types of jurisdiction required the presence in the action of at least one claim that met the standards of one of the statutory bases for subject-matter jurisdiction. Jurisdiction then could be allowed over some otherwise jurisdictionally insufficient claim if that claim arose out of the same core of aggregate fact or, stated alternatively, if both claims arose out of a common nucleus of operative fact, or the same transaction or occurrence. Given the liberal claim and party joinder provisions in the federal rules, see §§ 3–11—3–20, below, these bases for jurisdiction frequently were invoked.

Although the test governing the assertion of both ancillary and pendent jurisdiction was basically the same, the terms technically applied to different types of situations. Historically, pendent jurisdiction was invoked when the question presented was whether a state-law claim could be asserted by a party who already was asserting a federal-question claim. Ancillary jurisdiction pertained to all other situations in which the federal court retained jurisdiction over closely related claims that were jurisdictionally insufficient by themselves, but were attached to jurisdictionally proper claims.

The assertion of this jurisdictional power was deemed constitutional under Article III, § 2 because the courts were deemed to be defining what constituted "a case or controversy" in a multiple-claim situation. The rationale supporting the extension of federal court jurisdiction to ancillary and pendent claims was primarily one of judicial economy—to rule otherwise would require the filing of two suits, one in federal and the other in state court. Further, the availability of pendent jurisdiction made the federal court a viable alternative to the state courts in which all the claims could be joined.

The leading Supreme Court case setting out the standard for assessing whether ancillary or pendent jurisdiction could be asserted was United Mine Workers of America v. Gibbs, 383 U.S. 715 (1966). The Court set forth a two-part analysis, which remains relevant today.

The first question asked under the Gibbs analysis is whether the claim meets the standard for asserting this type of jurisdiction—is there a common nucleus of operative fact between the jurisdictionally sufficient and insufficient claims? Illustratively, an action asserting a federal antitrust claim and a state unfair-competition claim arising from the same alleged conduct usually will meet this standard. Many of the facts that must be proven to show unfair competition also will aid in demonstrating price-fixing or a monopoly, which would violate the federal law. On the other hand, a slander claim will often require proof of different facts than a personal-injury claim. This is true even if the defendant allegedly slandered the plaintiff immediately after their accident so that the events giving rise to the claims were part of a series of related events.

Once the court determines that it has the power to decide the entire case, it then must decide the second question: whether taking the otherwise jurisdictionally insufficient claim will foster judicial economy and will be fair to the parties. Thus, unlike other forms of jurisdiction, the actual assertion of ancillary or pendent jurisdiction was discretionary. A wide range of factors could be taken into account in deciding this discretionary issue and the court could review the exercise of its discretion throughout the case. For example, if the claims that independently met subject-matter jurisdiction requirements were dismissed at an early stage in a lawsuit, judicial economy might suggest that the ancillary or pendent claims also should be dismissed and the parties left to litigate those issues in the state courts. Similarly, if the state-law issues presented by a proposed ancillary or pendent claim were peculiarly difficult or novel, jurisdiction might be declined in order to allow the state courts to rule on those questions. If the presence of the additional claims or parties would produce jury confusion that could not be controlled in other ways, jurisdiction also might be refused. In any case in which pendent or ancillary jurisdiction was not allowed, only the additional claims were dismissed; the federal court continued to decide the jurisdictionally proper claims before it.

The expansion of pendent and ancillary jurisdiction to embrace situations in which additional parties as well as claims are involved presented serious difficulties for the courts. Ancillary jurisdiction traditionally included the introduction of claims by intervenors of right, see § 3–18, below, as well as the bringing in of third-party defendants by defendants, see § 3–16, below. Several lower federal courts also expanded pendent jurisdiction notions to include situations involving party joinder, developing what was referred to as pendent-party jurisdiction. Under this approach, a plaintiff could sue two defendants, asserting a jurisdictionally sufficient claim against one and a related but insufficient claim against the other. A similar result could occur when two or more plaintiffs joined in a suit against a single defendant.

The validity of pendent-party jurisdiction first was called into question by the Supreme Court in Aldinger v. Howard, 427 U.S. 1 (1976). There the Court stated that in addition to finding that the claims arose out of a common transaction, it was necessary to consider whether there was anything in the statute conferring jurisdiction over the proper claim suggesting that Congress would not approve the extension of jurisdiction over the additional party. Using this standard, the Court in a later case struck down an attempt to use ancillary jurisdiction concepts to authorize a plaintiff in a diversity case to assert a claim against a nondiverse third-party defendant, finding that attempt violated the diversity statute's requirement of complete diversity. Owen Equipment & Erection Co. v. Kroger, 437 U.S. 365 (1978). The Court distinguished cases allowing ancillary jurisdiction to be used to assert counterclaims, crossclaims and third-party claims on the ground that in those suits the additional claims were logically dependent on the main claim and were being asserted by defendants who had not chosen the forum in which to sue. In 1989, the Supreme Court in Finley v. United States, 490 U.S. 545 (1989), suggested an even narrower view of pendent-party jurisdiction, holding that although the extension of pendent-party jurisdiction might be constitutional, the courts were powerless to create it in the absence of statutory authorization. In response, Congress enacted the 1990 supplemental-jurisdiction statute.

The availability of supplemental jurisdiction under the statute is governed by the Gibbs standard of whether the jurisdictionally insufficient claims share a common nucleus of operative fact with the jurisdictionally sufficient claims so as to constitute the same case or controversy. 28 U.S.C.A. § 1367(a). Supplemental jurisdiction may be invoked even if additional parties are joined, although the statute limits supplemental jurisdiction with respect to additional parties in some diversity-jurisdiction cases. 28 U.S.C.A. § 1367(b). Like traditional pendent jurisdiction, the exercise of jurisdiction under this statute is discretionary and the court may decline to exercise it in certain circumstances. 28 U.S.C.A. § 1367(c).

The statute has introduced some important jurisdictional changes, as well as ambiguities, particularly for cases in which the sole basis for federal subject-matter jurisdiction is diversity of citizenship. See 28 U.S.C.A. § 1367(b). Supplemental jurisdiction is not permitted over claims by plaintiffs against any individual made a party to the action through the use of the joinder devices of Federal Rule 14 (impleader), Federal Rule 19 (compulsory joinder), Federal Rule 20 (permissive joinder), or Federal Rule 24 (intervention) if doing so would be incompatible with Section 1332's requirements for diversity of citizenship. See §§ 3-11—3-18, below, for a discussion of these joinder devices. Thus, although the language of the statute allows a nondiverse third-party defendant to invoke supplemental jurisdiction to assert a claim directly against the plaintiff, the plaintiff cannot invoke the statute to assert a counterclaim in response.

Section 1367(b) also excludes supplemental jurisdiction in diversity cases over claims by plaintiffs who seek to intervene under Rule 24 or who are proposed to be joined as required parties under Rule 19. Because the statute does not forbid supplemental jurisdiction with respect to plaintiffs joined permissively under Rule 20, some lower federal courts allowed it to be invoked to uphold jurisdiction over claims not meeting the jurisdictional minimum that are asserted in conjunction with related claims that do meet the amount requirement. Other courts disagreed, finding that that result would be contrary to prior law regarding aggregation, see § 2–4, above, and that there was no congressional intent to overrule that law. The Supreme Court resolved the issue in 2005, upholding supplemental jurisdiction if one plaintiff has a sufficient claim arising out of the same controversy as the insufficient claims. Exxon Mobil Corp. v. Allapattah Servs., Inc., 545 U.S. 546 (2005).

Finally, some confusion has arisen regarding the courts' discretion to dismiss a supplemental claim under Section 1367(c), because the statute omits any explicit reference to the judicial economy, convenience, and fairness factors that the Supreme Court identified in Gibbs. Many courts, however, have continued to consider these factors in deciding whether to decline to exercise supplemental jurisdiction under the new provision. A federal court has no discretion to exercise supplemental jurisdiction over state law claims if the plaintiff amends the complaint to delete all federal law claims that were the initial basis for original jurisdiction under Section 1367(a); in that circumstance, the state law claims must be either dismissed or remanded to state court. Royal Canin U.S.A., Inc. v. Wullschleger, 604 U.S. 22 (2025).

§ 2-6. Removal Jurisdiction

When concurrent jurisdiction is placed in the federal and state courts, the plaintiff may choose in which one to file suit. If the plaintiff opts for state court, the defendant may be able to remove the suit to the federal court in that district if the defendant can show that the case falls within the special federal statute designed for that purpose, 28 U.S.C.A. § 1441. Only defendants can remove. 28 U.S.C.A. § 1441(a). Plaintiffs cannot remove even if the defendant interposes a counterclaim so that they are then "defending parties." Shamrock Oil & Gas Corp. v. Sheets, 313 U.S. 100 (1941).

Under the general removal provision, removal is proper only if the federal court would have had jurisdiction had the plaintiff opted to begin the action there. 28 U.S.C.A. § 1441(a). The fact that venue, see § 2-7, below, would have been improper in the federal court will not preclude removal. 28 U.S.C.A. § 1390(c). Only jurisdictional defects will act as a bar. In light of the well-pleaded complaint rule, see § 2-2, above, this means that removal cannot be based on a federal question in the defendant's answer or on the fact that a federal counterclaim is being asserted. With respect to the amount-in-controversy requirement, a 2011 amendment to the removal statute provides that, in cases in which state law either does not permit a demand for monetary relief or allows damage recoveries beyond the amount demanded, the removing defendant may show by a preponderance of the evidence that the amount involved is greater than the statutory minimum. 28

U.S.C.A. § 1446(c)(2)(B). Removal jurisdiction in multiclaim or multiple party actions may be proper if the plaintiff could have utilized supplemental jurisdiction, see § 2–5, above, for claims over which there is no independent basis of jurisdiction. In cases in which jurisdiction is based solely on diversity of citizenship, however, the case cannot be removed if any defendants are citizens of the state where the case is filed. 28 U.S.C.A. § 1441(b)(2).

The removal statute also contains special authorization for removal in certain federal-question cases involving multiple parties or claims that otherwise would not be removable. 28 U.S.C.A. § 1441(c). The purpose of this provision is to prevent the plaintiff from blocking the defendant's option simply by including some nonremovable claims or parties and to make the defendant's choice of the federal court a viable one. Removal of the entire action is permissible if the defendant can show that a claim exists that could have been brought in federal court under general federal-question jurisdiction and the action otherwise could have been removed if the additional claims not within the court's original or supplemental jurisdiction were not included. 28 U.S.C.A. § 1441(c)(1). Once the action is removed, however, the federal court, under 2011 amendments to the removal statute, is required to sever and remand all unrelated jurisdictionally insufficient claims to the state court. 28 U.S.C.A. § 1441(c)(2).

Removal jurisdiction raises serious federalism concerns as it presents a situation in which the federal court is taking a case away from a state court, albeit at the request of a party. This fact is emphasized by the removal procedure itself. The defendant in the state court action files a notice of removal, containing a short and plain statement of the grounds for removal, in the federal court. 28 U.S.C.A. § 1446(a). A copy of the notice is filed simultaneously in the state court and written notice is given to the other parties. As stated in the federal removal statute, "the State court shall proceed no further unless and until the case is remanded." 28 U.S.C.A. § 1446(d). A plaintiff who wishes to challenge removal must do so by filing a motion to remand in the federal court. 28 U.S.C.A. § 1447(c). The desire to afford the defendant the opportunity to invoke federal jurisdiction is deemed to outweigh concerns about the potential impact of removal on federal-state court relations.

B. VENUE

§ 2-7. General Principles Governing

Venue is a statutory requirement designed to regulate the flow of judicial business within a particular court system and to identify a convenient forum for the parties to litigate their dispute. In the federal court system, venue provisions set out the district or districts in a given state in which suit may be brought, assuming subject-matter and personal jurisdiction requirements are met. In state court systems, venue statutes typically refer to the proper county in which to bring the action. Once it has been determined whether an action can be filed in state or federal court, §§ 2-1—2-6, above, and in which courts personal jurisdiction may be obtained over the defendant, §§ 2–10—2–20, below, the applicable venue statutes must be consulted in order to further identify which courts within those judicial systems are permissible fora.

Although the types of venue statutes vary, some discussion of their characteristics may be helpful. A common provision that is utilized places venue for transitory causes of action at the residence of the defendant. E.g., Cal.Civ.Proc.Code § 395(a). The residence of a corporation has been established statutorily in some states as the corporation's principal place of business. E.g., Cal.Civ.Proc.Code § 395.5. More specific venue provisions may be tied to the kind of action being brought (e.g., tort, contract) and may identify the locale of specific events (e.g., the performance of the contract, tortious injury) as a convenient place to bring suit. In cases in which more than one venue may be proper, the plaintiff can choose where to file suit.

In the federal system, the general venue statute was significantly rewritten in 2011. Prior to that time it contained different rules for determining venue depending on whether the action was based on federal-question or diversity jurisdiction. The new statute contains a single venue standard for all federal cases. It provides that venue is proper (1) in a district in which any defendant resides if all defendants reside in the same state, (2) in a district in which "a substantial part of the events or omissions giving rise to the claim occurred, or a substantial part of property that is the subject of the action is situated," or (3) if there is no district that satisfies those criteria, in any district in which any defendant is subject to the court's personal jurisdiction. 28 U.S.C.A. § 1391(b). Additionally, the amended statute provides that business entity defendants are deemed to reside for venue purposes in any district to which they are subject to personal jurisdiction. 28 U.S.C.A. § 1391(c)(2).

Venue is determined at the outset of the action. If additional claims are filed, such as third-party claims or intervention claims, the venue requirements typically will not be applied to those claims. Courts commonly invoke notions of waiver or ancillary venue in these circumstances. When a counterclaim is asserted against the plaintiff, it is said that by filing suit plaintiff consented to the convenience of the forum. These approaches to venue over additional claims rest on the sound premise that if the forum is established as a convenient one at the outset of the litigation, it will remain so for the parties and all their claims. Venue need not be tested each time a claim is added to the action.

Notably, the fact that the forum chosen meets statutory venue requirements does not guarantee that it necessarily will be the most convenient one for a particular dispute. Thus, as is discussed later, an action filed in compliance with the venue statute may later be dismissed or transferred to a more convenient locale. See § 2–30, below. Additionally, in a contract dispute in which the parties have entered into a forum selection clause, the Supreme Court has held that the proper way for the defendant to seek to enforce that clause within the federal court system is by a motion to transfer and not by a motion to dismiss for improper venue. Atlantic Marine Constr. Co. v. U.S. District Ct. for W. Dist. of Texas, 571 U.S. 49 (2013).

§ 2–8. Local Action Principle

A common distinction that has been drawn in venue statutes is the difference between a local and a transitory action. Local actions are those which involve ownership of, possession of, or injury to real property. Transitory actions encompass all other suits. Historically, because of the desire to have juries who were familiar with the facts of the case, local actions could be brought only in the county in which the land was situated. Transitory actions were not so restricted.

The local action principle may be viewed as a venue rule, regulating the business of the courts within a state. When applied across state lines its significance increases because it becomes entwined with notions of state sovereignty over real property within a given state's borders. Based on the local-action principle, the United States Supreme Court held that a court in the county or district in which land is situated may refuse to give full faith and credit to a judgment or decree of another state's court which affects the title to that land, even though the parties were within the personal jurisdiction of the forum court at the time the judgment was entered. Fall v. Eastin, 215 U.S. 1 (1909). This seems to elevate the local-action principle to one of constitutional magnitude, an anomalous result in our federal system. Whether it is appropriate to consider the local-action principle as grounded in jurisdictional concerns or merely as a specialized venue restraint is predominantly a matter of academic interest. All modern state decisions have ruled that full faith and credit will be given, even though it is not required, and the 2011 amendments to the federal venue statute explicitly provide that federal venue is to be determined without regard to whether the action is local or transitory. 28 U.S.C.A. § 1391(a)(2). Thus, the principle has not produced significant problems in modern times.

C. PERSONAL JURISDICTION

§ 2-9. Introduction

The doctrine of personal jurisdiction addresses the question whether a court has the power to render a binding, enforceable judgment defining or declaring the rights and duties of the parties. As to plaintiffs, the very act of seeking relief always has been supposed to constitute a submission to jurisdiction, warranting a judgment against them. When the proposed defendant resides in and is present in the state in which the court is sitting, the question has posed few problems; power is assumed to exist because each state has sovereign control over all things and persons within its borders. In those cases the question becomes whether jurisdiction has been obtained in compliance with proper procedural requirements and with adequate notification.

One difficulty in applying these territorial principles involved corporations, because corporations are only legal constructs and have no tangible existence and thus no visible situs. This problem first was solved by holding that a corporation always was subject to the jurisdiction of the courts under whose laws it was incorporated. The courts later added to this notion the rule that a corporation also was subject to suit when it had "consented" expressly or impliedly to be sued in a particular state. See § 2–15, below. This consent theory quickly verged on the fictitious, so courts added another concept seeking to equate corporations and natural persons. Because the physical presence of a person in a state was deemed enough to justify personal jurisdiction, a corporation was declared "present" and thus subject to personal jurisdiction when the extent and continuity of its business activities in the state seemed large enough to equate activity with presence. Under this "presence" approach, the discontinuance of corporate activities, like the departure of an individual, terminated the state's power to enter a binding, enforceable judgment. This limitation on the court's power would apply even though the defendant corporation was being sued on the basis of its earlier activities in the state.

Perhaps not surprisingly, the major jurisdictional problems and developments have centered on the issue whether and when a court can assert personal jurisdiction over a defendant not found within the state. To answer this question usually requires two inquiries. First, is there a statute authorizing the assertion of personal jurisdiction over persons outside the forum state's borders under circumstances similar to the case at hand? See §§ 2–10—2–12, below. Second, does the application of the statute to the case at hand meet constitutional standards? See §§ 2–16—2–20, below. Both these questions must be answered affirmatively for each and every defendant in an action, as well as any additional parties who later may be joined.

The development of state statutes and of the constitutional standard applied to extraterritorial assertions of personal jurisdiction has undergone several twists and turns, including a line of Supreme Court cases beginning with International Shoe Co. v. Washington, 326 U.S. 310 (1945), that continues to evolve to this day. Thus, a complete study of this area of procedure requires an analysis of Supreme Court decisions, a close look at a number of the statutes that have been adopted, and a review of lower court decisions that have applied and interpreted these developments. After an abbreviated review of the historic premises from which the modern law of personal jurisdiction developed, the primary focus in this Nutshell will be on modern jurisdictional theory.

Finally, in addition to finding an applicable statute and making certain that the use of that statute is consistent with the Constitution, procedural due process concerns also require that persons whose rights will be affected by any judgment be given adequate notice and an opportunity to be heard. See § 2–21 and § 6–4, below. This means that the method used to assert jurisdiction must be designed to comport with those requirements. Otherwise, any judgment that is entered may be invalid.

Necessarily, the discussion in this Nutshell of each of these elements of obtaining proper personal jurisdiction must be somewhat brief. Readers who would like a more complete treatment of these matters should refer to J. Friedenthal, M. Kane, A. Miller & A. Steinman, *Civil Procedure* Ch. 3 (6th ed.2021), or 4 & 4A C. Wright, A. Miller & A. Steinman, *Federal Practice and Procedure* §§ 1067–1069.2.

1. STATUTORY SOURCES OF JURISDICTIONAL POWER

a. State Courts

§ 2–10. Types of Statutes

There are two types of statutes that may be consulted to determine whether a state court may assert jurisdiction over a nonresident defendant who is outside the borders of the state. The first type (commonly called a long-arm statute) specifically authorizes the state courts to exert extraterritorial jurisdiction over defendants who meet the conditions set out in the statute. Alternatively, if the defendant owns property in the state, then it may be possible to assert jurisdiction based on the attachment of that property at the outset of the suit. In that situation, it is necessary to determine whether the state has an attachment statute authorizing jurisdiction on this basis. If no long-arm or attachment statute covering the case at hand exists, personal jurisdiction cannot be asserted over a nonresident defendant who remains outside the state's borders.

Although state long-arm statutes are many and varied, a brief description may be helpful. The primary differentiating characteristic between long-arm statutes is the amount of detailed requirements or categories that are set out. At one end of the spectrum are those statutes permitting the assertion of jurisdiction whenever the defendant has the necessary minimum contacts with the state so that jurisdiction would not be contrary to the constitution or laws of the United States. E.g., R.I.Gen.L. § 9–5–33, Cal.Civ.Proc.Code § 410.10. This general statutory standard allows the courts to stretch their jurisdiction to its furthest possible limits. This type of statute also is easy to apply in an era of increasing travel and changing business arrangements because the statute can be invoked for new and different situations without any need to fit the case into a definition or category that was included for other purposes. This fluidity has drawbacks, however. Every jurisdiction question becomes a constitutional one, and the prognosis for when jurisdiction will be upheld can be more difficult to make because of the sometimes ambiguous nature of the standard.

At the other end of the spectrum, some statutes list in great detail the kinds of activities on the part of nonresidents for which extraterritorial jurisdiction may be asserted. For example, all fifty states had nonresident motorist statutes, providing for the assertion of jurisdiction over nonresidents who drove into the state and caused an accident there. Other common acts for which long-arm jurisdiction may be asserted are: the transaction of business in the state, contracting to supply goods or services in the state, the commission of a tortious act in the state, the commission of a tortious act outside the state that causes injury in the state, coupled with some other business activity of defendant in the state, and the ownership, use or possession of real property in a state. E.g., N.Y.C.P.L.R. 302(a); Uniform Interstate & Int'l Pro.Act § 1.03. Other states have focused on the kind of action being brought (e.g., contract, tort) and have set out the conduct on the part of the defendant that will justify the assertion of long-arm jurisdiction in those types of suits. E.g., N.C.Gen.Stat. § 1–75.4. If an action does not fit into any of the categories listed in these more specific statutes, personal jurisdiction cannot be asserted.

State attachment statutes vary in the procedural requirements that are necessary to effectuate a proper attachment. Further, those requirements must meet the constitutional standards developed by the Supreme Court to ensure adequate notice and an opportunity to be heard. See § 6–4, below. Most states also have limited the applicability of their attachment statutes to certain prescribed situations, such as when the defendant, with the intent to defraud creditors, has assigned, secreted, disposed of, or removed property from the state, or is about to do so. E.g., N.Y.-McKinney's CPLR 6201. Thus, it is important to consult local law carefully to determine whether and how jurisdiction may be asserted by attachment.

b. Federal Courts

§ 2-11. General Rules Governing

Although Congress could enact legislation governing the assertion of personal jurisdiction by the federal courts, with few exceptions, see § 2-12, below, it has not done so. Absent specific statutory authorization, Federal Rule 4(k) governs when service of process will establish personal jurisdiction in a federal court. The Supreme Court has rejected arguments that federal courts have unfettered authority to extend their jurisdiction as a matter of federal common law. Omni Capital Int'l v. Rudolf Wolff & Co., 484 U.S. 97 (1987).

The federal rules allow federal courts to exercise personal jurisdiction in one of three circumstances. First, under Federal Rule 4(k)(1)(A), the court can refer to the statutes and rules governing personal jurisdiction in the state in which it is sitting. Federal courts may utilize state long-arm statutes or any state statute allowing the attachment of property owned by nonresidents in order to obtain jurisdiction over a nonresident defendant. Thus, the ability of a federal court to enter a binding, enforceable judgment against an out-of-state defendant often is the same as the state courts of the state in which it is sitting.

Second, Federal Rule 4(k)(1)(B) authorizes service of process within one hundred miles from where the summons was issued for certain additional parties to the action. In many instances this 100-mile bulge provision will not act extraterritorially as the court may be so situated that a one-hundred-mile radius is still within the state. In other cases, however, the application of the provision will result in long-arm jurisdiction being obtained, despite the absence of any applicable state long-arm statute.

The third situation when a federal court may be able to exert jurisdiction over parties outside the state in which it sits was added to Federal Rule 4 in 1993. It applies if the underlying claims in the action arise under federal law and the defendant is not otherwise subject to the jurisdiction of any state. Fed. Rule 4(k)(2). This would occur, for example, if the defendant is in a foreign country and defendant's conduct was not such that it fit within the scope of any existing state long-arm provisions.

§ 2–12. Specialized Provisions

The few federal long-arm provisions that exist are generally parts of statutes establishing particular federal causes of action. For example, in actions brought under the antitrust or the federal securities laws there are no geographic boundaries to the federal courts' jurisdiction. 15 U.S.C.A. §§ 4 and 78aa. Similarly, in federal interpleader actions in which a stakeholder with a limited fund to which there are conflicting claims is seeking a ruling as to how the fund should be distributed, a federal statute authorizes nationwide service of process, eliminating any limitations on the federal courts' personal jurisdiction. 28 U.S.C.A. § 2361. See § 8–7, below. Although these provisions are few in number, it is wise in actions asserting federal claims for relief to check the statute on which the claim is based to determine if a special long-arm provision is available. Federal Rule 4(k)(1)(C) confirms that service of process will establish personal jurisdiction in federal court when authorized by a federal statute.

2. STANDARD FOR ASSERTING PERSONAL JURISDICTION

a. Traditional Bases

§ 2-13. Sovereignty: The Territoriality Theory

Personal jurisdiction doctrine originally rested on notions of sovereignty. Since each state had exclusive power over all persons within its borders, it could render binding judgments in all suits brought against those persons. This jurisdiction typically was referred to as *in personam*. In personam jurisdiction was premised on the presence of the individual defendant in the state at the time the action was commenced. It mattered not whether the defendant's presence was temporary, as in the case of a transient, or more permanent. On the other hand, in personam jurisdiction was not allowed over persons outside the state borders because that would violate another state's sovereignty. A valid in personam judgment was entitled to full faith and credit in all the sister states under Article IV, § 1 of the United States Constitution.

The state also had sovereign power over all property within its borders, and it was held that a state court could render a valid and enforceable judgment concerning the ownership of or title to in-state property, regardless of the whereabouts of the defendant owner. This form of personal jurisdiction was termed *in rem*. Because of the state's exclusive control over the property, any judgment entered in such an action would "bind the world" and other states would be required to give it full faith and credit.

Notions of sovereignty were not as limited as the preceding description might suggest. For example, the Court upheld in personam jurisdiction based on the defendant's domicile and even a defendant's national citizenship. Milliken v. Meyer, 311 U.S. 457 (1940); Blackmer v. United States, 284 U.S. 421 (1932). It was reasoned that the sovereign could command certain obligations and duties from its citizens even when they were not physically present in the jurisdiction. Similarly, in cases involving the marital status of a resident plaintiff and a defendant who no longer was a resident, jurisdiction was upheld based on the notion that the state had sovereign power over the legal status of its domiciliaries and necessarily must be able to render a binding decree on the status of its resident plaintiff. Finally, nonresidents who owned property within a state were deemed within the state's in personam jurisdiction on causes of action arising out of that property. A nonresident landlord could be sued for injuries caused by the failure to maintain the property in a safe condition. The state's sovereign control over the property allowed it to enter an enforceable judgment against any landlord who had the privilege of owning property in the state.

Another important aspect of sovereignty as applied to personal jurisdiction is known as *quasi-in-rem* jurisdiction. In quasi-in-rem jurisdiction cases, property within a state was used as a vehicle to reach the defendant to adjudicate personal rights that might or might not be related to the property. Thus, a plaintiff might invoke quasi-in-rem jurisdiction to secure a preexisting claim to the property, such as in a suit for specific performance of a contract to convey land. When used this way, quasi-in-rem jurisdiction differed from in rem jurisdiction primarily because the property was important only to the remedy, it did not involve the underlying substantive right to relief, which was premised on contract law. Alternatively, quasi-in-rem jurisdiction could be used when the personal rights at issue were totally unrelated to the property. When used this way, this form of jurisdiction was sometimes referred to as attachment jurisdiction.

Under either form of quasi-in-rem jurisdiction, the state's sovereign power was asserted by attaching or seizing the property at the commencement of the action. Then, utilizing the fiction that the property was a manifestation of the defendant, the court adjudicated the personal claim before it. A defendant who appeared to defend thereby submitted to the in personam jurisdiction of the court, and a binding judgment for the full amount claimed could be entered in the event that the plaintiff prevailed on the merits. If the defendant did not appear and defaulted, the judgment was limited to the value of the property attached because, in keeping with the fiction, that was the limit of the state's sovereign power. No full faith and credit would be given to the judgment beyond that amount. The plaintiff had to begin an entirely new action in order to obtain further relief.

Attachment of the property at the commencement of the action was crucial to this form of jurisdiction. It substantiated the state's claim of power and, by preventing the property from being moved or sold during the lawsuit, it ensured the enforceability of any judgment the plaintiff might obtain. Pennoyer v. Neff, 95 U.S. 714 (1877). Attachment also served as a means of notifying the defendant of the proceedings.

Although the doctrine of quasi-in-rem jurisdiction originated in cases involving real property, where the state's sovereignty was deeply rooted in history, it gradually was expanded to apply to movable property, intangibles, and even contingent obligations. As discussed in the following section, these latter developments caused a great degree of controversy.

§ 2–14. Intangibles and Contingent Obligations

The assertion of quasi-in-rem jurisdiction based on the presence of intangibles and contingent obligations in the forum state raised the problem of how to identify their situs. For example, bank deposits were deemed to be located at the bank with which the defendant did business, and stock commonly was deemed to be present wherever the stock certificates were located. One of the most controversial applications of quasi-in-rem jurisdiction was the ruling by the United States Supreme Court in Harris v. Balk, 198 U.S. 215 (1904). The Court held that a debt resides with the debtor. By locating the debt with the debtor, a creditor (A) could obtain attachment jurisdiction over a nonresident debtor (B) if B were owed money by another person (C) and C came into A's state and was served with process there. If C contested the fact that a debt was owed to B, then A could not obtain quasi-in-rem jurisdiction over B. In personam jurisdiction over B would be needed in order to be able to enter a judgment declaring that the debt between B and C existed. New York Life Ins. Co. v. Dunlevy, 241 U.S. 518 (1916). Until that question was decided, there was no property within the state on which the court could base quasi-in-rem jurisdiction. If C conceded the obligation, then in-state service of process on C permitted the court to invoke the fiction that the debt as property of B was within its sovereign reach and, thus, it could render a judgment on the unrelated claim of A against B that would be enforceable against that property. Under this reasoning, B was subject to attachment jurisdiction wherever B's peripatetic debtor might wander. B was afforded some protection in this scheme by the fact that C had to notify B of the proceedings brought by A in order to escape being forced to pay again. However, notice did not affect the original court's jurisdiction; it merely protected C from double liability.

An even more controversial application of quasi-in-rem jurisdiction was developed in New York where the courts applied the analysis just described to allow jurisdiction based on an insurer's contingent obligation to defend and indemnify its insured. Seider v. Roth, 269 N.Y.S.2d 99, 216 N.E.2d 312 (1966). The approach taken was as follows. A, a New York resident, was injured in an automobile accident in some other state by B, a nonresident of New York. B was insured by I, a large corporation doing business in New York, as well as in other states. A sued B in New York by attaching I's duty to defend and indemnify. Quasi-in-rem jurisdiction was allowed because of the state's sovereign power over I. The controversy over this form of attachment lies in the contingent nature of the debt: if the insured is found to be free from negligence, then there is no debt; the debt exists only if the plaintiff wins. Thus, jurisdiction is extended on the basis of something that does not yet—and may never—exist. Again, some protection was afforded to ameliorate the apparent harshness of this doctrine by allowing the defendant to make a limited appearance and defend on the merits without consenting to full in personam jurisdiction. See § 2–28, below. The judgment remained limited to the face amount of the policy. Further, the New York courts ruled that the plaintiff had to be a resident or the cause of action had to arise in New York before this form of attachment jurisdiction could be asserted.

The two developments just described represent the furthest extensions by the courts using sovereignty as a basis for personal jurisdiction. Perhaps not surprisingly, a majority of states refused to follow the lead of New York in the insurance field, and other courts and commentators suggested that the fairness of asserting jurisdiction under these circumstances was of prime importance. In an era that emphasizes fairness as the lynchpin for the assertion of jurisdiction, see § 2–16, below, theories resting solely on sheer power and fictions regarding the situs of intangibles were problematic.

§ 2–15. Consent

A party always may concede a court's authority to render a binding, enforceable judgment against it. In some cases consent may be explicit, as when it is in a contract. In others notions of waiver act as implied consent. This may occur by the failure of the defendant to comply with the applicable rules governing the methods of raising jurisdictional objections. See § 2–27, below. In the case of a nonresident plaintiff faced with counterclaims, the entry into the forum to institute the action is deemed submission to the state's jurisdiction for purposes of the counterclaim.

Historically, finding that a nonresident defendant had impliedly consented to jurisdiction prior to the filing of a lawsuit served as a prime basis for asserting in personam jurisdiction over a mobile, business citizenry when a strict application of sovereignty principles would not permit jurisdiction. In the corporate field it was held that a state could exclude a nonresident corporation from doing business in the state. Thus, some states enacted legislation requiring out-of-state businesses to consent to jurisdiction as a condition of doing business in the state by appointing an agent in the state to receive process for them. Other states designated a state official in their statutes as the agent for receipt of process for nonresident corporations and provided that all corporations doing business thereafter impliedly consented to suit in the state in actions arising out of their activities there. The fact that a corporation no longer was doing business in the state at the time an action was commenced did not affect the court's jurisdiction because of the corporation's prior implied consent to suit.

But the consent theory had its limitations. For example, when implied consent was used, jurisdiction could be asserted only for causes of action arising out of the business done in the forum state. Jurisdiction based on express consent was not so limited. However, in that situation, the termination of corporate activities within the state acted as a negation of consent and jurisdiction no longer could be asserted even in suits directly arising out of forum state activities of the corporation before it left the state. It does not, however, violate due process to require a corporation to consent to personal jurisdiction in order to do business in that state. Mallory v. Norfolk Southern Railway Co., 600 U.S. 122 (2023).

In cases involving individuals, implied consent became an important justification for the assertion of jurisdiction over nonresident motorists who were alleged to have harmed resident plaintiffs. Utilizing their state police power (a direct manifestation of state sovereignty), states enacted nonresident motorist or single-act statutes, authorizing their courts to assert in personam jurisdiction over nonresident defendants when their sole contact with the state was the accident giving rise to the action and a resident plaintiff was injured. The fiction utilized was that the defendant had impliedly consented to jurisdiction by driving on the highways once the long-arm statute had been enacted. Hess v. Pawloski, 274 U.S. 352 (1927). Later decisions expanded the application of these statutes to cases involving nonresident plaintiffs. Despite the movement away from utilizing fictions as the basis for asserting jurisdiction, these statutes remain valid today because the limited type of jurisdiction they authorize should be permissible even under more modern jurisdictional theories. See § 2–20, below.

b. Modern Standards

§ 2–16. The In Personam Wing: Minimum Contacts, "Fair Play and Substantial Justice"

With the increasing movement of individuals between states and the expansion of corporate activities on a national scale, the limitations of the sovereignty and consent theories became apparent. Although courts continued to rely on expanding sovereignty notions as the means of supporting in rem and quasi-in-rem jurisdiction, increased emphasis was placed on more general due process principles as providing the major limitation on a court's power to assert in personam jurisdiction over a nonresident outside its state's borders.

The Supreme Court enunciated the principles underlying this due process approach for in personam jurisdiction in International Shoe Co. v. Washington, 326 U.S. 310 (1945). The Court's test was that the defendant should have sufficient "minimum contacts" with the forum state so that traditional notions of "fair play and substantial justice" would not be offended by the assertion of jurisdiction there.

This International Shoe standard evolved into a two-pronged test. First, minimum contacts must be shown; and second, the court must find that the forum is a fair one in which the defendant will have a full opportunity to be heard. While these two determinations necessarily overlap, they have independent significance and meeting one will not justify ignoring the other. For example, the fact that the forum state is convenient because many of the witnesses and parties are there does not in itself warrant the assertion of jurisdiction. The court still must find that the defendant has the requisite minimum contacts with the state to support jurisdiction. Indeed, the importance of the minimum contacts portion of the International Shoe standard was underscored in World-Wide Volkswagen Corp. v. Woodson, 444 U.S. 286 (1980), when the Supreme Court characterized the minimum contacts inquiry as a threshold question. The failure to cross that threshold meant that various facts suggesting that the particular forum chosen was fair or convenient were irrelevant.

Additional content has been given to the meaning of "minimum contacts" by numerous Supreme Court decisions since International Shoe. The Court has noted repeatedly that the defendant's contact with the forum must be purposeful—the court must be able to find that the defendant has purposefully availed himself of the privilege of conducting some activity in the state, thereby invoking the benefits and protections of state law. Hanson v. Denckla, 357 U.S. 235 (1958). The need to show purposeful conduct has proved a significant barrier to the assertion of jurisdiction in numerous cases. For example, a divorced father who cooperated with his children's desire to go to live with their mother was not subject to jurisdiction in the mother's state in a suit for child custody and increased child support. Sending the children to the mother was not deemed a purposeful act; it was mere acquiescence in their request. Further, the father derived no economic benefit from the forum state as a result of the change. Kulko v. Superior Court, 436 U.S. 84 (1978). And in an Oklahoma case arising out of a car accident in the forum state, the Supreme Court ruled that jurisdiction could not be asserted over the New York auto retailer and the regional distributor because neither of those defendants had purposefully attempted to serve the Oklahoma market. It was not sufficient that they might derive revenue and benefit from the fact that the cars they marketed were mobile and thus could be used in Oklahoma. The unilateral activity of the plaintiff car owners in driving to Oklahoma could not be used to suggest a benefit that would sustain jurisdiction—it was the defendant's conduct that was crucial. World-Wide Volkswagen Corp. v. Woodson, 444 U.S. 286 (1980).

On the other hand, although purposeful contact with the forum state is found most easily if the defendant actively conducts business in the state, deliberate activity outside the state that is aimed at obtaining some benefit, albeit indirect, from the forum state may satisfy this part of the International Shoe standard. The Supreme Court in the Volkswagen case stated that personal jurisdiction is proper over a defendant "that delivers its products into the stream of commerce with the expectation that they will be purchased by consumers in the forum State." However, in a later case, Asahi Metal Industry Co. v. Superior Court, 480 U.S. 102 (1987), the Court was evenly divided on the question whether it was necessary to show "something more than that the defendant was aware of its product's entry into the forum State through the stream of commerce." The Court again failed to develop an agreed-upon approach to contacts that occur via the stream of commerce in its more recent decision in J. McIntyre Machinery, Ltd. v. Nicastro, 564 U.S. 873 (2011).

Under either view, the rationale for finding sufficient contact is that the defendant's conduct outside the state is of such a character that the defendant should reasonably foresee that if its product malfunctions in the forum state, it may be subject to suit where the problem occurred. Thus, the conduct of the defendant outside the state must be examined carefully to determine if it was of such a character that defendant should have foreseen having to defend in the forum state.

The quality and purposefulness of the defendant's contact with the state is related not only to foreseeability, but also to the notion that the defendant has obtained some benefit or privilege from the forum state so that it is fair to require the defendant to defend suit there. For example, in a products liability setting such as the Volkswagen case, the local retailer might reasonably foresee that a purchaser may drive the car to another state. But, in contrast to the manufacturer, it has done nothing itself to try to benefit economically from business with other states' citizens. Consequently, it cannot be held accountable in distant fora where the product later malfunctions.

Although reference to the defendant's foreseeability in being sued in the forum state may seem to inject a complex subjective inquiry into the minimum contacts standard, this is not necessarily so. First, as just noted, foreseeability may be satisfied easily if it is coupled with purposeful conduct outside the forum designed to somehow derive benefits from the forum state. This may be true, for example, when an intentional tort is involved. E.g., Calder v. Jones, 465 U.S. 783 (1984). However, the fact that the defendant knew that the plaintiff resided in the forum state and suffered injury there is insufficient in itself if the defendant had no other contacts with the state and did not derive any benefits from the state. Walden v. Fiore, 571 U.S. 277 (2014). In contrast, when an out-of-state party deliberately seeks and negotiates a long-term contract, envisioning continuing contacts with the forum, it is foreseeable that it would have to defend a suit there involving a dispute arising out of that contract. Burger King Corp. v. Rudzewicz, 471 U.S. 462 (1985).

Finally, it must be remembered that even if the conduct of a defendant is shown to have crossed the minimum contacts threshold, jurisdiction still may not be upheld unless the court is able to find that its assertion is consistent with notions of fair play and substantial justice. No one factor is determinative. Keeton v. Hustler Magazine, Inc., 465 U.S. 770 (1984) (fact that plaintiff is a nonresident and chose the forum because of uniquely long statute of limitations is not determinative). Rather, the court will consider a number of factors, including the forum state's interest in regulating the activity involved or in providing a forum for its residents; the relative convenience to the parties of the tribunal chosen in terms of the witnesses, evidence and general location, as well as whether an alternative forum exists; the desire to avoid a multiplicity of lawsuits; and any other factor bearing on the fairness of the chosen forum. In one case, the Supreme Court found jurisdiction to be unreasonable in light of the special burdens imposed on foreign defendants, particularly when the forum state had only a minimal interest in the litigation. Asahi Metal Industry Co. v. Superior Court, 480 U.S. 102 (1987).

Necessarily, then, the International Shoe standard as refined by the Supreme Court in its later decisions requires a detailed analysis of the facts in each case in order to decide whether the assertion of jurisdiction is constitutional. The standard applies to both individual and corporate defendants. Because of its flexibility, it allows the courts to take into account the extra burdens that may result from broad extensions of jurisdiction, without requiring specialized rules for any particular defendant.

§ 2-17. Application of Minimum Contacts Test: Some Examples

The question of the kind and sufficiency of contacts needed to satisfy the International Shoe threshold as well as whether in a given case those contacts, when balanced against the other reasonableness factors, will support jurisdiction cannot always be answered precisely. Nonetheless, some examples will highlight the relevant considerations.

If a corporation or an individual is continuously and systematically entering the state and the cause of action arises out of those in-state activities, then jurisdiction is proper. International Shoe Co. v. Washington, 326 U.S. 310 (1945). Not only are the contacts substantial, but also the forum usually will be convenient for all concerned as the witnesses, evidence, and governing law will be there. This also may be true when the cause of action arises outside the state, but out of activities that occurred within the state. Cornelison v. Chaney, 127 Cal.Rptr. 352, 545 P.2d 264 (1976). At the opposite end of the spectrum, if the defendant's contacts are only sporadic and the cause of action does not arise out of them, whether it arises within or without the state, minimum contacts will not be found and jurisdiction will not be allowed regardless of the convenience of the forum. Hanson v. Denckla, 357 U.S. 235 (1958).

In evaluating cases that fall between these two extremes, the Supreme Court has articulated an important distinction between "general jurisdiction" and "specific jurisdiction." Helicopteros Nacionales de Colombia, S.A. v. Hall, 466 U.S. 408 (1984). General jurisdiction permits a defendant to be sued for any and all claims, regardless of whether the claim is connected to the defendant's activity in the forum state. Specific jurisdiction does not require as high a level of contacts with the forum state, but the claim must arise out of or relate to those contacts.

Specific jurisdiction has been upheld based on a single act of the defendant. This occurs, for example, in the case of nonresident motorists who have an auto accident in the forum state causing an injury there, or in a contract dispute in which one of the contracting parties resides in the forum state and the contract involved is the only one into which the nonresident defendant has entered. In the former case, the interest of the state in providing a forum for its resident plaintiff and regulating its highways coupled with the fact that the defendant purposefully entered the state, and the convenience of the forum insofar as the evidence is concerned, permits the assertion of jurisdiction consistent with notions of fair play. Hess v. Pawloski, 274 U.S. 352 (1927). In the latter situation, the type of contract involved, the amount of activities the defendant undertook in the state in connection with the contract, and a finding that the defendant purposefully entered the state in order to make the contract may justify the assertion of jurisdiction even though only a single contract is involved. McGee v. International Life Ins. Co., 355 U.S. 220 (1957) (insurance contract).

However, in contract disputes the decision whether the International Shoe standard has been met in single-act cases often requires a very complex inquiry. Thus, the Supreme Court has noted that in contract actions it is not appropriate to determine jurisdiction by attempting to identify an artificial locus of the contract. Rather, the question whether minimum contacts are satisfied depends upon an inquiry into the facts surrounding the prior negotiations and their contemplated future consequences, the terms of the contract, and the parties' actual course of dealing. Burger King Corp. v. Rudzewicz, 471 U.S. 462 (1985).

General jurisdiction requires a different analysis. In the International Shoe decision itself, the Supreme Court recognized that the continuous activity of a defendant in the forum state may be of such a nature that the defendant may be subject to jurisdiction even upon causes of action unrelated to the forum activity. But purposeful activities in or directed at the forum state are not necessarily enough for general jurisdiction. Helicopteros Nacionales de Colombia, S.A. v. Hall, 466 U.S. 408 (1984). Thus, the sales of a defendant's tires in North Carolina were not deemed enough to sustain general jurisdiction there over a claim for an injury caused in France by tires purchased in the European market.

Goodyear Dunlop Tires Operations, S.A. v. Brown, 564 U.S. 915 (2011).

The Supreme Court has clarified that general jurisdiction requires the defendant's contacts to be "so 'continuous and systematic'" that it is "essentially at home in the forum state." Daimler AG v. Bauman, 571 U.S. 117 (2014). Additionally, the Court stated that to determine whether a defendant is "at home" in the forum, the court must consider not only the defendant's in-state contacts, but all its corporate activities nationwide and world-wide because a corporation operating in many places cannot be deemed to be at home in all of them. BNSF Railway Co. v. Tyrrell, 581 U.S. 402 (2017) (interstate railroad not within general jurisdiction). And in cases involving parent and subsidiary corporations, the in-state activities of one of those entities will not be sufficient to subject the other entity to general jurisdiction on claims unrelated to the in-state forum activities. Goodyear Dunlop Tires Operations v. Brown, 564 U.S. 915 (2011); Daimler AG v. Bauman, 571 U.S. 117 (2014). When, however, a corporation has consented to general jurisdiction—such as through a state law requiring such consent to do business in the state—it does not violate the Due Process Clause to assert jurisdiction based on that consent, even if the corporation's contacts would not otherwise meet the "essentially at home" standard. See § 2–15, above (discussing Mallory v. Norfolk Southern Railway Co., 600 U.S. 122 (2023)).

The high bar for obtaining general jurisdiction has made it especially important to determine whether a defendant's contacts must be evaluated under a general-jurisdiction or a specific-jurisdiction standard. Specific jurisdiction is available only when there is an affiliation or connection between the forum and the lawsuit, such as when the suit arises out of our relates to the defendant's contacts with the forum. It is not appropriate to use a "sliding scale" approach to specific jurisdiction by which the strength of the relationship between the specific claim and the defendant's state contacts may be lessened if the defendant otherwise has numerous contacts with the state unrelated to the claim. Bristol-Myers Squibb Co. v. Superior Court, 582 U.S. 255 (2017). In the Bristol-Myers case, the Court found that specific jurisdiction did not exist in California over claims by out-of-state consumers against the defendant drug manufacturer, even though it had significant operations in California. The manufacturer's contacts with California were not sufficient to establish general jurisdiction, and the claims by out-of-state consumers lacked a sufficient relationship to California.

In Ford Motor Co. v. Montana Eighth Judicial District Court, 592 U.S. 351 (2021), however, the Court clarified that claims may "relate to" the defendant's contacts with the forum—and therefore justify specific jurisdiction—even if the plaintiff's claim was not caused by the defendant's in-state conduct. Specific jurisdiction requires a "connection" between the suit and the defendant's activities, but "a strict causal relationship between the defendant's in-state activity and the litigation" is not required. Thus, specific jurisdiction applied to a manufacturer that had systematically served the market for automobiles in the forum state, in a lawsuit arising out of an accident occurring in that state, even though the particular vehicle involved in the accident had been purchased initially in a different state.

Finally, it should be noted that even when suit is brought in a federal court, the assessment of whether sufficient minimum contacts exist often looks only to contacts related to the state where the federal court is located—not the defendant's nationwide contacts. Omni Capital Int'l v. Rudolf Wolff & Co., 484 U.S. 97 (1987). This is because—absent independent statutory or rule-based authority for personal jurisdiction—personal jurisdiction in a federal district depends on the principles that would govern in state court. See Fed.Rule 4(k)(1)(A).

Contacts with the state are not required, however, when jurisdiction is based on a federal rule or statute—for example, when a federal long-arm statute authorizes nationwide service of process, see § 2–12, above, or if the action arises under federal law and the defendant is not otherwise subject to the general jurisdiction of any state, see § 2–11, above (discussing Fed.Rule 4(k)(2)). In these situations, the constitutionality of personal jurisdiction is governed by the Fifth Amendment Due Process Clause, not the Fourteenth Amendment Due Process Clause that applies to state courts. The Supreme Court has declined "to import the Fourteenth Amendment minimum contacts standard into the Fifth Amendment," holding instead that the Fifth Amendment "necessarily permits a more flexible jurisdictional inquiry commensurate with the Federal Government's broader sovereign authority." Fuld v. Palestine Liberation Organization, 606 U.S. 1 (2025). The Fuld decision did not specify a particular test for determining the "outer bounds" of permissible jurisdiction under the Fifth Amendment.

§ 2-18. Minimum Contacts as Applied to In Rem and Quasi-In-Rem Cases

In 1977 the Supreme Court decided Shaffer v. Heitner, 433 U.S. 186 (1977), and adopted minimum contacts, fair play, and substantial justice as the constitutional standard governing in rem and quasi-in-rem jurisdiction. No longer is it sufficient to invoke jurisdiction merely by attaching property in the forum state. Instead, the focus is on whether the defendant's due-process rights are infringed by the court's assertion of jurisdiction. A close look at how the Court applied due process to the facts of Shaffer helps to understand how the standard operates in other cases.

The case was a shareholder-derivative action brought in Delaware against a corporation, Greyhound, and several of its present and former officers and directors. The corporation was incorporated in Delaware, but its principal place of business was Arizona. None of the individual defendants resided in Delaware. The plaintiff alleged that the corporation, while under the guidance of the individual defendants, had engaged in some activities in Oregon that had resulted in damages and fines against it for violating the antitrust laws.

Those damages and fines were to the ultimate detriment of the corporation and the plaintiff, as a shareholder, sought relief for the damage caused to the corporation by the individual defendants' authorization of the illegal activities. In order to obtain jurisdiction over the nonresident individuals, the plaintiff utilized the state sequestration statute and, invoking a Delaware law declaring the situs of all stock in Delaware corporations to be in that state, seized approximately 82,000 shares of stock belonging to those individual defendants by placing stop-transfer orders on the books of the corporation. The lower Delaware courts upheld this assertion of quasi-in-rem jurisdiction, but the Supreme Court reversed.

Applying the International Shoe standard, the Court ruled that the presence of property in the state was not sufficient in and of itself to support jurisdiction. The cause of action was deemed not related to that property because the defendants' stock ownership was not directly tied to their fiduciary relationship to the corporation. Therefore, additional contacts were necessary. The Court noted that Delaware had not manifested any particular state interest in regulating the defendants' conduct by asserting jurisdiction over them because its sequestration statute was a general one, not designed specifically for the regulation of its corporations and their officers. Finally, it concluded that even if Delaware had manifested a strong state interest and minimum contacts were established, Delaware was not a fair forum in which to hear the dispute. The individual defendants had never purposefully availed themselves of the opportunity to conduct activities in the state or had anything to do with the state. They had no reason to expect to be brought before a Delaware court since the ownership of stock could not be deemed to imply consent to suit in the state of incorporation. In addition, there was an alternative forum that would not be unfair; presumably the suit could be filed in Arizona, the principal place of business of Greyhound, or Oregon, where the allegedly illegal activity took place.

Although the Shaffer Court made clear that the mere presence of property in the forum no longer suffices to confer jurisdiction there, that fact is not wholly irrelevant. Rather, its presence in the forum may suggest other contacts that are sufficient to permit jurisdiction to be exercised. In particular this is so when the property is directly related to the plaintiff's claim for relief. For example, if the in-state property is itself the subject matter of the dispute, the Shaffer decision indicated that jurisdiction would be proper in light of the close relationship that necessarily exists among the defendant, the forum, and the litigation. The same would be true when the plaintiff's claim relates to rights and obligations arising out of the defendant's ownership of that property—such as when a plaintiff suffers a tortious injury on the defendant's property.

In both of these scenarios, at least with respect to real property, the state's traditional interest in regulating all matters relating to its land is well recognized. Further, because of the tangible, immovable nature of the property, it will be clearly foreseeable to the defendant that jurisdiction might be asserted. The ownership of the property itself will demonstrate that the defendant benefitted from the protection of the laws of the state.

As acknowledged by the Shaffer Court itself, the main impact of applying the International Shoe standard is in those cases in which movable or intangible property is involved, or in which, as in Shaffer, the property is viewed as totally unrelated to the claims being asserted. The nature of the property may suggest that the defendant may not knowingly have entered the state or invoked the protection of its laws and that the defendant's contact with the state is minimal. In these cases the jurisdictional decision must rest on a careful inquiry into the type of contacts the defendant has had with the state, the interest of the forum in the underlying controversy, whether the plaintiff has another forum available that might be more fair, and the actual burden on the defendant in having to litigate in the forum. Similarly, even if the property is secure in the state, it is necessary to find other ties between the defendant, the forum, and the litigation before the assertion of jurisdiction will be deemed fair.

Applying the minimum-contacts standard, it is quite clear that the attachment of a wandering debtor in order to reach another nonresident debtor, without more, no longer will be permissible. For a few years after Shaffer, there was some dispute over whether quasi-in-rem jurisdiction could be asserted in suits brought against a nonresident tortfeasor through the attachment of the defendant's insurance policy. Courts continuing to uphold jurisdiction in this situation focused on three things: (1) the insurance company was clearly doing business in the forum state and actually would be the one conducting the defense of the action; (2) the interest of the state in providing a forum for its injured resident; and (3) the protection afforded the named defendant by allowing a limited appearance restricting defendant's potential liability to the insurance coverage. Ultimately, however, the Supreme Court overruled this form of attachment jurisdiction based on the defendant's lack of minimum contacts with the forum state. Rush v. Savchuk, 444 U.S. 320 (1980).

§ 2-19. Current Utility of the Three Jurisdictional Categories

Although the minimum-contacts standard must be applied to all types of jurisdiction, the tripartite division of jurisdiction into in rem, quasi in rem, and in personam still serves some useful purposes. On a purely practical level, it helps to identify what is in issue and what contacts may be most relevant. Illustratively, in the pure in rem suit an analysis of whether the facts of the case fit the traditional quiet-title pattern typically will demonstrate simultaneously that the constitutional standard has been met.

Quasi-in-rem jurisdiction also remains a separate and useful jurisdictional category. In those states that do not have long-arm statutes authorizing the assertion of extraterritorial jurisdiction to the furthest constitutional limits, the plaintiff's case may not fit within the specific categories set out in the statute. Even though sufficient minimum contacts could be found to meet due-process concerns, the absence of an applicable long-arm statute prohibits the assertion of in personam jurisdiction. But if an attachment statute exists and the defendant owns some property that is in the state, quasi-in-rem jurisdiction will be permissible. In quasi-in-rem actions the judgment is limited to the value of the property, and, in many instances, the defendant will be allowed to enter and defend on the merits without submitting to the in personam jurisdiction of the court. See § 2–28, below.

Having said that quasi-in-rem jurisdiction still may have some independent use, it must be acknowledged that the expansion of in personam jurisdiction since International Shoe and the imposition of a minimum-contacts standard in Shaffer has diminished its utility. Indeed, in the federal courts, 1993 amendments to the federal rules authorize quasi-in-rem jurisdiction only when personal jurisdiction cannot be asserted utilizing regular service of process. Fed.Rule 4(n)(2).

§ 2–20. Current Viability of Consent, Domicile, and Transient Jurisdiction Theories

Given the sweeping language in Shaffer v. Heitner to the effect that all forms of jurisdiction must meet the International Shoe standard, some questions can be raised about the viability of some of the other traditional bases of jurisdiction that do not rest on a minimum-contacts analysis. In particular, can jurisdiction continue to be premised on the defendant's consent, domicile, or transient presence in the forum state without any additional contacts?

In the case of jurisdiction resting on consent or domicile, the answer is clearly yes. The Supreme Court's invocation of minimum contacts is for the purpose of establishing constitutional limits on the states' assertions of jurisdiction; essentially the standard balances the rights of the forum state and the defendant and suggests when a defendant legitimately may object to defending in a particular forum. But the defendant need not object if the defendant does not want to. Thus the right of the defendant to consent to jurisdiction is not incompatible with the Shaffer Court's pronouncements.

For different reasons jurisdiction premised on the defendant's domicile also remains constitutional. The premise of domicile jurisdiction is that it always is fair to make a person amenable to suit where domiciled; the very determination of domicile suggests that the defendant has some continuing and permanent ties to the state and thus could foresee being sued there. Although there may be cases today in which an individual may be changing domiciles and the invocation of the traditional rule might seem unfair, in the vast majority of cases, domicile will remain a sufficient contact on which to base jurisdiction. The Supreme Court has referred to domicile as the "paradigm" forum for general jurisdiction over a natural person. Goodyear Dunlop Tires Operations, S.A. v. Brown, 564 U.S. 915 (2011).

The traditional form of jurisdiction that seems most incompatible with the minimum-contacts approach is that premised on the mere transient presence of the defendant. Transient jurisdiction rests on the territoriality principles espoused in Pennoyer v. Neff and the state's sovereign power over all persons and things within its borders. After Shaffer, those principles generally were viewed as rejected. Thus, although the temporary physical presence of a person within the forum is a contact with the state, in the absence of any other contacts between the defendant, the forum, and the litigation, the propriety of jurisdiction in those cases was questioned.

The Supreme Court addressed the continued viability of transient jurisdiction in Burnham v. Superior Court, 495 U.S. 604 (1990), unanimously upholding California's assertion of jurisdiction over a New Jersey resident who was served with process in a divorce action while in the state to conduct business and visit his children. The justices did not all agree as to why due process was satisfied, however. Some found it sufficient to rely on the strong history and tradition supporting transient jurisdiction, and others determined that the in-state service rule satisfied fairness standards. Regardless, it now is clear that tagging the defendant in the forum state, without more, remains a legitimate and constitutional means of obtaining jurisdiction over a nonresident defendant—at least if the defendant is voluntarily present in the forum when service occurs.

3. OTHER JURISDICTIONAL CONSTRAINTS

§ 2-21. Notice

Even if a case meets both the statutory and constitutional requirements for personal jurisdiction, the suit may be dismissed or the judgment collaterally attacked if insufficient notice was given to the defendant. The defendant can claim that the proceeding violated due process because without proper notice there was no effective opportunity to be heard. What constitutes sufficient notice to satisfy the Constitution involves an inquiry into both the type of notice utilized and the timing of the notice. The latter element ensures that the opportunity to be heard is a realistic one; it is discussed in § 6–4, below. The type of notice goes to the heart of whether a defendant has any opportunity to defend at all.

In in personam cases, individual service of process is the best means of ensuring actual notice and thus a favored way of obtaining jurisdiction. Similarly, although the historic rule in in rem proceedings was that attachment of the property plus publication was a sufficient means of notifying the defendant, the modern rule is that individual notice must be sent when the identity and location of the defendant is known. Walker v. City of Hutchison, 352 U.S. 112 (1956).

Individual notice is not a constitutional prerequisite to all actions; the type of notice that must be utilized is decided on a case-by-case basis. The key in all cases, regardless of the type of jurisdiction involved, is what is practicable, with the emphasis on utilizing the means of notice that is most likely to reach the defendant. When determining what type of notice to require, the court also may consider the difficulties (cost, as well as impracticability) of locating the defendant and the need for the adjudication. Mullane v. Central Hanover Bank & Trust Co., 339 U.S. 306 (1950). Applying this standard, the Supreme Court has held that if the defendant's address may be ascertained by reasonably diligent efforts, publication will not suffice and individual notice must be utilized. Tulsa Professional Collection Servs., Inc. v. Pope, 485 U.S. 478 (1988); Mennonite Bd. of Missions v. Adams, 462 U.S. 791 (1983). Posting notice on residential property rather than using first-class mail also has been deemed insufficient when mailed notice was more likely to reach the defendant. Greene v. Lindsey, 456 U.S. 444 (1982).

Finally, although the defendant may attack a judgment on the ground that insufficient notice was given, a defect in the mere formalities or techniques of giving notice will not render the judgment constitutionally suspect. See § 2–31, below. Further, a party always can waive the right to notice by contract. National Equipment Rental, Ltd. v. Szukhent, 375 U.S. 311 (1964). In the absence of some evidence that the waiver was unknowing or involuntary, it will not be deemed violative of due process. D.H. Overmyer Co. v. Frick Co., 405 U.S. 174 (1972) (waiver to jurisdiction, notice, and service of process deemed constitutional).

§ 2-22. Other Constitutional Limits

Most of the decisions in the area of personal jurisdiction have involved an elaboration of the meaning of due process as contained in the minimum-contacts standard and as required to provide adequate notice and an opportunity to be heard. A few other constitutional limits on what otherwise would be a proper exercise of jurisdiction have been suggested, however.

An essential element of due process is the notion that the court before whom the parties are appearing has the power to assure that once a judgment is rendered the defendant will not be subject to double or multiple liability in another court. If the court cannot provide this assurance, and an alternative forum exists where all the interested parties can be joined, then the suit must be dismissed on the defendant's motion even though all other jurisdictional prerequisites are met. For example, a Pennsylvania action to escheat funds held by Western Union as uncollected money orders was dismissed when the Pennsylvania court could not obtain jurisdiction over all the other states that also might claim the funds and thus could not protect the defendant against subsequent liability to those states for the same funds. An alternate forum, the Supreme Court, was available and could provide this protection. Western Union Tel. Co. v. Pennsylvania, 368 U.S. 71 (1961).

A serious problem is presented when no forum exists in which all interested litigants may be joined. The Supreme Court has ruled that the desire to protect the defendant from multiple liability does not permit the court to bind absent persons to a judgment, if they are not otherwise within the court's personal jurisdiction reach. If personal jurisdiction is not obtained over those absent parties, then the defendant may suffer having to pay twice. New York Life Ins. Co. v. Dunlevy, 241 U.S. 518 (1916). In order to avoid this occurrence, some courts have applied the minimum-contacts standard so as to stretch their personal jurisdiction reach to ensure that all the pertinent parties are before the court. E.g., Atkinson v. Superior Court, 316 P.2d 960 (Cal.1957). Notice requirements also have been construed in a more flexible manner when requiring individual notice would prevent the suit from being maintained and there is no alternative means of settling as a final matter defendant's potential liability. See, e.g., Mullane v. Central Hanover Bank & Trust Co., 339 U.S. 306 (1950).

A few lower courts relied on the interstate commerce clause as a separate limitation on the exercise of extraterritorial jurisdiction by a state. An attempted assertion of jurisdiction was held to have a direct and negative impact on interstate commerce—discouraging it because of a liberal long-arm statute. Thus, jurisdiction was denied even though the forum appeared to be a fair one under a due-process standard. Erlanger Mills, Inc. v. Cohoes Fibre Mills, Inc., 239 F.2d 502 (4th Cir.1956). A majority of courts have not adopted this standard, however, and it has not had any significant impact on the expansion of personal jurisdiction. In the Supreme Court's decision in Mallory v. Norfolk

Southern Railway Co., 600 U.S. 122 (2023) (discussed in § 2–15, above), one Justice argued that "there is a good prospect" that a state law requiring that a corporation consent to general personal jurisdiction in order to do business in that state would violate the Commerce Clause. The Supreme Court did not decide that question, however, leaving it for consideration on remand.

Some lower courts also invoked the First Amendment to limit assertions of jurisdiction in libel actions against nonresident publishers. E.g., New York Times Co. v. Connor, 365 F.2d 567 (5th Cir.1966). These courts held that a higher than ordinary threshold of minimum contacts had to be crossed in libel actions against the media because of the danger that forcing publishers to defend in a distant and inconvenient forum could have a chilling effect on free speech. The Supreme Court subsequently made it clear, however, that First Amendment concerns are not properly part of the jurisdictional inquiry. Calder v. Jones, 465 U.S. 783 (1984).

Thus, jurisdiction limitations arising out of constitutional clauses other than the Due Process Clause have not really developed. Rather, the Supreme Court has restricted jurisdiction primarily through additional refinements to its minimum-contacts standard.

4. SERVICE OF PROCESS—THE MEANS OF ASSERTING JURISDICTION

§ 2–23. Types of Service

Local statutes of the state in which suit is brought determine what type of service may be authorized in the state courts. Federal Rule 4 sets out the general rules governing how process is served in federal court actions, and it also authorizes the federal courts to make use of any applicable state law methods. Fed.Rule 4(e)(1). Federal courts may utilize the procedure set out in state long-arm statutes, or in state attachment statutes for actions based on quasi-in-rem jurisdiction. Special rules are provided in Federal Rule 4(f) and in treaties with specific countries as to how service is to be accomplished outside United States borders.

In general there are three types of service—actual, substituted, and constructive. When actual service is utilized, in-hand delivery of the summons and complaint is made. In the case of a corporate or governmental defendant, the statutes frequently denominate the person who is authorized to receive actual service. For corporations this often is the company's general or managing agent, Fed.Rule 4(h)(1)(B); for governments it may be a designated official, such as the United States attorney in the district in which suit is brought, Fed.Rule 4(i)(1).

Substituted service embraces a wide variety of means of notifying the defendant of the action without personal delivery of the summons and complaint. Most state long-arm statutes, for example, provide for process to be sent to the defendant by registered mail. Attachment statutes also provide a means of substituted service in that they typically authorize the seizure of the property, with notice being mailed to the owner. More directly, a defendant may denominate an in-state person to receive actual process, with mailed notice being sent to the defendant. Process also may be delivered to the defendant's home and left with a person "of suitable age and discretion who resides there." Fed.Rule 4(e)(2)(B). Finally, in an effort to avoid costs associated with service, Federal Rule 4(d) provides a procedure by which the plaintiff can simply notify the defendant of the commencement of the action and request the defendant to waive service of a summons. If the defendant does not comply with the request and cannot show good cause for that failure, the court must impose the costs incurred in effecting service.

Constructive service—service by publication—historically was the primary means of service of process on out-of-state defendants in in rem jurisdiction cases. Since the main purpose of service of process is to ensure that the defendant is notified of the action, constructive service may be permitted only when other more direct means of notice, such as mailing, are not possible. McDonald v. Mabee, 243 U.S. 90 (1917). Thus, if the defendant's whereabouts are unknown, and there is no domicile to which process can be delivered, then service by publication may be allowed. E.g., Cal.Civ.Proc.Code § 415.50.

§ 2–24. Impermissible Use of Service

In general the courts have allowed process servers to employ whatever means necessary to complete personal service on recalcitrant defendants. However, if the means used not only induced the defendant to accept service, but also enticed the defendant into the forum state and the only basis for the court's personal jurisdiction is transient jurisdiction resting on service in the state, then the suit may be dismissed. Further, if a default judgment is entered, it may be collaterally attacked on the ground that jurisdiction was obtained by fraud. This challenge will be upheld even though it does not involve a constitutional defect in the original judgment because the courts will not validate jurisdiction that is obtained by improper or false means.

§ 2–25. Immunity from Process

There are certain circumstances when service of process cannot be effectuated on a potential defendant who is physically present in the state. In order to encourage active participation in judicial proceedings so as to have full and fair trials, courts typically have granted immunity from process to all trial participants who otherwise would be outside the court's jurisdictional reach. The one exception to this rule is in the case of counterclaims against a nonresident plaintiff. Immunity is not given in that situation because, by instituting the action, the plaintiff has submitted to the court's jurisdiction. Immunity protects nonresident attorneys, parties, and witnesses from being served with process in an unrelated action while in attendance or in transit to a trial—criminal or civil—within the state. It also has been extended to cover persons who were within the state for the sole purpose of discussing an out-of-court settlement.

Since immunity from process is premised on a desire to encourage nonresidents to enter the state voluntarily when they otherwise could remain outside, it does not apply if the potential defendant entered the state before any action was brought but subsequently was detained involuntarily and then served with process. Similarly, the doctrine is of no utility if the person is subject to the extraterritorial long-arm jurisdiction of the court because, under the circumstances, the defendant could not prevent service merely by staying outside the state's borders. Thus, with the great expansion of long-arm jurisdiction in recent years, immunity from process has become a doctrine of decreasing utility for parties wanting to resist jurisdiction, although it still may play an important role for witnesses.

D. CHALLENGE TO THE PLAINTIFF'S SELECTION

1. DIRECT ATTACK

§ 2–26. Subject-Matter Jurisdiction

Because issues of subject-matter jurisdiction address the court's constitutional or statutory power to entertain a particular controversy, they involve questions concerning the very nature of the court itself and are not matters of personal right. Thus, an objection to subject-matter jurisdiction can be made at any time throughout the proceedings; it even may be raised for the first time on appeal. Consistent with this flexibility, a party may raise this defense either in the responsive pleading or by a separate motion to dismiss. Fed.Rule 12(b). Further, the court has an independent obligation to inquire into its subject-matter jurisdiction and may raise any issues relating thereto on its own at the trial or appellate level. In sum, there are no real restrictions on raising a subject-matter jurisdiction defense during the course of the proceedings to which the objection is being made.

When a subject-matter jurisdiction objection is combined either with a personal jurisdiction challenge or an attack on the merits, the court must decide the jurisdictional issues prior to ruling on the merits. Steel Co. v. Citizens for a Better Environment, 523 U.S. 83 (1998). The court may determine a personal jurisdiction challenge and dismiss the action without ruling on the subject-matter jurisdiction question, at least where the case involves "a straightforward personal jurisdiction issue presenting no complex question of state law, and the alleged defect in subject-matter jurisdiction raises a difficult and novel question." Ruhrgas AG v. Marathon Oil Co., 526 U.S. 574 (1999).

§ 2-27. Personal Jurisdiction

Because issues of personal jurisdiction are tied to the personal due-process rights of the defendant, the defendant can waive objections to the court's jurisdictional power. Consent to jurisdiction may occur prior to any suit being filed. See § 2–15, above. After an action is brought, however, except in the rare circumstance in which the defendant makes a formal statement waiving all personal jurisdiction objections, it is necessary to establish some means by which the court can ascertain when the defendant has participated in the proceedings to such a degree that it would be appropriate to hold that the defendant impliedly has waived any objections and consents to jurisdiction. The method commonly used is to establish special rules governing how defendants can object to personal jurisdiction. The failure to comply with the procedures established is deemed consent.

One method of challenging the court's personal jurisdiction is by special appearance. Many states require a defendant who wishes to object to personal jurisdiction to enter a "special appearance" prior to answering on the merits. In order to preserve this objection, the defendant typically is not permitted to introduce any other defenses prior to or at the time of making the special appearance. A defendant who does so will be deemed to have made a general appearance and to have waived the right to object to jurisdiction. The sole exception involves objections to the court's subject-matter jurisdiction; the defendant may join objections to the court's subject-matter jurisdiction with personal jurisdiction objections without making a general appearance.

If, when ruling on defendant's jurisdiction objection, the court finds that personal jurisdiction does not exist, the suit will be dismissed. However, if it rules against the defendant, then the question presented is whether the defendant waives the right to object on appeal by continuing to defend on the merits. In states allowing appeals only from final judgments, the defendant's objection is preserved by making the initial special appearance and the defendant may raise the objection anew on a direct appeal from any adverse final judgment on the merits. In other states that provide for some sort of interlocutory appeal, the defendant waives the objection by failing immediately to appeal the court's ruling before defending on the merits and, in that event, will not be allowed to raise the jurisdiction issue on an appeal from the final judgment. In either case, once the defendant enters a special appearance and receives an adverse ruling, the only means of obtaining further review is by a direct appeal; the defendant cannot subsequently default and attempt to collaterally attack the judgment on personal jurisdiction grounds. See § 2–31, below.

The distinction between general and special appearances has been abolished in the federal courts and in those states that have adopted the federal rules. Instead of requiring the defendant to make a special appearance in order to object to personal jurisdiction, the defendant may raise the objection either in a pretrial motion to dismiss or in the answer, Fed.Rule 12(b). Further, other objections may be raised at the same time. The defendant's options are circumscribed primarily by timing constraints. Failing to include a personal jurisdiction defense in a pretrial motion raising other defenses, Fed.Rule 12(g), or failing to include the defense in the answer when no pretrial motions have been made, Fed.Rule 12(h)(1), will result in the waiver of the defense. As in the case of a special appearance, however, once a timely objection has been made, it may be raised again on a direct appeal, but it cannot be the basis for a collateral attack.

§ 2-28. Limited Appearances

In actions based on quasi-in-rem jurisdiction, a desire to give the defendant an opportunity to protect the property seized without forcing the defendant to submit to the court's in personam jurisdiction poses a special problem. A number of states adopted the device of a limited appearance in response to this problem. In those states, the defendant making a limited appearance is allowed to defend the action on the merits; if defendant loses, only the property will be forfeited; if defendant wins, no binding effect will be given to the judgment so the plaintiff may sue again in another court in which jurisdiction may be obtained. In states not authorizing a limited appearance, a defendant faced with a proper quasi-in-rem action has two options: (1) default and thereby forfeit the property, or (2) enter to defend on the merits and thereby submit to the court's in personam jurisdiction. Which option is preferable will depend on the value of the attached property as compared to the amount of damages being sought by the plaintiff.

The federal rules do not address the propriety of limited appearances. Thus, in actions brought in the federal courts the availability of the procedure depends on whether the court refers to state law as the governing law on that issue. See § 9–2, below. Because state courts are split on the propriety of making a limited appearance (with the slightly more prevalent view allowing it), it is most important to check the local law where the action is brought to determine its availability.

Perhaps because of the seeming wastefulness of a second trial when the first was fully litigated, a few courts have suggested that binding effect should be given to the specific issues actually decided in the first quasi-in-rem action. However, giving even this limited binding effect to the judgment effectively treats it as in personam, to the detriment of the defendant.

The significance of the limited appearance as a major protection against the seeming harshness of quasi-in-rem jurisdiction clearly has decreased. This form of jurisdiction now must be premised on more than the mere presence of property within the forum state; the court must find that the assertion of jurisdiction, even of this limited scope, satisfies the minimum contacts and fair play and substantial justice criteria. See § 2–18, above. Consequently, the availability of a limited appearance no longer is the sole safeguard against unfairness to a defendant in a quasi-in-rem action.

§ 2–29. Venue and Service of Process

Objections to the court's venue or the means or form of service of process must be made at the outset of the action or they will be waived. Because venue restrictions are designed primarily to identify a convenient forum, the failure of the defendant to raise the lack of venue either in a pretrial motion to dismiss or in the answer will be deemed acquiescence. Indeed, in many instances the remedy for improper venue is not dismissal, but transfer. See § 2–30, below. Service-of-process objections that do not involve the failure to give actual notice or to obtain personal jurisdiction present primarily technical problems dealing with the form or method of process. Thus, defects of that character are waivable unless raised by pretrial motion or in the answer. Further, although it is important to comply with the statutory requirements for service of process, the court often will not dismiss the action if the defect can be corrected by amending the process. As a result, most commonly, motions to quash service or to dismiss because of improper service are joined with motions to dismiss based on a lack of personal jurisdiction. When filed alone, they frequently are dilatory tactics.

§ 2–30. Forum Non Conveniens and Transfer

Even if the forum chosen by the plaintiff meets jurisdictional and venue requirements, there may be circumstances in which a better, more convenient forum exists. Recognizing this, the judicial doctrine of *forum non conveniens* developed, under which the defendant may make a motion to dismiss the action even though the plaintiff's choice of forum meets all statutory and constitutional requirements. The motion is addressed to the court's discretion and will be granted only infrequently, typically when the plaintiff's forum is clearly inconvenient and an alternative forum exists that is a vast improvement. In several states a forum non conveniens dismissal is not allowed whenever the plaintiff or one of the parties is a resident of the forum state; Idaho does not have a forum non conveniens doctrine at all. However, in most instances no single factor will authorize or preclude dismissal as long as an alternative forum exists. There is a strong presumption to honor the plaintiff's forum choice, but the court will balance against that presumption any factors relating to the convenience to all the parties, as well as to the judicial system, in determining whether to honor the plaintiff's forum choice or grant a forum-non dismissal. Piper Aircraft Co. v. Reyno, 454 U.S. 235 (1981). Further, the presumption is much weaker if a foreign plaintiff is involved. Finally, in order to protect the plaintiff, a court granting the motion often will do so only on condition that the defendant consent to suit in the alternative forum.

In the federal court system and within several states, forum non conveniens has been codified in a transfer statute. E.g., 28 U.S.C.A. § 1404. These statutes permit the court to transfer the case to another court where it might have been brought within the same judicial system. Thus, the transferee forum also must meet jurisdiction and venue requirements. Transfer between federal courts also may be to a district to which all the parties have consented. Unlike what occurs on a forum non conveniens motion, however, either party may move to transfer, and the action does not need to be dismissed and then recommenced in the new forum. Indeed, the court can transfer a case on its own motion. Transfer often may be obtained on a lesser showing of inconvenience than would be necessary to grant a forum non conveniens motion. Nonetheless, even in those systems having transfer statutes, forum non conveniens remains an important tool because transfers are limited to courts within the same system. If the defendant wants to change from a federal forum to a court in another country or from one state court to the state courts in another state, a motion to dismiss for forum non conveniens is the appropriate method.

One further difference between forum non conveniens and transfer should be noted. Forum non conveniens is premised on the fact that both the original court and some other court meet all the applicable jurisdiction and venue requirements. Special statutory provisions in the federal system, however, permit transfer even when the original forum was not a proper venue. 28 U.S.C.A. § 1406(a). In addition, the Supreme Court has upheld a transfer when the transferor court had no personal jurisdiction and the statute of limitations had run so that to dismiss the suit for lack of jurisdiction would have resulted in forfeiting the claim. Goldlawr, Inc. v. Heiman, 369 U.S. 463 (1962). This application of the transfer statute typically has been restricted to situations in which the lack of personal jurisdiction was not clear at the outset, so that dismissal would be unduly harsh to the plaintiff.

For both forum non conveniens and transfer, the Supreme Court has adopted a different approach when the defendant bases the motion on a valid forum-selection clause in a contract. In that situation, a federal court must give the plaintiff's forum choice no weight; it must disregard arguments about the parties' private interests; and it must grant the motion to allow the case to proceed in the contractually-selected forum "unless extraordinary circumstances unrelated to the convenience of the parties clearly disfavor a transfer." Atlantic Marine Constr. Co. v. U.S. District Ct. for W. Dist. of Texas, 571 U.S. 49 (2013).

2. COLLATERAL ATTACK

§ 2–31. Principles Governing

When a defendant interposes an objection to the plaintiff's choice of the forum in action A in an action to enforce the judgment obtained in A, or in some other proceeding before another trial court, B, this is called a collateral attack on the judgment in A. The availability of collateral attack is severely restricted because it erodes the finality and stability of judgments. In situations in which action B is in a different court system than A, it violates statutory, 28 U.S.C.A. § 1738, and constitutional principles, Art. IV, § 1, providing that full faith and credit should be given to sister-state judgments. Thus, collateral attack may be available only when the type of objection the defendant raises is of a constitutional dimension; venue objections being merely matters of convenience or service-of-process objections that involve merely the form of the service never can be raised on collateral attack.

The following rules apply to determine when a collateral attack is permitted as a means of raising a subject-matter or personal jurisdiction defense. If the defendant never appears in action A and a default judgment is entered, then the judgment may be collaterally attacked on either ground. If the defendant appears and raises the jurisdiction objections, fully litigating them in the trial court in A, then collateral attack is barred; defendant's only remedy is a direct attack on appeal from the judgment in A.

Special rules apply if the defendant appears in A and defends on the merits without ever challenging either the court's subject-matter jurisdiction or its personal jurisdiction. If defendant fails to raise any objections to personal jurisdiction, collateral attack is not available to later raise the defense. The personal jurisdiction defense was waived by the failure to make a timely objection. See § 2–27, above. The problem of whether to allow collateral attack on subject-matter jurisdiction grounds when the defendant has fully participated in the first proceeding, but failed to raise any objection there, is more complicated because parties cannot consent to the subject-matter jurisdiction of the court.

The few cases that have considered the problem suggest that typically collateral attack will not be available. However, if the policy against the court's acting beyond its jurisdiction is strong, such as when a state court improperly hears matters confined to the exclusive jurisdiction of the federal courts, or when the jurisdictional defect raises problems of sovereign immunity, then a collateral attack may be permitted. Additionally, the court may consider whether the jurisdiction determination depends on a question of law rather than fact or whether the lack of subject-matter jurisdiction was clear. These and other factors designed to aid in balancing the conflicting policies of finality and limited jurisdiction are suggested in Section 10 of the *Restatement Second of Judgments* (1982).

CHAPTER 3

PRETRIAL: FRAMING THE LITIGATION

A. PLEADING

§ 3–1. General Theory of Pleading

The pleadings are the papers by which the litigants first set the case before the court. A thorough study of the art of pleading embraces both procedural and substantive concerns. *How* you plead is a procedural question, depending on the specific rules of the court in which the case is filed. *What* you plead is determined by considerations of substantive law and the knowledge of what facts are legally significant in each context. The primary focus in this book is on the first question. For a more detailed discussion of the art of pleading, see J. Friedenthal, M. Kane, A. Miller & A. Steinman, *Civil Procedure*, Ch. 5 (6th ed.2021).

There have been four historic functions associated with pleading: (1) notice giving; (2) fact revelation; (3) issue formulation; and (4) screening to constrict or expand the flow of litigation in a particular court system. Different procedural systems rely on the pleadings for one or a combination of these purposes. Depending on which of these functions is emphasized, more or less detail may be required and a given pleading may be deemed sufficient or insufficient and subject to dismissal. Thus, it is important to understand the philosophy underlying the pleading system for the court in which suit is brought in order to better understand the level of specificity or degree of flexibility that exists.

§ 3-2. History: Common Law Pleading

Although it is virtually nonexistent in American courts today, common law pleading is the direct antecedent of modern code and federal rule pleading and is important to consider in order to better evaluate the present pleading rules. Pleading in common law courts was characterized by rigid formality and precision; its object was to produce through the pleadings a single issue for trial. A plaintiff could plead only a single cause of action (claim) in each case and the defendant could make only one response. Alternative or multiple defenses were not permitted. The failure to comply with the pleading rules resulted in the dismissal of the action, with no leave to replead. Thus, the course of pleading was perilous and great attention was given to that portion of the proceedings because the pleadings truly acted as a screening device, preventing many cases from going forward. Suits in equity courts were not governed by the same rigid, complex system. Because those proceedings were solely before a judge, joinder of claims and parties was allowed, some discovery was available, and the pleadings did not act as the primary screening device.

A brief description of how common law pleading operated illustrates its formality, as well as pitfalls. In order to bring an action, the plaintiff had to determine which of the existing forms of action best suited the facts of the case and obtain the proper writ (summons) for that form of action. Examples of the historic forms of action are detinue, debt, replevin, covenant, trespass, and trespass on the case. The forms of action were essentially categories of legal liability; if no form of action existed to meet the plaintiff's needs, there was no remedy for the alleged wrong. The use of an improper writ for the alleged wrong resulted in a dismissal with prejudice. Defense counsel were faced with a similar array of carefully defined responses. The defendant could: (1) deny that the facts alleged gave the plaintiff a legal right to relief (a demurrer); (2) enter a dilatory plea challenging the plaintiff's right to have the case heard by the court before whom it was lodged; or (3) enter a plea in bar, denying that the alleged facts were true (a traverse) or arguing that even if the facts were true, other facts rendered the right unenforceable (confession and avoidance). These alternatives were mutually exclusive, even though they are not necessarily contradictory. If the defendant pleaded in confession and avoidance, no issue was joined on the facts and the plaintiff had to respond to the newly introduced facts by demurrer, traverse, or another confession and avoidance. The exchange of pleadings continued until a single issue remained to be tried.

As time passed, the common law pleading system became encrusted with requirements so that actions were won or lost not on the merits, but due to pleading technicalities. The objective of producing a single, clear issue for trial became outweighed by the desire to develop a system more responsive to the needs of the parties and less filled with pitfalls for the unwary. These concerns underlay the development of state pleading codes and ultimately federal rule pleading.

1. PLAINTIFF

§ 3-3. The Complaint: Code Pleading

Following the lead of New York, which adopted the Field Code in 1848, several states enacted statutes to govern the procedures in their courts. These statutes were particularly important because they abolished the common law forms of action and unified law and equity to provide for a single form of action for all claims. The pleading requirements included in those statutes commonly are referred to as code pleading.

Code pleading eradicated much of the extreme formality and resulting pitfalls of common law pleading. It eliminated pleading distinctions between cases at law and those in equity and adopted a uniform set of pleading rules for all actions, regardless of the nature of the substantive cause of action. The function of the pleadings was transformed from one of issue formulation to fact revelation. Under code pleading, it typically is said that the plaintiff has only to plead the facts constituting a cause of action; in other words the plaintiff must plead the facts showing a legal right and wrong. If the allegations fit into some pattern of an established right, the case can continue. But the plaintiff need not identify the precise right involved. This standard is designed to provide notice to the opposing party, as well as to give the court sufficient information to allow it to strike or dismiss legally insufficient claims and avoid useless trials.

Under code pleading, the plaintiff can plead alternatively and even inconsistently, at least when the facts are not all within the plaintiff's knowledge, as long as the pleading is made in good faith. The only other restraint on alternative allegations is that they must be placed in separate counts in the complaint so as to give adequate notice to the defendant. Multiple causes of action may be alleged, as long as they too are placed in separate counts.

Although the codes abandoned the rigid formality of the common law, fact pleading presented its own problems. First, it is difficult to define what constitutes a cause of action. Two views prevail. One, called the primary-rights theory, defines the cause of action in terms of the nature of the injury allegedly suffered. The focus is on the harm caused rather than on the acts that produced the harm or the remedy; the pleader must set forth only all the facts showing each injury. The other view defines a cause of action by the events that give rise to a right to relief and requires the pleader to set forth the "aggregate of operative facts" for which relief is demanded. Difficulty in applying these two views arises because under the primary-rights approach courts do not always agree as to what constitutes a single harm, and under the operative-facts approach there is no focus provided to determine what facts may be sufficiently related, creating the potential for long and complex pleadings.

Another problem under code pleading is determining the level of detailed facts that must be pleaded. It usually has been said that the plaintiff need plead only ultimate facts, not evidentiary facts or legal conclusions. Attempts to delineate the difference between these three terms filled the case reports in code-pleading jurisdictions. In practice, the distinction is primarily one of how much detail is involved. Thus, ultimate facts are those essential to show that the plaintiff has a cause of action. Under a theory of cause of action as the breach of a primary right, the complaint must allege a primary right possessed by the plaintiff, a corresponding duty on the defendant, and the facts showing a wrong by the defendant constituting a breach. Any special damages also must be alleged. Evidentiary facts provide greater detail and legal conclusions are necessarily more general and vague. The pleading of additional evidentiary facts, while improper, generally is harmless and will not result in dismissal. A pleading that is filled only with legal conclusions will be fatally defective, however.

The use of the common counts in some contract cases also is authorized under code pleading, and it provides an exception to the normal degree of specificity that is required. Under the common counts the only allegations that must be alleged are that the pleader is suing for unjust enrichment (money had and received), for labor performed (quantum valebant) or for goods sold and delivered or services rendered but not paid for (quantum meruit). No further facts need be alleged. Thus, in an action based on a common count, there is much less emphasis on the pleadings; indeed, the common counts remain somewhat anomalous in the code-pleading system. One explanation for the tolerance of this general pleading standard is that the type of action involved is really one for restitution, premised on a desire to prevent the defendant from being unjustly enriched; consequently, an action based on the common counts is equitable in nature and historically did not fall within the common law pleading system.

§ 3–4. The Complaint: Federal ("Notice") Pleading

When the Supreme Court promulgated a uniform set of procedural rules for all federal cases in 1938, a key feature of that reform was the adoption of Federal Rule 8, which closely followed the simple equity rules of pleading. The key provision is Rule 8(a)(2), requiring a party to set forth "a short and plain statement of the claim showing that the pleader is entitled to relief." Consistent with this liberal approach, the plaintiff can plead alternatively and inconsistently, even within the same count. Fed.Rule 8(d). Similarly, although the plaintiff must include a demand for relief, Fed.Rule 8(a)(3), the court is not bound by the demand in a contested case and can award whatever relief ultimately is deemed appropriate in light of the evidence. Fed.Rule 54(c). The ad damnum clause limits recovery only in default-judgment situations. Finally, the rules require courts to construe the pleadings so as to do substantial justice. Fed.Rule 8(e).

The only exception to these generally liberal pleading requirements of the federal rules is in some very specific types of cases in which, by special rule, more detail is required. See Fed.Rule 9(b). For example, in fraud actions it is not enough to allege merely that the defendant committed a fraud. Rather, the pleader must allege with particularity the circumstances constituting the fraud. Fraud was a so-called "disfavored" action, which courts had traditionally scrutinized rigorously because of the potential for harassment. To discourage frivolous suits in these areas, a higher pleading threshold applies.

The Supreme Court has made clear that heightened pleading standards may only be applied to those actions identified in Rule 9(b); all other cases are covered by the more general pleading standard of Rule 8. Swierkiewicz v. Sorema N.A., 534 U.S. 506 (2002); Leatherman v. Tarrant County Narcotics Intelligence & Coordination Unit, 507 U.S. 163 (1993). Rule 8's approach came to be known as "notice pleading." In Conley v. Gibson, 355 U.S. 41 (1957), the Supreme Court explained that a plaintiff's complaint does not need "to set out in detail the facts upon which he bases his claim." Rather Rule 8's "short and plain statement" must merely "give the defendant fair notice of what the plaintiff's claim is and the grounds upon which it rests." With this standard, the rulemakers sought to eliminate some of the pleading-motion practice that occurs under the code system in which significant amounts of time and money are spent on technicalities before reaching the merits of the case. In the federal system, the burden of fact revelation is placed on the discovery process, see §§ 3–21—3–33, below, eliminating what often are definitional squabbles at the pleading stage. Of course, one necessary effect of liberalizing the pleading requirements is to lower the threshold for bringing an action in the federal courts.

More recent Supreme Court decisions have created uncertainty about the federal pleading standard, however. In Bell Atlantic Corp. v. Twombly, 550 U.S. 544 (2007), the Court stated that a complaint must allege facts showing that recovery was not merely "conceivable" but that it was "plausible." Two years later, in Ashcroft v. Iqbal, 556 U.S. 662 (2009), the Court noted that "conclusory" allegations in a complaint need not be accepted as true at the pleading phase; a complaint therefore could be dismissed if the nonconclusory allegations failed to "plausibly suggest an entitlement to relief."

The utilization of this new pleading standard, which the Court stated applied in all federal actions, suggests that careful attorneys should provide as much detail as possible and not simply rely on giving the defendant general notice of what is being claimed in order to survive dismissal. It is unclear, however, whether Twombly and Iqbal entail a full rejection of notice pleading. The decisions disavowed some of the Supreme Court's earlier reasoning in Conley, but they did not directly reject Conley's "fair notice" standard. Questions remain regarding what kind of allegations can be disregarded as merely "conclusory." And what constitutes a "plausible" statement of a claim as opposed to one that is "implausible" or "inconceivable"? Ultimately, courts retain considerable discretion when applying the federal pleading standard to particular cases. As the Iqbal decision stated, deciding "whether a complaint states a plausible claim for relief" is "a context-specific task that requires the reviewing court to draw on its judicial experience and common sense." The Court's reconstruction of the Rule 8 pleading standard is not binding on state courts, however. For a more detailed discussion of the Twombly and Iqbal decisions and their impact, see J. Friedenthal, M. Kane, A. Miller & A. Steinman, *Civil Procedure* §§ 5.9 and 5.10 (6th ed.2021).

§ 3–5. The Reply

Under both code and federal procedure, pleadings beyond the complaint and answer are generally disfavored or forbidden. This development reflects the de-emphasis on pleadings in modern legal systems. In certain limited circumstances, the plaintiff may be allowed, or even required, to file a reply. For example, most pleading rules require the plaintiff to file a reply to counterclaims made by the defendant; in the federal system, that pleading is called an answer to a counterclaim. Fed.Rule 7(a)(3). However, a majority of courts do not permit a reply to affirmative defenses, treating them as automatically denied. When a reply is filed, the plaintiff is in a defensive posture, responding to the defendant's allegations, and the general rules governing responsive pleading apply. See § 3–6, below. No pleadings beyond the reply are permitted.

2. DEFENDANT

§ 3-6. The Answer

The defendant has several options as to how to respond to the plaintiff's complaint under both the state codes and the federal rules. As is discussed later, see § 3-8, below, the defendant can enter what has traditionally been called a plea in abatement either by motion or in the answer. The defendant also can enter a denial, can introduce an affirmative defense, and can seek independent relief from the plaintiff. Each of these last three options may be used alternatively or in combination. In addition, the defendant may admit the allegations in the complaint, either by specifically acknowledging their truth or by failing properly to deny them. All of these responses should be included in the defendant's responsive pleading—the answer.

There are five different types of denials that may be used. Each one places in issue the matter denied. The major problem in deciding which to utilize is that the denial must be truthful and cannot be misleading; the defendant should only place in issue those matters that actually are in dispute. A *general denial* puts in issue all matters set forth in the complaint, and thus typically cannot be utilized truthfully. Alternatively, the defendant can enter a *specific denial,* denominating those paragraphs that are in dispute. The failure to deny the other paragraphs results in their admission. See Fed.Rule 8(b)(6). Similarly, a *qualified denial* may be used, denying only specific averments within a given paragraph. These three types of denials are the most common. Most judicial systems also allow a denial on the ground that the defendant has *insufficient knowledge to form a belief* as to the truth or falsity of a given allegation in the complaint. This form of denial must be used with caution. The issue must be one outside the defendant's knowledge and, further, one about which the defendant could not easily have become informed. It is unclear exactly what burden is placed on the defendant to gain the requisite knowledge, and the court will decide on a case-by-case basis whether a defense based on insufficient knowledge is legitimate. If the denial is found inappropriate, the matter that was denied will be deemed admitted. The last form of denial that may be utilized is a *denial on information and belief.* This approach is used most often by corporate or institutional defendants who are being sued because of the activities of their employees. It is permitted because the information available to the corporation at the time of filing the answer may be only secondhand. This form of denial allows them to protect themselves should later information reveal the truth of some of the plaintiff's allegations.

In addition to pleading some form of denial, the defendant may include affirmative defenses in the answer. Affirmative defenses are descendants of the common law plea in confession and avoidance: the defendant admits the truth of the plaintiff's allegation but alleges new facts that require the dismissal of the action. Unlike common law practice, however, affirmative defenses may be used in conjunction with denials. The defendant may assert the defense without admitting the plaintiff's allegations; and that defense may allow the defendant to avoid liability even if the plaintiff proves its allegations. Examples of affirmative defenses are statute of limitations, res judicata, assumption of the risk, and release. Any defense that seeks to avoid the plaintiff's allegations by introducing new facts, rather than challenging the allegations in the complaint, may be deemed an affirmative defense. This definition is an important one to understand; the failure to include an affirmative defense in the answer can result in its waiver. The rationale for this rule is that because the defense introduces new facts, its omission from the pleadings fails to notify the plaintiff so that it would be unfair to allow its assertion at a later time. Although the courts sometimes will allow amendments to raise these defenses, see §§ 3–9—3–10, below, the ability to amend is not guaranteed. Thus, a good rule of thumb is: when in doubt as to whether a given defense is affirmative, plead it.

The final matter to consider including in the answer is a request for some affirmative or independent relief from the plaintiff. This is referred to either as a counterclaim or a cross-complaint. The rules regarding when a defendant is permitted to seek affirmative relief in this manner are discussed elsewhere. See § 3–20, below. For pleading purposes, a defendant in this position is treated like a claimant and the same pleading requirements that govern the complaint control the assertion of a claim in the answer.

3. ASSURING TRUTHFULNESS IN PLEADING

§ 3–7. Signature and Verification Requirements

The two most common methods used to promote truthfulness in pleading and to discourage the filing of frivolous claims and defenses are an attorney signature requirement and verification. In many jurisdictions, the attorney is required to sign the pleadings and that signature stands as a certification that the claim or defense is filed in good faith—that there are good grounds to support it and that it is not interposed for purposes of delay. Although these provisions stand as a reminder to attorneys of their obligations to the legal system, they have not been very effective as control devices because, among other things, judges have been reluctant to impose sanctions for violation of the signature requirements unless there is a finding of subjective bad faith—a most difficult element to prove.

Recognizing these enforcement problems, the federal rules were amended in 1983 to provide that the attorney signature is to be affixed only after "a reasonable inquiry" as to whether there are sufficient grounds in law and in fact to support the pleadings. Fed.Rule 11. Sanctions for noncompliance were made mandatory. These changes were designed to allow the court to apply objective criteria as to the attorneys' reasonable inquiry and to enlarge the use of the sanction power to deter marginal conduct. Considerable litigation involving Rule 11 occurred after its amendment, and questions were raised concerning very basic features of the revised requirement, as well as whether the amended rule was achieving its purpose or was breeding a new form of satellite litigation. Amendments were made in 1993 to try to respond to some of the criticism.

The revised rule continues to utilize an objective, rather than a subjective, bad-faith standard for assessing whether the signer made a reasonable inquiry and concluded that the pleading was well-grounded in fact and law. See Business Guides, Inc. v. Chromatic Communications Enterprises, Inc., 498 U.S. 533 (1991). The attorney's certification also is expanded to cover all written motions and other papers filed in the litigation, and a continuing duty is imposed throughout the litigation so that all subsequent positions advocated must meet that standard. Sanctions for violations are discretionary, however, and the rule now imposes a number of limitations on what sanctions can be used. Fed.Rule 11(c)(4), (5). A "safe harbor" provision also is included by which parties desiring to request sanctions must serve the sanction motion papers on their opponent and wait at least 21 days before filing the motion with the court. If the alleged violation is cured in that period, no sanction motion can be filed. Fed.Rule 11(c)(2).

Verification requirements differ from the attorney certification prerequisites in that the pleader by verifying swears under oath as to the truth of all the allegations in the pleading. Thus, this requirement has practical utility only in situations in which facts are pleaded on which it would be useful to have the pleader attest to the truth thereof at the outset. Most judicial systems have abolished mandatory verification, except in certain special cases, such as in shareholder-derivative suits, see Fed.Rule 23.1. Some states retain an optional verification scheme—the plaintiff has discretion whether to verify the complaint, but if the plaintiff does, the defendant then must verify the answer. Cal.Civ.Proc.Code § 446; Ill.-Smith-Hurd Ann. 735 ILCS 5/2–605. This prevents the defendant from using a general denial. Although the application of strict verification requirements has the potential of being a trap for the unwary, courts generally have refused to apply sanctions for technical violations of these rules when the interests of justice would not be served thereby. See Surowitz v. Hilton Hotels Corp., 383 U.S. 363 (1966).

4. CHALLENGES TO THE PLEADINGS

§ 3–8. Methods of Challenging the Pleadings

There are a wide range of challenges that may be made to the pleadings. Most commonly, challenges are made by the defendant who seeks to dismiss or delay the action on grounds unrelated to the merits. The plaintiff also may attempt to challenge the defendant's pleadings, however. Objections that delay the time when a responsive pleading must be filed are referred to in some systems as dilatory pleas.

The types of pleading challenges that may be made are generally the same in code-pleading and federal-rule jurisdictions. The major difference between the two systems is in form. Objections to the pleadings in code states typically are made either by a motion to quash or by general or special demurrer, whereas objections under the federal rules are made by a specifically denominated motion or they may be included in the responsive pleading.

In general, the kinds of challenges available can be divided into four categories. In the first category, the defendant may object to the court's power to entertain the action—for example, objections to personal jurisdiction, subject-matter jurisdiction, venue, or some defect in the parties. In the second category, the defendant's challenge is to the complaint itself. By general demurrer or a motion to dismiss under Federal Rule 12(b)(6), the defendant can argue that the plaintiff has failed to state a claim for relief or a cause of action. This challenge can be directed to the entire complaint or to only some counts in the complaint. It points only to defects on the face of the complaint: the plaintiff actually may possess a claim, but simply has not properly pleaded one. Thus, most often dismissals on this ground are with leave to amend. Both of these types of challenges are directed toward claims for relief rather than defenses and consequently are utilized most frequently by defendants. However, when the defendant has included a claim for relief (a counterclaim) in the answer, the plaintiff may raise either challenge as well.

The third type of challenge that may be made also is based on pleading defects. The object is not to obtain a dismissal, but to cure alleged deficiencies in the pleadings. Either a plaintiff or a defendant may make a motion to strike specific paragraphs or sentences. Objections operating as the basis for a motion to strike may challenge matter that is redundant or immaterial or matter that is sham or scandalous. The motion to strike acts to prune the pleadings and generally is disfavored, given the de-emphasis on the pleadings in modern litigation. Turning to another pleading deficiency, however, the defendant can question any matter that is ambiguous, unintelligible, or generally uncertain in the complaint by special demurrer or by a motion for a more definite statement. This challenge cannot be used merely as a fishing device and is only available to a party who is required to file a responsive pleading. Given the few situations in which the plaintiff is allowed to file a reply, see § 3–5, above, this objection is one made most typically by defendants. The general standard used by the courts in deciding whether to grant these motions is whether the defects are such that the defendant cannot respond adequately unless a more definite statement is made. If a responsive pleading could be made without any additional information, then the challenge will be rejected and the defendant must rely on discovery to flesh out or clarify the case further.

The fourth and final pleading challenge that occurs is when the parties seek to attack the substantive sufficiency of the allegations by making a motion for judgment on the pleadings. This motion differs from a motion to dismiss in that, as its title suggests, it cannot be made until the pleadings are closed—that is, after both the complaint and answer are filed. In essence, a request for a judgment on the pleadings challenges not only the pleading sufficiency of the opponent, but whether a substantive right to relief or a legally sufficient defense exists on the facts as presented in the pleadings. Thus, its use typically is limited to situations in which the facts as shown in the complaint and answer reveal an affirmative defense absolutely barring plaintiff's claim, such as the statute of limitations. Conversely, it may be used when the sole defense relied upon by defendant in the answer is insufficient as a matter of law, such as if a defendant were to plead the statute of frauds in a case in which the plaintiff alleged a written contract.

B. AMENDED AND SUPPLEMENTAL PLEADINGS

§ 3-9. General Standards and Practice

At common law the pleadings assumed a dominant and controlling role and the ability to amend was virtually nonexistent. No variance was tolerated between the pleadings and the proof at trial, and a departure in the evidence from the issue as framed in the pleadings resulted in the dismissal of the suit.

Modern code and federal practice differ radically from this approach. Amendments to the pleadings are allowed quite freely in an effort to decide cases on their merits, rather than on technicalities, and a variance between the pleadings and the proof is permissible. Amendments have been allowed at trial and even after judgment in an effort to render justice. Courts generally will exercise their discretion to refuse an amendment only if allowing it would cause undue prejudice to the opposing party. This may occur, for example, if an amendment is sought so late that evidence that might disprove the new allegations no longer is available or it would require delaying the trial to allow the opposing party to prepare how to respond to the issue. When a party wishes to reopen a judgment in order to amend its pleading but more than one year has passed since the entry of judgment, it must show "extraordinary circumstances" to justify relief under Fed.Rule 60(b)(6). BLOM Bank SAL v. Honickman, 604 U.S. 204 (2025).

An amendment to conform the pleadings to the proof that is introduced at trial also may be utilized. If evidence is presented at trial on an issue not raised in the pleadings and no objection is raised, the court may deem the pleadings amended by the implied consent of the opposing party. Fed.Rule 15(b)(2). The overriding concern in deciding whether to allow this type of amendment is the existence of knowing consent on the part of the opponent.

In addition to the ability to amend, a number of jurisdictions authorize the filing of supplemental pleadings. E.g., Fed.Rule 15(d). As distinguished from amended pleadings, supplemental pleadings seek to present matters that actually have occurred since the original pleadings were filed; amendments, by contrast, present omitted matters that occurred prior to the time suit was filed. For example, a supplemental pleading might be used to add related claims that have newly arisen in a case involving a continuing nuisance. Their availability eases the burden on the pleader who otherwise would be forced to file an entirely new action to present the newly arising claims.

§ 3-10. Statutes of Limitation: Relation Back

The most difficult problem involving amendments arises when a proposed amendment seeks to add a new claim or party after the statute of limitations has run. This problem commonly is described in terms of whether the amendment will be allowed to relate back to the institution of the action. Whether the amendment may relate back often hinges on notice: did the opposing party have notice within the statutory period that this new claim could be asserted? If not, the amendment generally should not relate back.

Relation back is handled differently depending on whether the amendment proposes to add a new claim between already existing parties or seeks to add new parties themselves. In the first situation, the amendment typically will be allowed if the new facts or theories being alleged are part of the same cause of action (code states) or arise out of the same transaction or occurrence (federal rules practice) that is presented in the original pleadings. This standard is designed to assure that the new claim bears a close relationship with the claims already in the action.

Notice is presumed because of the relationship of the amendment to the original pleadings.

The addition of new parties does not allow the same presumption. Thus, under the federal rules not only must the amendment present a transactionally related claim, but the new party must have received actual notice of the claim within a set period of time and known that it would have been named as a party but for a mistake about its identity. Fed.Rule 15(c)(1)(C). The focus is not on whether the plaintiff made a mistake or a deliberate choice in failing to name the party, but on whether the new defendant understood that the plaintiff may have been mistaken regarding the proper party's identity. Krupski v. Costa Crociere S.p.A., 560 U.S. 538 (2010). Notice need not mean service of process, but must involve more than general knowledge that the plaintiff was injured. The federal court can also allow an amendment adding a new party to relate back if doing so would be permitted under state law, Fed.Rule 15(c)(1)(A).

Practice in code pleading states is somewhat more ambiguous. There is no separate test for amendments adding parties; the cause of action test governs all amendments. Typically, the presence of a new party means that there is a new cause of action because different rights and duties are at issue. Thus, relation back of party amendments is strictly limited.

In some states, such as California, John Doe complaints are allowed and an issue arises as to whether the substitution of a real party for the fictitious one can be accomplished through an amendment relating back to the filing of the complaint. The courts have interpreted cause of action in these circumstances to mean the same facts, which would appear to allow unlimited amendments to substitute actual persons for John Does. However, the court will look carefully at the complaint to make certain that the claim being asserted against the newly named party was clearly contemplated in the original complaint. Totally new claims against new parties cannot be accomplished by using the John Doe device, even though they arise out of the same facts. On the other hand, if the claim was clearly within the scope of the complaint, the amendment will be allowed even though there was no actual notice to those parties.

C. JOINDER OF PARTIES AND CLAIMS

1. PARTY JOINDER

§ 3-11. Parties Who Must Be Joined

Although generally the plaintiff decides where, when, and whom to sue, the plaintiff is not given complete freedom. Rules denominating who are real parties in interest and who are necessary or indispensable parties to the action restrict the plaintiff's options to a limited extent. See §§ 3-12—3-13, below.

The rules governing who must be joined serve several important functions. As the name suggests, real-party-in-interest rules assure that the named plaintiff is the person who possesses the substantive right being sued upon. (Compare the rules regarding who has standing to sue in § 9–1, below.) If the suit is not brought by a real party in interest, it may be dismissed unless a proper plaintiff can be joined. In this way, the defendant is protected from potentially harassing and duplicative litigation. Historically, real-party-in-interest rules provided a means of identifying the actual owner of the right being sued upon when there had been an assignment or some other transfer in interest prior to the action. In modern times, the rule simply clarifies who is a proper party plaintiff. See, e.g., Fed.Rule 17(a).

In the federal courts the designation of the real party in interest traditionally denominated the person whose citizenship controls for purposes of diversity jurisdiction. This latter function of the rule posed some problems in cases in which it was alleged that a nonresident administrator was appointed or an assignment was made so as to create or destroy federal diversity jurisdiction. Thus, the Supreme Court struck down an assignment of interest solely for collection purposes that was made to create diversity. Kramer v. Caribbean Mills, Inc., 394 U.S. 823 (1969). Further, as was discussed in § 2–3, above, Congress amended the diversity statute to provide that administrators and guardians are deemed to be citizens of the same state as the state of the decedents, infants, or incompetents they represent. Thus, although the administrator remains the real party in interest and is the proper party to file suit, that fact does not affect whether diversity jurisdiction may be established.

The required party rules compel party joinder in order to protect persons who might be harmed by a judgment entered in their absence or, conversely, to protect existing parties who might be prejudiced or be unable to obtain complete relief without the presence of those absent persons. The focus is on the impact of the judgment if the absentees are not joined. The difference between a "necessary" and an "indispensable" party has posed some problems for the courts. See § 3–13, below. Nonetheless, the rules serve the important function of protecting existing parties, as well as absent persons, from piecemeal or harmful litigation. For a more complete exploration of the various rules surrounding mandatory party joinder, see J. Friedenthal, M. Kane, A. Miller & A. Steinman, *Civil Procedure* §§ 6.3 and 6.5 (6th ed.2021).

§ 3–12. Real Parties in Interest and Capacity to Sue

Real-party-in-interest rules should be distinguished from rules governing a party's capacity to sue or be sued. The former attempt to assure that the named plaintiff possesses the substantive right on which the suit is based. Capacity rules focus on whether a party is qualified to appear as a named party in an action. They are dependent upon the character of the parties, not the rights involved. Typically, rules denying legal capacity are designed to protect certain classes of persons who might not be able to protect their own interests adequately, or they derive from the regulation of certain organizations or legal relationships. Criteria such as age and mental ability often determine a person's capacity to sue or be sued. For example, a minor child who is harmed in an automobile accident has no capacity to sue, although the minor does possess a cause of action. The child's guardian or parents will be deemed real parties in interest and, having capacity, may sue on the child's behalf. In this way, the capacity rules allow the person in the best position to pursue the child's rights to do so. In contrast, certain organizations, such as nonresident corporations, may be deprived of capacity because they have not registered to do business in the state and no one else may sue or be sued in their behalf. Because capacity rules focus on the abilities of certain classes of persons, rather than the question whether they possess a claim for relief, they apply both to plaintiffs and defendants.

§ 3-13. Compulsory-Party Joinder

Compulsory-party joinder can be divided into two categories—"necessary" parties who must be joined if feasible but whose nonjoinder will not result in dismissal, and "indispensable" parties whose joinder is compelled even at the cost of dismissing the action. In the federal system the rulemakers in 1966 abandoned the terminology "necessary" and "indispensable," requiring courts instead to consider specific pragmatic factors in order to balance the equities of the situation and reach a decision. But the labels continue to be used as a shorthand.

To determine whether an absentee's joinder should be compelled—whether the party is "necessary"—

courts must address three questions: (1) In the absence of joinder, can complete relief be accorded those already parties to the action? (2) Will a judgment in the absence of the nonparty as a practical matter impair that individual's interest in the subject matter of the action? and (3) Will those already parties be subject to a substantial risk of incurring inconsistent obligations in separate suits? Fed.Rule 19(a)(1). If the answer to any of these questions is affirmative, the nonparty must be joined "if feasible." Efficiency concerns alone, however, do not merit a finding that an individual is a necessary party. Temple v. Synthes Corp., 498 U.S. 5 (1990) (joint tortfeasors are merely permissive parties and do not meet the Rule 19(a) standard).

After it has been determined that a nonparty's joinder should be compelled and that joinder is feasible, the party seeking joinder usually is given a reasonable opportunity to serve the nonparty and bring it into the action. Dismissal of the action for nonjoinder should be the last resort.

In some cases, however, joinder may be impossible because the person may not be within the personal jurisdiction reach of the court. And in the federal courts, subject-matter jurisdiction may prevent joinder—for example, if the new party would destroy diversity of citizenship. In these situations, the court must decide whether "in equity and good conscience" it should proceed with the action in the nonparty's absence. If the court concludes that proceeding would be so prejudicial to the rights of either the nonparty or those persons already in the action that the case should not go forward, then the action will be dismissed; in the colloquial terminology, that absentee is "indispensable."

Because of the serious effects of a finding of indispensability, courts evaluating this question will look carefully at several factors: (1) the extent of any prejudice caused if a judgment is rendered without the absentee's presence; (2) whether the relief can be shaped in such a way to avoid or lessen any prejudice to the absentee or the existing parties; (3) whether a judgment rendered in the person's absence would be adequate (even if not complete); and (4) whether the plaintiff would have an adequate remedy if the action were dismissed for nonjoinder. Fed.Rule 19(b). Although the federal rules do not dictate what weight to give each of the four factors, the Supreme Court has suggested that the trial courts should attempt to apply Rule 19(b) in such a way as to avoid dismissal unless it is absolutely required, such as when the absent party is a foreign government that has foreign sovereign immunity. Republic of Philippines v. Pimentel, 553 U.S. 851 (2008). If the absentee seeks to intervene in the action, see § 3–18, below, none of these concerns need be addressed.

The equitable concerns behind the compulsory party joinder rule are so important that the failure to join an indispensable or Rule 19(b) party may be raised by the court on its own motion, or it may be raised on appeal even though the issue never was addressed at trial. Thus, some courts have characterized this defect in parties as constituting a lack of subject-matter jurisdiction. However, the defect is not jurisdictional, but equitable, and it cannot be invoked to collaterally attack an otherwise valid judgment. Further, when raised for the first time on appeal, the court may take into account the untimeliness of the objection when considering the prejudice that will accrue if joinder is not ordered; delay in making the motion effectively may be grounds for denial.

§ 3-14. Parties Who May Be Joined

Various rules exist governing who may be joined by the plaintiff in a lawsuit, who may be added to the lawsuit by the defendant or who may enter a lawsuit of their own volition. The addition of parties to an ongoing action is restricted by rule requirements, as well as by jurisdictional restraints. The court must be able to assert personal jurisdiction over each of the parties in the suit and, in the federal courts, subject-matter jurisdiction must be established over each of the claims between the various parties. The rules authorizing party joinder do not alter or affect the court's jurisdictional authority. The following sections will explore the requirements imposed by the rules on party joinder. A more detailed treatment may be found in J. Friedenthal, M. Kane, A. Miller & A. Steinman, *Civil Procedure* §§ 6.4 and 6.9–6.10 (6th ed.2021).

§ 3-15. Permissive-Party Joinder

The term proper parties refers to those persons whom the plaintiff may join as parties to the action when it is commenced. The joinder of a proper party is totally permissive so that the failure to join an otherwise proper party will not result in the dismissal of the suit. Under most code systems, which follow equity practice, any person who has an interest in the subject matter of the suit or the relief may be joined in the action. Unfortunately, under the early codes most courts ruled that any person joined must have an interest in all the relief being sought. Under this restrictive interpretation, a husband and wife could not join as plaintiffs in a suit arising out of a car accident when they each were asserting personal-injury claims because neither plaintiff would have a legal interest in the personal-injury recovery of the other. Most modern state courts interpret this requirement liberally not literally, however, encouraging joinder.

Under modern joinder practice, as exemplified by the federal rules, the joinder of proper parties is determined by a standard designed to promote judicial economy and to prevent the action from becoming unwieldy or cluttered with unrelated parties and claims. If the claims for relief by or against the persons sought to be joined arise out of the same transaction or occurrence or series thereof and the joined parties share *any* common question of law or fact, then joinder is proper. Fed.Rule 20. The issue of what constitutes a transaction is within the court's discretion and frequently depends upon the number and centrality of the common questions that exist. The greater the overlap in evidence, the more efficiency that will be gained by allowing joinder. In the case of defendant joinder, the courts also may be inclined to construe transaction broadly because to disallow joinder may require multiple lawsuits, produce inconsistent verdicts, and ultimately leave the plaintiff remediless.

§ 3-16. Impleader (Third-Party Practice)

In order to provide defending parties an opportunity to protect themselves more fully, most procedural systems provide some mechanism by which the defendant can bring in (implead) a third-party defendant. E.g., Fed.Rule 14. The defendant thereby becomes a third-party plaintiff. The two requirements for impleader are that the person to be joined is not already a party to the action and that the person "is or may be liable" to the defendant if the defendant is found liable to the original plaintiff. Thus, the most common theories for impleader are that the third-party defendant has a duty to indemnify the defendant or to contribute to the payment of the plaintiff's damages. It is irrelevant whether the impleaded party is directly liable to the plaintiff; the third-party defendant must have some legal liability toward the defendant. In the absence of impleader, the defendant would have to wait to file suit against the third party until after losing the main action in order to be reimbursed for part or all of its loss to the plaintiff. Impleader avoids this time lag between judgments and, because all the issues are decided in one action, it increases the likelihood of consistent results.

A third-party defendant who has been joined to the action is allowed to assert not only defenses to the impleader claim, but also defenses to the main action that the original defendant may have omitted. Personal defenses, such as a lack of personal jurisdiction, may not be asserted on behalf of the original defendant. The third-party defendant is allowed to assert defenses to the main action, so as to protect himself from liability should the original defendant be lax in this regard. This also protects the third-party defendant from potential collusion between the original plaintiff and defendant. Subject to jurisdictional limitations, see § 2–5, above, the third-party defendant also may assert claims against any of the other parties to the action. Conversely, the other parties to the suit can assert additional claims directly against the impleaded defendant if those claims meet the jurisdictional requirements. This free assertion of claims between the parties is permitted under the rules to allow a single action to decide the entire dispute, thereby promoting judicial economy.

An impleader claim may be asserted without leave of court if the defending party files the third-party complaint within 14 days after serving its original answer. Fed.Rule 14(a)(1). Otherwise, the defending party must file a motion seeking the court's leave, and the decision whether to permit an impleader claim is left to the court's discretion. The basic rule is that impleader should be permitted unless it clearly will prejudice the plaintiff or third-party defendant either by complicating unduly the original suit or by delaying its resolution.

§ 3-17. Other Additional Parties

The assertion of a proper counterclaim or crossclaim between the existing parties to an action, see § 3-20, below, may suggest the addition of another party whose presence would further the adjudication of that claim. See Fed.Rule 13(h). In some instances the party may be deemed necessary to an adjudication of the new claim so that joinder will be ordered or the claim will be dismissed. See § 3-13, above. Other parties who have lesser interests also may be joined, as long as they meet the standard of permissive-party joinder. See § 3-15, above. When testing the propriety of joinder, the court will look at the relationship or interest of the additional parties to the counterclaim or crossclaim involved, rather than their relationship to the main action.

§ 3-18. Intervenors

An intervenor is a person who is not already a party to an ongoing action but who seeks to be made a party. In the federal courts a distinction is drawn between intervention as of right, Fed.Rule 24(a), and permissive intervention, Fed.Rule 24(b). Under the former provision, if the intervenor demonstrates an interest in the action that might be impaired if intervention is not allowed, and the opposing parties do not show that that interest is already adequately represented, intervention will be allowed.

In general, courts have interpreted these requirements liberally to accommodate multi-party litigation that will resolve completely a particular controversy. Thus, an intervenor has been found to have a sufficient interest under Rule 24(a) even though the interest is not an economic one—such as parents seeking to intervene in a suit challenging the way in which a school board administers the schools. And, although inadequate representation will be found when there are clearly conflicting interests between the intervenor and the existing parties, it also may be established when the intervenor's claim is sufficiently different from those already in the action that no one currently in the action is likely to vigorously pursue it. The courts have considerable leeway in deciding what constitutes a sufficient interest or whether the interest is already protected, but their discretion is not boundless. Once the standard is met, intervention cannot be denied simply because it would delay the action or prejudice the existing parties. If the rule's requirements are satisfied, intervention must be granted so long as federal subject-matter jurisdiction exists with respect to the intervenor. Subject-matter jurisdiction could pose an obstacle to intervention, however, if federal subject-matter jurisdiction is based on diversity and the intervenor is a citizen of the same state as an opposing party. The 1990 supplemental-jurisdiction statute specifically excludes intervenors from supplemental jurisdiction in diversity-jurisdiction cases, 28 U.S.C.A. § 1367(b), even though prior to its enactment courts routinely held intervenors of right to be within their ancillary jurisdiction. See § 2–5, above.

The premise for permissive intervention is merely that the intervenor's claim or defense shares a common question of law or fact with the pending action. Even when that requirement is met, the court is given discretion whether to allow intervention. The decision whether to allow intervention is based on a balancing of the needs or interests of the intervenor against the possible burdens on the existing parties if intervention is permitted. The more the intervenor is attempting to inject new issues, the greater the potential prejudice and delay to the original action.

The timeliness of a motion to intervene also is important because the greater the delay by the intervenor, the greater the likelihood of prejudice to the existing parties. Although timeliness may be taken into account for intervention under both Fed.Rule 24(a) and Fed.Rule 24(b), the courts are much more inclined to grant a late motion to intervene as of right than one for permissive intervention. The difference between permissive intervention and intervention as of right also is important in the federal courts in other contexts. For example, courts have applied different rules to determine the appealability of orders denying intervention as of right and permissive intervention. The former may be appealed immediately; the latter are appealable only if the appellate court finds that the trial court abused its discretion in denying intervention.

2. CLAIM JOINDER

§ 3–19. Claim Joinder—in General

The ability to join several claims in one suit depends upon rules authorizing joinder and whether the claims are within the court's jurisdictional power. This latter prerequisite is important primarily in the federal courts as they have only limited subject-matter jurisdiction and the application of a joinder rule cannot operate to extend their power. In the state courts the primary concern is whether joinder is authorized under the procedural rules governing the judicial system where suit is brought.

There are two types of rules governing claim joinder that should be distinguished. The first authorizes defending parties to introduce certain claims against opposing or co-parties, such as counterclaims and crossclaims. These are discussed in the next section. The second and more general provisions deal with whether a party with authorization to interject some claims into the action may join with those claims additional claims against the same party. Most commonly, these rules are invoked by a plaintiff seeking to join several claims against a defendant, but they also may be used by defendants desiring to assert multiple counterclaims or crossclaims. For simplicity's sake, the remainder of this section will speak of these latter rules as plaintiff claim-joinder rules, but it should not be forgotten that they also control the joinder possibilities of any party seeking to assert multiple claims against an opponent.

The rules governing joinder of claims by the plaintiff fall into three categories. The first is derived from the Field Code and lists a series of categories, permitting the plaintiff to join any claims that fall into a single category. E.g., Cal.Civ.Proc.Code § 427. In all but one category, claims are joined by subject matter (e.g., injury to the person, injury to property, contracts). In the remaining category, joinder is permitted because of a unity of occurrence—claims "arising out of the same transaction or transactions connected with the same subject of the action." Further restrictions in some code pleading systems require that the joined claims must affect all the parties to a dispute and must present consistent, not alternative, theories of recovery. The misjoinder of claims may be challenged by demurrer and the suit dismissed until properly pleaded.

The second category of claim-joinder rule places no limitations on the plaintiff. E.g., Fed.Rule 18(a). Plaintiff is permitted to join as many claims, related or unrelated, as the plaintiff may have against the defendant. Concerns about potential prejudice due to jury confusion or the convenience of trying all the claims in one suit are decided at the trial stage, when the court may order a severance of one or more of the claims for a separate trial. Misjoinder under these rules is impossible at the pleading stage.

The third type of joinder provision allows the plaintiff the same freedom to join unrelated claims, but includes a compulsory joinder provision, requiring the joinder of all claims arising out of the same transaction or occurrence. See, e.g., Mich.Ct.R.

2.203. In this way judicial economy is assured and the defendant is protected against a series of potentially harassing suits. Notably, although both of the other approaches speak only of permissive joinder, the plaintiff's options under any system may be restricted by the judicial doctrines of res judicata and collateral estoppel, see §§ 6–5—6–14, below. The potential application of those doctrines to prevent a second or third action may create some compulsion on the plaintiff to join all related claims in one action. The inclusion of a compulsory joinder provision in the rule itself clarifies the hazards of failing to join those claims and also simplifies the second court's inquiry as to whether a subsequent action should be barred.

§ 3–20. Defendant Joinder: Counterclaims and Crossclaims

The constraints placed upon the defendant's freedom to assert and to join claims stem both from rule and jurisdictional limitations. Thus, even though the joinder of the defendant's claims may be permissible under the rules, each new claim also must have some jurisdictional basis. Before considering the rule requirements, a few terminological remarks are necessary. In some states all claims asserted by a defendant are denominated "cross-complaints." Other states, as well as the federal courts, distinguish between claims asserted against opposing parties ("counterclaims") and claims between co-parties ("crossclaims"). Different limitations are placed on the defendant in each of these two situations. Thus, it is important to be careful to distinguish between cross-complaints and crossclaims, as the latter is a term of art referring only to a very specific situation under the applicable rules.

There are three questions to address when considering the propriety of defendant claim joinder. The first is what claims the defendant has the power to assert against the other parties to the action. The second question is whether the defendant can join additional claims to those specifically authorized under a particular rule. The third is whether the defendant can join additional parties against whom the defendant wishes to assert a claim. It is the first question that will be addressed in this section. The defendant's ability to join additional claims is governed by the same rules and principles applicable to plaintiff claim joinder, see § 3–19, above. The addition of parties to the action is discussed in §§ 3–16—3–17, above.

All judicial systems permit the defending party, as a matter of rule practice, to assert any claims the defendant may have against the opposing party, typically the plaintiff. The modern-day counterclaim traces its roots to the historic practice of recoupment and set-off. Recoupment allowed the defendant to reduce the plaintiff's recovery by proving a transactionally related claim. Set-off permitted the defendant to assert unrelated, liquidated claims against the plaintiff. In either case, no affirmative relief beyond the plaintiff's claim was allowed and the defendant waived the right to claim any excess in a subsequent action.

Modern systems typically allow a defending party to assert any claims that party has against an opponent. E.g., Fed.Rule 13. Additionally, most systems distinguish between counterclaims that are related to the opposing party's claim and those that are not. The defendant is required to assert any transactionally related claims, e.g., Fed.Rule 13(a), and is permitted to assert any others, e.g., Fed.Rule 13(b). This distinction between compulsory and permissive counterclaims is important because the failure to interpose a compulsory counterclaim will prevent the defendant from raising that claim in a separate action due to notions of waiver or estoppel.

The general standard for determining whether a counterclaim is compulsory is whether the claim arises out of the same transaction or occurrence as the main action. This test typically will be met if there is a logical relationship between the claims, such as if they arise out of the same event, or if some of the same evidence must be used to prove both the claim and the counterclaim. There are a few exceptions to the compulsory counterclaim rules that act to protect the defendant from being under too great a burden. Thus, the defendant must assert only those transactionally related claims that are mature when the original complaint was served, that are not already the subject of pending litigation, and that do not require the presence of other parties over whom the court may not have jurisdiction. Fed.Rule 13(a). Other rule provisions allow supplemental pleadings to assert counterclaims that matured or were acquired after the defendant's initial pleading, Fed.Rule 13(e), and amendments prior to judgment to include omitted or newly discovered counterclaims. Fed.Rule 15(a). Additional exceptions have been created by the courts in order to protect the defendant further. For example, a person who is defending two separate actions and whose counterclaim is transactionally related to both may choose in which action to assert the counterclaim and need not file it in the first proceeding that was brought. Of course, a defendant who wishes to assert any of these excepted counterclaims may do so permissively.

Although a few states provide for the unrestricted assertion of crossclaims, e.g., N.Y.C.P.L.R. 3019(b), the ability of a defendant to assert claims against co-defendants typically is more limited than the ability to claim against an opposing party. In general, only crossclaims that are transactionally related to the main action are permitted under the rules. Fed.Rule 13(g). A party who has filed a proper crossclaim, however, may join any additional claims against that co-defendant, even if they are unrelated. This is because the power to join claims is governed by the general claim joinder rules which typically are open-ended, see § 3–19, above, not by the crossclaim provisions.

The rationale for restricting a party's initial right to crossclaim to transactionally related claims reflects a concern that the litigation of claims not directly involving the plaintiff may delay the plaintiff's action. Further, to the extent it complicates the litigation, it may prejudice the resolution of the original suit. In contrast to the broader authority for counterclaims, the crossclaim limitation recognizes that complete justice between the plaintiff and the defendants can be accomplished without the adjudication of any crossclaims, whereas complete justice may not be achieved without adjudicating counterclaims. Thus, crossclaims are always permissive; the defendant may assert a transactionally related claim against a co-defendant in a separate action.

Although proper crossclaims, like compulsory counterclaims, are governed by a transaction test, there is greater disagreement among the courts as to what constitutes the same transaction for crossclaim purposes. This reflects the fact that crossclaims bring into play two conflicting concerns. Some courts emphasize the desire to decide an entire dispute in one action, even though it involves a series of claims between different parties. These courts define the transaction very broadly. A good example of this broad joinder philosophy is the allowance of crossclaims in a dispute arising out of a large construction project involving claims of breach of contract between the contractors, subcontractors, architects, and the sureties. Other courts are concerned about unnecessarily complicating and delaying the plaintiff's action and, in order to prevent that from happening, interpret transaction narrowly to include only claims in which the rights of the original plaintiff are implicated in some way.

D. DISCOVERY

1. IN GENERAL

§ 3-21. General Principles Governing

The discovery phase of litigation serves several important purposes: it can be used to preserve evidence of witnesses who may not be available at the time of the trial; to reveal facts; to aid in formulating the issues; and to freeze testimony so as to prevent perjury. Discovery may serve to prepare a case for summary judgment, see § 4-1—4-5, below. It also may promote settlements insofar as parties are able by careful inquiry to test the strength of their opponent's case. Even if it does not result in obviating the need for a trial, if properly utilized, discovery should aid in producing a crystallized trial. With full revelation of facts between the parties, the trial becomes less of a "game of wits" and more of a probing into the actual truth of certain facts. This results in a savings for the judicial system, as well as in a fairer or more just trial. Thus, it is not surprising that the federal courts and most states have provided for very liberal discovery.

The effectiveness of any discovery system depends in great measure on whether it can operate extrajudicially. Otherwise, the amount of time saved at trial is lost in litigation over discovery orders. In recognition of this fact, under the federal discovery rules, as well as in several states, the only time the parties appear before the court during discovery is when some problem or disagreement arises concerning the valid scope of an inquiry.

The provision of broad discovery is tied to the move away from special or rigid pleading rules. It represents a shift in the time at which parties must be able to prove their cases. Liberal pleading and discovery rules allow the parties to build their cases up to the point of trial, or at least summary judgment. Systems maintaining more rigid pleading rules limit discovery and typically permit it only with tight court supervision. The parties are required to know more and be able to show more about their case at the time suit is filed or they will not be allowed into court. Obviously these two approaches represent very different philosophies and strong arguments can be made as to which is the better approach or where a proper balance is struck. What is important to be aware of is how and why discovery operates as it does.

The scope of discovery provided in the rules of most judicial systems illustrates the modern philosophy toward full disclosure. Generally, a party may seek any information that is relevant, as long as it is not privileged. (See the exception for attorney work-product information in § 3–31, below.) Relevance typically had been defined broadly as meaning the material is related to the "subject matter of the action." Amendments to the federal rules made in 2000 and 2015, however, restricted general party-initiated discovery to matters "relevant to any party's claim or defense." Fed.Rule 26(b)(1). Those amendments do not necessarily undermine the norm of broad discovery, however. Discovery into matters that are relevant to claims or defenses remains quite expansive. Under the federal rules and their state counterparts it is proper to discover facts not necessarily admissible themselves, so long as they may lead to admissible evidence. Federal Rule 26(b)(1) states explicitly that information "need not be admissible in evidence to be discoverable."

The prohibition on discovery of privileged matters refers to information that is transmitted between individuals in certain relationships, such as doctor-patient and lawyer-client. The law regards encouraging the confidence of persons in those relationships as more important than discovering what has been discussed between them. The law of privileges is part of the Rules of Evidence and thus outside the scope of this volume. What is important here is merely to note how few restrictions exist on the scope of what may be discovered.

Prior to 2015, the scope of discovery in federal court did not include an explicit reference to proportionality. Rather, a lack of proportionality was a basis for limiting the use of discovery that was otherwise relevant and non-privileged. The 2015 amendments to the federal rules transplanted those concerns into the scope of discovery, requiring that discovery be "proportional to the needs of the case, considering the importance of the issues at stake in the action, the amount in controversy, the parties' relative access to relevant information, the parties' resources, the importance of the discovery in resolving the issues, and whether the burden or expense of the proposed discovery outweighs its likely benefit." Fed.Rule 26(b)(1). Considerations relevant to the proportionality of discovery are discussed in § 3–30, below.

The discussion that follows will describe the various types of discovery devices available, using the federal system as the model. The federal procedures have been adopted in whole or in part in most states. However, the reader should be careful to check the specific rules of the jurisdiction in which suit is brought, as the amount of freedom in this area may vary somewhat from forum to forum, and many of the states have not yet adopted some of the recent federal discovery rule amendments. For a more complete discussion, see J. Friedenthal, M. Kane, A. Miller & A. Steinman, *Civil Procedure* Ch. 7 (6th ed.2021).

§ 3–22. Mandatory Disclosure

In response to various criticisms of the existing federal discovery regime, see § 3–34, below, Federal Rule 26(a) was amended in 1993 to provide for the mandatory disclosure of certain information at the outset of the case to be later supplemented by further discovery. Fed.Rule 26(a). The main purpose of the inclusion of mandatory disclosure was to accelerate basic information exchanges between the parties, eliminating the paperwork otherwise involved in requesting the information. This change was very controversial and opposed by most of the practicing bar, and districts were allowed to opt out of this mandatory disclosure regime by local rule, which many did. Amendments to the rule in 2000 eliminated the local opt-out authority and restored national uniformity, listing only eight specific categories of cases exempted from disclosure. This list was based on experience gained by the courts under the 1993 amendments.

The rule requires three waves of disclosures. In the first wave, each party must provide its opponents with the names of individuals likely to have information, as well as all relevant documents, electronically stored information, and tangible things "that the disclosing party may use to support its claims or defenses"; a computation of the damages being sought by the disclosing party; and any insurance agreements indicating that an insurer will satisfy all or part of any judgment entered. Fed.Rule 26(a)(1)(A). In the second wave, parties must disclose information regarding any experts they may use at trial. Fed.Rule 26(a)(2). Third, shortly before trial, the parties must disclose information regarding any evidence that may be used at trial, such as names of witnesses and documentary or exhibit evidence intended to be used. Fed.Rule 26(a)(3). The debate over the wisdom of this mandatory disclosure regime continues, but it remains the controlling federal law.

2. DISCOVERY DEVICES: THE MECHANICS AND TACTICS

§ 3–23. Depositions

Depositions are probably the most useful and most costly of discovery devices. They can be taken of a party or a witness. A deposition acts as a sort of minitrial. The person deposed (the deponent) appears before a court officer or another individual designated by the parties and gives sworn testimony in response to questions by the attorneys from both sides of the case. The scope of the examination is not limited by the rules of evidence; the attorneys may inquire of anything relevant, as long as it is not privileged. Examination and cross-examination occurs with the opportunity to pursue new lines of inquiry as new facts are revealed and to test the deponent as a witness, not only as to the probable substance of the testimony, but also as to demeanor, quickness, confidence, etc. The testimony is transcribed, signed, and sworn to.

Although depositions may be taken anytime after an action is commenced, most rules provide that the plaintiff cannot begin a deposition until some time after the defendant is served with process, usually twenty to thirty days. This allows the defendant to obtain a lawyer and to ready the case so as to be prepared at the deposition. The one exception to this restriction is a special provision authorizing a deposition to be taken to perpetuate the testimony of persons who most likely will not be available at trial. See, e.g., Fed.Rule 27. It only can be invoked when the requesting party states why the action has not been or cannot be filed first.

The adversarial nature of the deposition permits its use at trial for a variety of purposes. It can be used to impeach a witness whose trial testimony varies from that of the deposition. It can be used for witnesses who are dead or outside the court's subpoena power at the time of trial. In the federal system, depositions can be introduced for witnesses more than 100 miles from the place of trial, see Fed.Rule 32(a)(4)(B). This willingness to allow "paper witnesses" because of inconvenience illustrates the strength of the deposition.

One major drawback to depositions is their cost. Attorneys' fees for both sides, witness' fees, stenographers' fees, and transcription costs can be extremely expensive, if not prohibitive. Further, although a party may be deposed wherever the suit is lodged, a nonparty can be commanded to appear only if the nonparty is within the subpoena power of the court, see Fed.Rule 45(a)(1)(A)(iii), and the deposition must occur within 100 miles of where the nonparty resides, is employed, or regularly transacts business in person, see Fed.Rule 45(c)(1)(A). If a deposition is desired of a distant witness, the parties and their attorneys typically must travel to the witness, adding travel costs to this already expensive procedure. Recognizing that in some cases multiple-day depositions may have the potential of harassing witnesses, amendments to the federal rules in 2000 provide that, unless the parties stipulate or the court orders otherwise, "a deposition is limited to 1 day of 7 hours." Fed.Rule 30(d)(1).

§ 3-24. Depositions upon Written Questions

The major difference between depositions and depositions upon written questions is that the latter are scripted in advance. The scope of the examination in terms of who may be deposed and what information may be sought remains the same. Similarly, depositions upon written questions are governed by the same rules as oral depositions regarding their use at trial.

The side requesting this procedure sends a proposed list of questions to the opposing counsel, who in turn submits a series of cross-examination questions. Redirect and recross questions also may be exchanged. The deponent then appears before a court reporter and responds to this set of prepared questions, with all answers being transcribed, signed, and sworn to.

The chief advantage of this procedure is that it is less costly than a deposition, particularly when dealing with a distant witness. Because the examination is limited to questions submitted in advance, none of the attorneys need be present and, by definition, the procedure takes place wherever the deponent is located. Further, since the testimony is delayed until questions are exchanged, there is no fear of the witness being unprepared, and the procedure can be used by either party immediately after commencement of the action. However, the loss in spontaneity and flexibility regarding what questions are asked suggests that it never should be used when deposing a hostile or key witness or when the subject under examination is very complicated. Thus, not surprisingly, this device is not often utilized.

§ 3-25. Interrogatories

Interrogatories consist of a series of written questions to which written answers are prepared and signed under oath. They differ from depositions on written questions in that they may be directed only to parties, not to non-party witnesses, and the answers may be composed by the party working with an attorney. Although technically the scope of proper inquiry is the same—relevant, but not privileged, information—the requestor is not limited to things within the respondent's personal knowledge. Facts may be solicited that require the party to search records in order to answer. The responding party has no duty, however, to investigate into matters outside the respondent's direct control. Thus, interrogatories are most useful to discover organizational knowledge that requires searching corporate records. Compared to depositions, they are a less expensive means of obtaining information; the requesting party typically bears no burden or cost except the cost of phrasing the questions. Although traditionally interrogatories were not limited as to the number that could be served, charges that they were subject to abuse and had become too burdensome resulted in several judicial systems placing some restrictions on their use. For example, in 1993 the federal rules were amended to provide that a party may not serve more than 25 interrogatories, including all discrete subparts, on an adverse party except with leave of court or by written stipulation. Fed.Rule 33(a)(1).

Interrogatories usually are not used as evidence at trial. Their admissibility depends on the rules of evidence in the trial court and this means, because of the hearsay and best-evidence rules, that they ordinarily will be excluded. Thus, the primary use of interrogatories is as a start-up device. Based on the facts revealed in the answers to the interrogatories, the attorney better can determine what issues are presented and how to frame depositions, see §§ 3–23 and 3–24, above, or requests for discovery of documents and things, see § 3–26, below.

As noted earlier, interrogatories can be burdensome and subject to considerable abuse. This is one reason why their exchange is limited to parties. In an effort to curtail some of these abuses in the business context, when response to interrogatories may require an investigation of business records, the federal rules and several states have provisions designed to allow the responding party to shift some of the burden onto the requesting party. Under these provisions a corporation can designate the records in which the answer to the interrogatories can be found and the requesting party then must search out the answer, see Fed.Rule 33(d). The respondent cannot use this protection to hide information, however, and must designate with some specificity what documents or files contain the information sought so that the party seeking discovery should be able to find it.

§ 3–26. Discovery of Documents and Things

Discovery rules also allow parties to obtain access to documents and other items not in their possession. The requesting party may seek to inspect files or examine premises or other things in order to reach conclusions regarding the facts, rather than to propound interrogatories requiring the opponents to prepare answers after reviewing their own records. The party seeking discovery may make copies of those documents of interest, take photographs, or make whatever record is appropriate.

Modern discovery rules generally provide for document discovery between the parties as soon as the action is commenced. No court order is needed. The requesting party simply asks the opponent for access to the documents or things that it wishes to investigate. Any document that is relevant, not privileged, and within the possession, custody, or control of a party may be discovered. See Fed.Rule 34.

One of the main problems involved in obtaining discovery relating to property is determining when items are within the control of a party. Control does not mean legal control. If a party is in a position to influence the person or organization possessing the documents, the party will be deemed to control them. In the one case to reach the United States Supreme Court on this issue, Societe Internationale v. Rogers, 357 U.S. 197 (1958), the Court ruled that the defendant would be required to deliver documents to the plaintiff even though under Swiss law the revelation of those documents could result in a criminal penalty. The party still possessed and controlled the documents, and the Court noted that the party had the ability to influence the Swiss government to change the law or to create an exception to it.

Although the specific discovery rules relating to documents and things generally authorize discovery only from parties, nonparties also may be subject to document discovery under the subpoena power of the court. See Fed.Rule 45(a)(1)(A)(iii). Court control over this type of discovery from witnesses assures that it will not be too burdensome or intrusive—a charge often made regarding party document discovery. Further, in the case of nonparties, the court may order production only on specified conditions designed to alleviate any resulting hardship, such as reasonably compensating the answering party. See Fed.Rule 45(d)(3)(C).

§ 3–27. Physical and Mental Examinations

The one discovery device that remains under the complete control of the court is a request for the physical or mental examination of parties. This discovery device has survived constitutional attack and challenges that it violates the doctor-patient privilege. Sibbach v. Wilson & Co., 312 U.S. 1 (1941). Its use is strictly limited, however, to parties or persons under the custody or legal control of parties and to situations in which the need for information outweighs the right to privacy of the person being examined. See Fed.Rule 35(a).

A court will order a physical or mental examination only upon a showing that the party's health is an actual issue in the case and that there is "good cause" for granting the request. Good cause under these circumstances means more than relevance. The requesting party must show why the information is necessary and that it cannot be obtained otherwise. There must be some basis for believing that the party is suffering from some relevant physical or mental disability. Further, although it now is settled that this discovery device may be utilized against both plaintiffs and defendants, the court may be more stringent in applying the "good cause" requirement when defendants are being examined. This distinction reflects an awareness that typically it is the plaintiff who shapes the controversy and thus easily could place the defendant's health in controversy. See Schlagenhauf v. Holder, 379 U.S. 104 (1964). Despite these concerns, it is fair to say that in personal-injury litigation today requests for physical and mental examinations are granted rather routinely. It is only in other litigation areas that these requests pose difficulties.

In recognition of the intrusion a court-ordered examination may represent, the rules provide some reciprocal privileges to the examinee. Upon request, the person examined must be given a copy of the doctor's report. This opportunity contrasts sharply with the generally more limited access allowed to expert witnesses. See § 3–32, below. However, if such a request is made, the opposing party then may obtain a copy of any similar reports by doctors retained by the examinee. By making the initial request, the examinee has waived the doctor-patient privilege.

§ 3–28. Requests for Admissions

Requests for admissions are designed to frame the issues or facts actually in controversy. An admission obtained during discovery will establish conclusively that issue at trial, unless the court allows its later amendment or withdrawal—a very uncommon practice. In this way, admissions help to expedite the trial and relieve parties of the cost of proving facts not in dispute. Admissions made in response to a discovery request will not control in any other lawsuit. They are limited to the parties and essentially operate by means of an exchange of papers between the parties. A party may request an admission on either an issue of law or fact concerning all matters relevant, but not privileged, and within the knowledge of the opposing party. The responding party can either (a) remain silent, in which case the issue will be deemed admitted; (b) specifically admit or deny each request; (c) object on the ground that a request concerns irrelevant or privileged matter; or (d) refuse to answer, stating in detail why it is not possible to deny or admit as requested.

It is this last option that has posed the greatest difficulty for the courts. What are sufficient grounds for refusing to answer? Two problems surface immediately. First, when is some matter appropriately deemed outside the knowledge of the party so that no answer can be made? The respondent clearly need not conduct a detailed search for information in order to answer because that would place the party in the position of proving the other side's case. Nonetheless, some inquiry must be made.

Second, can a party refuse to answer on the ground that the issue concerned is the essential issue in dispute and to answer would be to concede the case? Some state courts prohibit admissions on basic issues. Under the federal rules, a party cannot object to an admission solely on the ground that it involves a core issue in the case. See Fed.Rule 36(a)(5). However, a party may in good conscience deny such a requested admission thereby placing the matter "at issue" for trial. In this way, at the least, the main issues for trial are framed.

§ 3–29. Objections to Discovery Requests

With the exception of requests for physical or mental examinations, discovery proceeds without court intervention unless some dispute arises. A party objecting to an inquiry made using any of the discovery procedures described in the preceding sections may pursue one of two routes. The first is to answer all non-objectionable questions, registering an objection to those the party refuses to answer. The party seeking discovery then can move for a court order compelling a response, at which time the examinee can explain the basis for the objections. Under this alternative the need for court intervention never may materialize, as the requesting party, after reviewing the responses that the party is willing to make, may decide that it is not necessary to pursue the unanswered questions. The other alternative is for the examinee to move for a protective order to avoid responding.

If the court orders a response to be made and the examinee continues to refuse, sanctions may be imposed. See § 3–30, below. However, if the court upholds the objection, it may enter a wide range of protective orders, ranging from forbidding inquiry into certain matters, to allowing discovery but only under certain circumstances (e.g., a deposition placed under seal and allowed to be opened only by court order). A good listing of the types of protective orders available to the court can be found in Federal Rule 26(c)(1).

The question of how to object to a particular discovery request raises another important problem—how to obtain immediate appellate review of court orders requiring or limiting discovery. In most judicial systems, appeals are permissible only after a judgment on the merits has been reached. See §§ 7–1—7–5, below. Interlocutory orders, such as discovery orders, must await the final judgment in the underlying action before being appealed. In many cases this will mean that the order is never reviewed by an appellate court because it will be most difficult to demonstrate that the discovery order, even if erroneous, was so prejudicial to the ultimate result as to justify a reversal. Any error the trial court made may be deemed harmless error, not subject to reversal.

There are two possible means available to an attorney to obtain immediate review under these circumstances. The first is to petition for the extraordinary writ of mandamus. See § 7–5, below. Mandamus provides only very limited relief, however, because it is restricted to situations in which some gross miscarriage of justice or abuse of discretion occurred in the trial court. For example, mandamus was granted to review an order requiring the defendants to submit to nine physical examinations; the challenge to the order alleged the violation of the constitutional rights of the defendants. Schlagenhauf v. Holder, 379 U.S. 104 (1964).

The second means of obtaining review is to refuse to obey the court order, be adjudged in contempt, and appeal from the final contempt judgment, challenging the bases on which it was entered. This approach is risky, however. No immediate appeal will be allowed if civil, rather than criminal, contempt is found. On the other hand, if criminal, rather than civil, contempt is involved, the scope of appellate review in some courts is so narrow that the court will not consider the objection to the underlying order that resulted in contempt. Further, in either case, if the appellate court upholds the lower court's discovery order, the contempt penalty will remain in effect. For these reasons, in most situations the trial court's discovery orders are final and binding.

§ 3-30. Proportionality, Protective Orders, and Sanctions: Controlling Abuses

The potential for the discovery process to be abused is apparent: continual requests for information that is not essential, but that fits within the broad notion of relevance, can be made to harass the opposing side; and obdurate refusals to respond to legitimate requests requiring court intrusion can be costly, as well as result in delay. Modern discovery provisions thus include several tools by which the courts are encouraged to protect against abuse and ensure that discovery is used for its legitimate purposes.

As mentioned in § 3–21, above, Federal Rule 26(b)(1) limits the scope of discovery to what is "proportional to the needs of the case, considering the importance of the issues at stake in the action, the amount in controversy, the parties' relative access to relevant information, the parties' resources, the importance of the discovery in resolving the issues, and whether the burden or expense of the proposed discovery outweighs its likely benefit." Federal courts are particularly encouraged to identify and discourage discovery abuse through provisions authorizing them to limit discovery that is too cumulative, that might be obtained in a less burdensome or expensive fashion, or that are outside the scope of discovery—including its proportionality requirement. Fed.Rule 26(b)(2)(B). In addition, Federal Rule 26(c) gives the court the power "to protect a party or person from annoyance, embarrassment, oppression, or undue burden or expense" by forbidding discovery, limiting it to certain matters, or specifying the terms of discovery or the methods to be used.

These provisions empower courts to block or limit certain discovery requests. Courts also may control the time and place of discovery to protect parties from extremely inconvenient discovery demands. As noted by the Supreme Court, this power to limit discovery when appropriate provides courts with flexibility to protect against overreaching in discovery without resorting to tightening the pleading rules. Crawford-El v. Britton, 523 U.S. 574 (1998). More recently, however, the Court's opinions in Twombly and Iqbal, see § 3–4, above, expressed skepticism about whether judicial management of the discovery process could adequately control discovery burdens.

The federal rules also include a signature requirement for all discovery documents; the signature constitutes a certificate by the attorney that the request or response is not being made for an improper purpose and is not unreasonable. Sanctions, including attorney fees, are authorized for any violations. Fed.Rule 26(g). In this way, attorneys are encouraged to consider seriously the legitimacy of each discovery request and response.

In addition to these protective devices, discovery rules contain a general provision for sanctions in the event court intervention is invoked to force a party to cooperate with a legitimate inquiry. See, e.g., Fed.Rule 37. Sanctions are available because of the violation of a specific court order, not because of the failure to comply with a party's discovery request. Most commonly, the court is permitted to assess expenses. A party who forced an adjournment of a deposition, or who fails to appear for a properly noticed deposition or to answer or respond to an otherwise proper discovery request, may be required to pay any expenses incurred by the opponent because of those tactics. In cases of willful disobedience, the court may dismiss the case or enter a default judgment. Similarly, it may deem established all matters about which the party refused to respond or strike those matters from the pleadings. Finally, when the court has ordered a party to respond to certain inquiries and the party has refused to do so, a contempt judgment may be entered, including a possible jail sentence and fine. The possibility of sanctions acts as a deterrent to attorneys who otherwise might be reluctant to cooperate fully in discovery. In general, courts have used their sanctioning power carefully, reserving the harshest sanctions for flagrant abuses. The trial judge's decision to impose sanctions is also difficult to overturn on appeal, because appellate courts will review it using a deferential abuse-of-discretion standard.

3. SPECIFIC PROBLEMS

§ 3–31. Attorney Work-Product

One of the serious problems that has faced courts having liberal discovery rules is how to prevent legal parasitism, by which one side in the litigation lessens its own investment and preparation by allowing the opponent to fully prepare the case and then discovering that attorney's work-product. To allow this kind of occurrence would undermine the adversary nature of the proceedings and debilitate the quality of lawyering in the courts because it would inhibit maximum trial preparation.

Generally, attorney-client privilege rules protect only direct communications between the attorney and the client. They do not protect information gathered from witnesses, investigative reports, internal memoranda, etc. Thus, the United States Supreme Court developed the work-product rule for the federal courts. It totally exempts from discovery the mental impressions, conclusions, opinions or legal theories of the opposing attorney. Further, the attorney's other work-product is not discoverable unless the person requesting access shows both need and that refusal to allow discovery would prejudice or cause extreme hardship to the requesting party. Hickman v. Taylor, 329 U.S. 495 (1947). The person requesting discovery must be able to show that there are no alternative means of obtaining the information and that it is vital to the preparation of the case. Several states have enacted the work-product rule as part of their discovery statutes, and the Hickman rule is now incorporated in the federal rules. See Fed.Rule 26(b)(3).

Some problems have arisen in defining what constitutes work-product. First, does it cover material gathered by persons other than the attorney, such as photographs or a surveillance report by an investigative agency? Second, is it limited to materials gathered solely in anticipation of trial or might it protect matter collected before it was reasonable to assume suit would be brought? The federal discovery rule answers these questions for the federal courts. It provides protection for all materials collected by the attorney or the attorney's agent but is limited to material gathered in anticipation of trial. Matter falling within this definition may be discovered only upon a showing of substantial need and undue hardship.

Instead of absolutely prohibiting the disclosure of any mental impressions of the attorney, as is done in some state rules, the federal rules provide that the court must guard against the disclosure of that matter. This difference still recognizes that the highest degree of protection must be given to the attorney's mental impressions, but it allows the court to order response to a discovery request when the information sought is necessary for the requesting party and can be provided in a way that will protect the attorney's impressions of the case.

One unique feature of the federal rule is the exception that allows witnesses and parties to obtain their own statements, made at an earlier time, without showing any need or prejudice. Fed.Rule 26(b)(3)(C). This exception is designed to allow a witness to avoid the potential embarrassment of being confronted at trial with inconsistent statements made earlier. It was not part of the common law Hickman rule and many state rules that otherwise have followed the federal approach have not adopted this exception on the ground that the concerns underlying it are unwarranted.

Finally, the difference between attorney work-product protections and attorney-client privilege should be noted. In contrast to attorney work-product as just described, the attorney-client privilege prohibits access to information communicated by the client to the attorney during the course of their confidential relationship. The client's information need not be given to the attorney in anticipation of actual litigation, but may be divulged merely in order to seek legal advice. There are no exceptional circumstances allowing access.

In the large corporate context, in which corporate counsel regularly consults and is consulted by numerous employees about various aspects of the business, it often becomes important to identify when counsel merely is gathering information because of anticipated litigation and therefore may claim only the limited work-product protection, and when the attorney has obtained information under a pledge of confidentiality and for the identified purpose of giving legal advice so that the absolute attorney-client privilege may be invoked. See, e.g., Upjohn Co. v. United States, 449 U.S. 383 (1981). Merely transferring all internal corporate documents to the general counsel's office is not sufficient to qualify for protection.

§ 3-32. Expert Witnesses

Discovery involving expert witnesses poses special problems. At the outset they appear protected by the work-product rule because it may be only through the ingenuity and hard work of the attorney that the expert witnesses were uncovered and their testimony developed for the case. Further, discovery of these witnesses may reveal in substantial part the theories and conclusions of the side retaining them. On the other hand, because of the complex or technical nature of most expert testimony, there is a definite need for the opposing side to have some idea of what to expect so it can cross-examine adequately and introduce an effective rebuttal. Concerns about fair and effective trials appear to outweigh fears about parasitism in this context.

In recognition of the special nature of this problem, most discovery rules explicitly permit discovery of the name and the substance of the testimony of any expert retained for use at trial. Indeed, under the 1993 amendments to the federal rules, parties are required to disclose the identity of all trial experts, as well as to provide a written report including the expert's opinions and supporting reasons that will be offered at trial. See § 3–22, above. After the report has been disclosed, the opposing party may then take the deposition of the expert. Fed.Rule 26(b)(4)(A). Most discovery rules also allow discovery of experts who are retained by counsel, but who will not testify at trial, if there are exceptional circumstances why the requesting party cannot obtain like evidence by other means. Fed.Rule 26(b)(4)(D). In this way one party cannot effectively control the case by retaining all the noted and available authorities in a field, using only those who support the client's case. To avoid a possible windfall to the requesting party who obtains discovery under this exception, however, the court is authorized to require the requesting party to pay a portion of the fees and expenses related to the experts discovered. Fed.Rule 26(b)(4)(E).

The special expert rule does not cover all categories of experts. Experts who have an informal relationship with an attorney, acting as sources of information without being retained, do not fall within the expert rule and are protected within the general work-product rule. See § 3–31, above. Similarly, in states not having a special expert rule, discovery will be governed by the work-product rule and permitted only when it would prejudice the requesting party to deny it. Finally, experts who also are employees of corporate parties and who were not hired for purposes of the particular litigation at hand are fully discoverable as witnesses by either side.

§ 3–33. Insurance Agreements

In most states the fact of insurance is not admissible at trial and direct actions by injured parties are not permitted against the insurance companies of alleged tortfeasors. Injured parties must sue the insured and then seek reimbursement. These limitations are designed to protect the insurance industry from possible inflated verdicts entered by juries influenced by the deep pockets of the insurer rather than the merits of the plaintiff's case. Nonetheless, most states authorize the injured party to obtain discovery of the defendant's insurance coverage and, in the federal courts, insurance is one of the things that must be disclosed at the outset. See Fed.Rule 26(a)(1)(A)(iv). Although not relevant to the trial, discovery is permitted in order to allow the parties an opportunity to assess adequately the settlement value of the case. While this information may result in tougher bargaining for larger settlements, it is felt that a fair settlement process requires full disclosure.

§ 3–34. Electronically Stored Information

The increasing reliance on electronically stored information by individuals and business entities has created one of the major challenges to the open-ended discovery regime fostered by the federal rules. These problems occur because electronically stored information is retained in much greater volume than its hard-copy counterparts; it also is dynamic, rather than static; and finally the information itself may be incomprehensible if it is separated from the system that created it. These unique features create special problems that the federal rules were amended to address in 2006.

The approach taken by the amended rules encourages early attention to electronic discovery issues by the courts and parties, see Fed.Rules 16(b)(3)(B)(iii) and 26(f)(3)(C); provides increased guidance on how to manage discovery into electronically stored information that is not reasonably accessible, see Fed.Rule 26(b)(2)(B); adds a new procedure for assertions of attorney-client privilege after the inadvertent production of privileged electronically stored information, see Fed.Rule 26(b)(5)(B); clarifies the application of the rules on interrogatories and document requests to that sort of information, see Fed.Rules 33(d) and 34; and amends the discovery sanction rule to authorize sanctions in a narrow set of circumstances that is peculiar to electronically stored information, see Fed.Rule 37(e). Although some of these changes generated considerable debate, there was broad support for those dealing with requiring early attention by the court and the parties to electronic discovery and with problems related to the form in which electronically stored information was to be produced.

§ 3-35. Abuses and Proposals for Reform

The liberal, wide-open discovery rules used in most state and federal courts have accomplished much in the way of eliminating verdicts won primarily by surprise tactics. They also have been subject to abuse. The costs of discovery, if not carefully controlled, can become a tactical weapon that has a significant effect on the outcome of a case regardless of the facts and the law. A litigant of little means may not be able to afford compliance with required disclosures and may have to avoid involvement in depositions and orders to produce materials directed to nonparties. Even a wealthy or well-resourced party may decide to give up a claim or to engage in an unfavorable settlement because of the costs involved.

When parties and their lawyers use discovery as a tool of delay and harassment, the ethics of these tactics should be seriously questioned. Attorneys are officers of the court as well as adversaries, and have the duty of seeking, not side-stepping, justice. Several judges, bar associations, and commentators have urged reforms to curb these abuses. Suggestions range from limiting the quantity of discovery to returning to special pleading and simultaneously limiting the scope of discovery.

In the 1980s, the trend in federal discovery reform was away from precise limits and hard and fast rules and toward adding means by which the judges could control abuses. The federal discovery rules were amended in 1980 and 1983 to require discovery conferences, Fed.Rule 26(f), and to encourage the greater use of protective orders and sanctions to deter marginal practices. See § 3–30, above. An attorney signature requirement also was added to further encourage lawyers to consider the propriety of their requests and responses. Fed.Rule 26(g).

Despite these changes, criticisms continued in the 1990s and a series of reforms made in that decade have attempted to reduce the adversary character of some discovery by mandating early disclosure of certain information, see § 3–22, above; narrowing the scope of both discovery and disclosures, see § 3–21, above; and confirming the judge's discretion to tailor or limit discovery to the needs of the particular case, see § 3–30, above. Additionally, absolute limits on the number of interrogatories and depositions in the absence of a court order have been introduced into both the federal and several state discovery rules. Problems dealing with electronically stored information were addressed in federal amendments in 2006. See § 3–34, above. More recently, the 2015 amendments to the federal rules sought to reinforce the role of proportionality in discovery. See § 3–21, above. The success of these reforms remains a matter under study and further changes most likely will appear as courts grapple with how to achieve an appropriate information exchange without abusive litigation tactics.

E. PRETRIAL CONFERENCE

§ 3–36. In General

Because of the liberal pleading requirements, the use of pretrial conferences has become the mechanism by which the case becomes crystallized and structured. Indeed, it typically is at a pretrial conference after discovery is completed that counsel, talking informally with the judge, are able to agree as to what issues are in dispute. They can plan the course of the trial because they know what evidence and witnesses they intend to introduce. In many instances, a series of conferences may be used to schedule discovery and to set deadlines for pretrial motions, as well as to structure the trial. There is no limit on the number of conferences that may be ordered in a particular case.

Judges have discretion to schedule pretrial conferences in both the state and federal systems, although some courts have provided by local rules that conferences are mandatory in all cases. The question whether pretrial conferences should be mandatory or discretionary is tied to the perennial debate on their ultimate usefulness. In simple cases, is more time wasted in the conference than is saved at trial or is it really a means of coercing settlement? In complicated cases, are the trials actually simplified and better organized and therefore speedier or does the pretrial conference merely add another hurdle and more time to the case?

In recognition of the frequent complexity of modern litigation and that leaving the attorneys with sole responsibility to organize and move along their cases has not been satisfactory, the federal courts have moved toward increased judicial management at the pretrial stage. This kind of intensive judicial management has been especially critical in class actions and multidistrict litigation. See §§ 8–1—8–8, below. In 1983, Federal Rule 16 was entirely rewritten to encourage federal judges to manage the cases before them, utilizing pretrial conferences to schedule the pretrial process, including pleading amendments, discovery, and motions, and to keep apprised of the attorneys' progress in the case.

In 2025, the Supreme Court adopted Rule 16.1, which governs management of cases that are transferred and consolidated for pretrial proceedings under the Multidistrict Litigation (MDL) statute. See § 8–8, below. Among other things, Rule 16.1 addresses issues such as the appointment of leadership counsel, the direct filing of new actions in the MDL court, coordinating with actions pending in other courts, and whether consolidated pleadings should be prepared.

§ 3–37. The Judge's Role

It is truly the judge who controls the effectiveness of the pretrial conference. The judge's interest, familiarity with the case, and belief as to the need to reach some agreement between the parties generally determines whether the parties actually will work toward some accord. The judge treads a careful line between coercing the parties and helping them to reach reasonable conclusions. This role has produced a difference of opinion as to whether the pretrial judge also should be assigned to try the case. If the pretrial and trial judges are different, then the expertise the judge gained during the pretrial is lost at trial. Conversely, the incentive of the pretrial judge to become totally familiar with the case is lessened, which may result in a less effective pretrial. On the other hand, using different trial and pretrial judges lessens the coerciveness of suggestions made by the pretrial judge; the parties need not fear that a failure to agree to some concession proposed by the judge will be prejudicial at trial. The pretrial judge functions more as an arbitrator or outside expert. Courts differ as to how they resolve this dilemma.

Regardless of whether the pretrial and trial proceedings are before the same judge, there are certain questions regarding the proper exercise of the judge's power at a pretrial conference that continue to surface. The first is the propriety of the judge urging the parties to settle the case out of court. Courts and commentators are split on this issue. Most judges seem to feel that it is proper to suggest that a settlement may be appropriate once the actual issues are revealed, and that one of the purposes of a pretrial conference is to see if an agreement can be reached and trial avoided. However, it is improper to coerce the parties into the settlement. The problem is one of degree. This view essentially is embraced in the federal rules, which specifically include in the objectives of pretrial conferences the desire to facilitate the settlement of the case. Fed.Rule 16(a)(5). Further, the judge may require that someone with settlement authority be available during the pretrial conference. Fed.Rule 16(c)(1).

The second issue regarding judicial power concerns whether the judge may force the parties to stipulate as to the issues. One of the purposes of a pretrial conference is to formulate the issues for trial, stipulating as to agreed-upon non-issues. However, if a party refuses to concede that something is a non-issue, should the court be able to force the stipulation? Most courts answer no; the court may require the parties to enter a formal stipulation only when they agree on specific issues.

The final question involving the pretrial judge's power concerns what sanctions may be applied if the parties fail to appear at a conference or refuse or fail to reveal certain information requested by the court, such as the witnesses who will be called or the evidence that will be introduced at trial. It generally is recognized that the court may enter a default judgment or, in the case of a delinquent plaintiff, an involuntary dismissal with prejudice against parties whose counsel fail to appear at a scheduled conference. However, this sanction is so powerful that, as a practical matter, its use is strictly limited to situations in which the party has been exceptionally dilatory. This usually means that the counsel not only has failed to appear at the conference, but also generally has delayed the course of the litigation. A more common sanction is to limit the evidence to be used at trial to only that which was revealed at the conference pursuant to the court's request. Typically, the issue arises in the context of a motion to amend the pretrial order and the court's "sanction" for the earlier failure is to deny that motion. Federal Rule 16(f)(2) expands on these traditional sanctions by including that the judge must require the party or attorney who failed to appear at a conference or otherwise did not cooperate as required under the rule to pay the expenses, including attorney fees, incurred by the opposing party as a result of that noncompliance, unless the court finds that the failure was substantially justified.

§ 3–38. Pretrial Orders

At the conclusion of the pretrial conference, the judge enters a pretrial order incorporating all the parties' stipulations, the list of witnesses and evidence agreed upon, and any other matters that were decided at the conference. The order supersedes the pleadings and controls the remainder of the proceedings in that action. If the attorneys wish to introduce a new issue or additional evidence at trial, they must petition the court for relief. Relief will be allowed to prevent manifest injustice, but it is within the discretion of the court to require adherence to its original order. Thus, the trial judge will weigh carefully the possible prejudice to the opposing party (who may have relied on the order when preparing for trial), the importance of the proposed change, and whether the moving party was dilatory in not introducing the proposed matter at the conference. If the movant succeeds, the relief typically will take the form of an amendment to the pretrial order.

CHAPTER 4

ADJUDICATION WITHOUT TRIAL

A. SUMMARY JUDGMENT

§ 4–1. In General

Summary judgment is a procedure by which a party can obtain a final binding determination on the merits without the necessity of a full trial. It differs from trial motions, such as the directed verdict, which also result in a final judgment, primarily because it is made earlier. A motion for summary judgment is distinguished from other pretrial motions to dismiss, demurrers, or motions for judgment on the pleadings, because outside evidence is produced and the court is not limited to the pleadings in making its decision. Indeed, it is common for the rules governing demurrers or motions for failure to state a claim for relief to provide that, if the movant introduces outside matter, the motion automatically is converted into one for summary judgment. A wide variety of outside material may be used, including affidavits, depositions, admissions, and even interrogatories. The key in deciding whether the material is properly before the court is whether it can be presented in a form that would be admissible under the rules of evidence at trial. See § 5–2, below.

Although the main purpose of summary judgment is to avoid unnecessary trials, it also can function to simplify the trial. Most judicial systems provide for some form of partial or interlocutory summary judgment by which only liability may be determined summarily or certain issues or claims may be eliminated from the case on summary judgment. See, e.g., Fed.Rules 56(a), (g). In addition, a party may move for summary judgment in order to force the opponent to reveal some of his case in resisting the motion.

Although summary judgment obviates the need for a trial, it does not impinge upon any jury trial rights. This is because the standard for obtaining summary judgment requires in part a finding that there is no material fact issue to send to the jury. See § 4–2, below. The court on summary judgment does not weigh the evidence and decide that one party would succeed if the case went to a jury. The court cannot try issues of fact. Rather, it determines that there are no factual questions for the jury to decide and that therefore summary judgment is warranted as a matter of law.

§ 4–2. Grounds for Obtaining

A party may obtain summary judgment when there is no *genuine dispute as to any material fact* and the movant is entitled to a judgment *as a matter of law*. Fed.Rule 56(a). The movant must satisfy that standard by citing to material in the record showing that a material fact cannot be disputed or by showing that the opposing party has not produced or cannot produce admissible evidence to support a material fact. Fed.Rule 56(c)(1). Similarly, the opposing party cannot successfully resist a summary judgment motion simply by alleging general disagreement with the movant's statement of facts. There must be a genuine or real dispute over certain key factual issues. This typically requires the opposing party to introduce contradictory evidence, not merely to make conflicting allegations or arguments. Further, the facts in dispute must be central or material to the case. Disputes over irrelevant or minor facts will not bar summary judgment because, by definition, their determination will not affect the outcome even if a trial is had. Finally, the law governing the case must mandate a judgment for the movant given the undisputed facts. If any one of these three criteria is not met, the motion will be denied and the case may proceed to trial.

§ 4-3. Burden of Proof

A very important factor on summary judgment motions is the placement of the burden of proof. A party moving for summary judgment necessarily has the initial burden of showing that the summary judgment standard has been met. This is true regardless of who would bear the burden of proof at trial. Most commonly, that burden is met by introducing outside evidence establishing that there is no genuine dispute about any material fact. But that evidence must be viewed in the light most favorable to the party opposing summary judgment. Tolan v. Cotton, 572 U.S. 650 (2014).

In cases in which the opposing party would bear the burden of proof at trial, the party moving for summary judgment also may succeed by claiming that the opponent has insufficient evidence to satisfy its ultimate trial burden. Celotex Corp. v. Catrett, 477 U.S. 317 (1986). Exactly what the movant must do to show there is no evidence in support of the nonmovant's claim remains a bit unclear, however.

The one thing that is clear is that when determining whether to grant the motion, the court will evaluate the evidence in light of the substantive evidentiary standard of proof that will be applied at trial. For example, in a libel suit requiring actual malice to be proved in order to recover, defendant will prevail on summary judgment unless there is sufficient evidence to establish a genuine dispute about a material fact under the clear and convincing evidence standard, rather than the more general preponderance of the evidence standard. Anderson v. Liberty Lobby, Inc., 477 U.S. 242 (1986).

Another important question that arises is what burdens are placed on the nonmovant in resisting the motion. In the federal courts, the opposing party is not permitted to survive summary judgment on the basis of the pleadings, alone, unless the movant did not meet the initial burden of showing the absence of any genuine dispute as to any material fact. If the movant's papers show that no genuine dispute of material fact exists, then the burden shifts to the opposing party to introduce outside evidence rebutting this conclusion. If the opposing party fails to introduce any outside evidence, then the movant's evidence will be taken as true and in most cases this will result in summary judgment being granted. This approach of shifting the burden to the opposing party was adopted so that summary judgment could act to pierce the pleadings and allow the court to assess the sufficiency of evidence. To ameliorate some of the burden on the nonmovant, another provision authorizes the opposing party to meet its responsive burden by showing why the party is unable at that time to present evidence in opposition. See Fed.Rule 56(d). If the court finds those reasons to be valid, it may deny or postpone summary judgment.

§ 4-4. Credibility as a Fact Issue

One of the most difficult problems on a motion for summary judgment is when to allow a party to overcome an otherwise properly supported summary judgment motion on the ground that material facts will have to be proven by the testimony of witnesses whose credibility can be determined only by a jury. To the extent that this argument is accepted without reservation, summary judgment is almost impossible to obtain if any of the key evidence introduced on the motion consists of depositions or affidavits of witnesses or parties.

The decision to deny summary judgment when a credibility issue is raised varies from system to system and even from judge to judge, depending, at least in part, on the level of their concern that the procedure not be allowed to impinge on jury trial rights. In some states there is a specific provision in the summary judgment rule granting the court discretion to deny summary judgment whenever "the only proof of a material fact offered in support of the summary judgment is an affidavit or declaration made by an individual who was the sole witness to that fact." Cal.Civ.Proc.Code § 437c(e). This type of provision tips the balance in favor of a full trial. There is no comparable provision in the federal rules, and the federal courts generally have held that an unsupported allegation that credibility is in dispute will not suffice to overcome summary judgment. The party opposing summary judgment must introduce facts showing why a witness's credibility is in question. This typically requires evidence that the witness is not disinterested (i.e., is a party) or that the determination of an issue of fact rests on the state of mind or motive of the actor so that it ultimately must turn on that person's credibility as to what was in the individual's mind at a given time. The court will not weigh or assess the actual credibility of any witness—that is the jury's role. Rather, it will decide if there is reason to believe that credibility may be determinative. If it finds that to be the case, then summary judgment will be denied.

§ 4–5. Procedure

Although the exact timing of summary judgment motions varies in each judicial system, a few general observations about the procedure on these motions can be made. Any party may move for summary judgment; cross-motions are possible. In that event, the court decides each motion separately. The fact that both parties are seeking summary judgment does not establish that there is no genuine dispute as to any material fact.

In some situations, the court's review of the papers submitted in connection with one party's summary judgment motion will reveal that—although there are no genuine, material factual issues—as a matter of law judgment should be for the opposing party. Although some courts have been reluctant to grant summary judgment under these circumstances, the clear trend supports the judge's authority to do so and the federal rules were amended in 2010 to make explicit that authority. Fed.Rule 56(f). However, the court must make certain that the party against whom judgment is to be entered has a full opportunity to present additional information showing what factual issues exist. The same problem of surprise is presented in an even more heightened fashion when the court decides on its own that summary judgment may be appropriate. Although several courts have been reluctant to enter summary judgment without a motion by at least one of the parties, as long as the opposing party is given a full opportunity to show why the summary judgment standard is not met, the court may enter judgment even without any formal motion.

Typically, the court will hold a hearing before deciding to enter summary judgment, although this is not required and the court may decide the motion on the basis of the papers alone. If there is a hearing, the parties will be allowed to engage in oral argument supporting their positions.

B. DEFAULT JUDGMENT

§ 4–6. Types of Default

There are essentially three types of defaults. In the first, the defendant never appears or answers in response to the plaintiff's complaint. In the second, the defendant makes an appearance but fails to file a formal answer or appear at trial. Both of these situations are specifically dealt with in specially designed rules present in each court system. In the third, the defendant fails to comply with some court order during the pretrial proceedings and the court enters a default judgment as a penalty. Authority for penalty defaults may be found in most discovery rules and they have been recognized as part of the inherent equitable power of the court to force compliance or cooperation at the pretrial discovery and conference stage.

The denomination of a particular case as falling into one of these three default situations has important consequences on the procedure that is utilized for obtaining the judgment, see § 4–7, below, and on the party's ability to set aside the judgment, see § 6–1, below. However, all three situations have the same impact on the defendant, insofar as they all treat the default as a concession on liability. The immediate effect of a ruling that a default has occurred typically is to find for the plaintiff on the merits.

§ 4-7. Procedure

When the defendant defaults at the outset of a case and the plaintiff moves for the entry of a default, the clerk must enter it on the record. However, one of two procedures applies in converting that entry into a formal judgment. If a sum certain (i.e., liquidated damages) is being sought, the clerk may enter a default judgment. If not, the judge must enter the default judgment after holding a hearing at which plaintiff will be required to prove the amount of damages, not liability. The plaintiff's ad damnum sets the ceiling on damages but does not guarantee that that amount will be recovered. The defendant may appear at the damages hearing and may even demand a jury trial on damages. This right is largely chimerical, however, because the defendant is not given any formal notice of the damages hearing and thus typically will not appear.

When the defendant has made an appearance and then defaulted, only the court may enter a default judgment and notice must be sent to the defendant prior to the damages hearing. Further, the defendant has the right to be personally served with all the subsequent papers in the action. A failure to send the prescribed notice is an automatic ground for setting aside the judgment. The damages hearing is the same as in the case of a default by nonappearance. The rationale for including a mandatory notice requirement in this situation is that the defendant has shown some interest in the litigation by making the initial appearance. The later default may have occurred as a result of the lawyer's failure to comply with various procedural provisions, rather than as a result of the conscious decision of the party. The notice provides some protection against this occurrence and further assures the defaulting party the opportunity of making a timely appeal.

In some situations, the defendant may be found to have appeared and defended, not to have defaulted under the rules. This may occur, for example, if the defendant participates in the pretrial, but simply does not show up for trial. That is not a default as the term is used in the rules and special notice that a judgment is about to be entered need not be sent. Further, a motion to reopen the judgment and have a trial on the merits under those circumstances often will be viewed less favorably than it would if a default were involved. This is because, unlike true defaults, the issues have been framed in an adversary fashion and judgment will be entered only after the court evaluates the strength of the plaintiff's case on liability, as well as on damages, albeit that there will be only an ex parte presentation of the evidence. See generally § 6–1, below. Thus, it is important to determine what constitutes an appearance sufficient to invoke the default judgment rule's protections, but not so active as to be deemed a full defense.

In general, if the defendant files any pretrial motions short of an answer, or even more informally advises the court and opposing party of the intention to make an appearance, the court will treat the case as one in which the defendant has appeared and then defaulted. More difficult is the problem of how to treat the situation when the defendant has filed a responsive pleading but then failed to appear. On the one hand, the defendant has placed the case in issue, not conceding liability, and the court should require the plaintiff to prove liability as well as damages before rendering judgment. On the other hand, because the defendant is not present at the trial, there is not a truly adversarial presentation and perhaps the court should treat it as a default with liability conceded and hold a hearing on damages after notice has been sent to the defendant. There is no uniform treatment of this problem. If classifying the defendant's failure to be present at trial as a default will provide grounds for reopening the judgment, the filing of an answer frequently will be deemed an appearance and the defendant's subsequent conduct a default. This reflects courts' general preference for a full adversary presentation.

The penalty default situation has posed special procedural concerns. Some courts have treated it as a default after an appearance. Others have ruled it outside those protections. Notice is not usually a concern because the court in ordering the penalty to be imposed typically notifies the parties. Rather, the more pressing issues are whether the court can rule that the defendant has conceded the entire case—liability and damages—and whether the court can award the plaintiff in excess of the ad damnum. If the situation is treated as falling within the general default provisions, the answer to both of these questions is no; but the answer is yes if a default entered as a penalty or sanction is not within those protections. The courts are split on these matters and the Supreme Court has not ruled on them.

C. VOLUNTARY AND INVOLUNTARY DISMISSAL

§ 4–8. Voluntary Dismissals

All judicial systems provide some means by which a plaintiff may voluntarily dismiss the case without court approval. This may occur when upon further investigation the plaintiff determines that the claim is not worth pursuing or when the parties have settled the suit out of court. Countervailing considerations suggest that some limitations be placed on this procedure. People should be encouraged to file suit only when they are serious about pursuing the case to judgment. Unrestricted voluntary dismissals would allow plaintiffs to harass defendants and present serious potential for abuse.

The federal rules provide the plaintiff only one automatic right to a voluntary dismissal without prejudice. See Fed.Rule 41(a). If the same suit is filed again and another voluntary dismissal is sought and granted, it will be entered with prejudice, thereby preventing the action from being filed a third time. Further, the plaintiff can voluntarily dismiss an action after the defendant has answered only with the consent of the defendant or by obtaining court approval. Similar restrictions exist in most state provisions.

§ 4–9. Involuntary Dismissals: Failure to Prosecute

A court can enter an involuntary dismissal for failure to prosecute. The defendant typically moves for this dismissal on the ground that the plaintiff has failed to take appropriate steps to move the case to trial, has failed to appear at scheduled hearings or conferences, or continually has delayed or sought continuances to lengthen normal time periods. If the court grants the motion, the case will be dismissed with prejudice on the merits and that decision will have preclusive effect, see Chapter 6, below, unless the court specifically stipulates otherwise—a very rare occurrence. Thus, involuntary dismissals are granted sparingly and usually only when the plaintiff has been particularly dilatory and the delay has resulted in prejudice to the defendant.

Some provisions, such as Federal Rule 41(b), leave the decision to enter an involuntary dismissal totally within the discretion of the trial court. Others, such as the California Code, give some further direction to the court, permitting a dismissal for delay in prosecution only if service is not made within two years after the filing of the complaint or if the action is not brought to trial within a designated period of time. Cal.Civ.Proc.Code §§ 583.410–583.420.

CHAPTER 5
THE TRIAL

A. THE PROCESS

§ 5–1. A General Description

Once a case has proceeded through discovery and survived any pretrial motions that may have been made, it will be placed on the court's trial docket and a date for trial assigned. At that time, if no continuances or postponements occur, the parties and their counsel must appear to begin the trial.

Both jury and non-jury trials follow the same general pattern, although the outset of the trial differs in a jury case as time must be spent choosing a jury for the case. See § 5–9, below. The order of presentation may vary slightly from court to court, but the general rules are as follows. Plaintiff's counsel followed by defendant's attorney each make opening statements, explaining what they intend to prove. The plaintiff's witnesses and evidence are examined and cross-examined. Then the defendant's witnesses and evidence are introduced, with similar rights of examination and cross-examination. The plaintiff and defendant then may be allowed to introduce rebuttal evidence. After all the evidence has been submitted, each side makes closing arguments summarizing the evidence supporting their respective positions. The plaintiff again typically summarizes first, but has a right of rebuttal after the defendant's closing remarks have been made. If there is no jury, the judge will evaluate the evidence and render a decision. If a jury is present, the judge instructs the jurors as to the law to be applied. Most commonly, the judge will require the parties to submit possible jury instructions in advance and will choose from among those submissions, edit them, or substitute his or her own. In some jurisdictions, pattern instructions have been approved for various types of legal issues and the parties will not need to prepare special drafts for their particular cases. In a few jurisdictions and in the federal courts the judge also may comment on the evidence. However, in most states this is deemed improper and the judge is authorized only to give an impartial summary of the evidence and to instruct the jurors on the relevant aspects of the law and the jurors' duties.

The jury then retires to deliberate until the jurors are ready to render their verdict. If the jurors report that they are deadlocked, the judge may send them back for additional deliberations. But if that fails to break the deadlock, a mistrial will be declared. When the jury returns with a verdict, the judge will enter a judgment on it.

§ 5–2. Rules of Evidence

The trial process is governed by rules of evidence. Each court system has its own set of evidentiary rules and the character of the trial may vary somewhat depending on what types of evidence are permitted to be introduced. Most generally, proper evidence or testimony is that which is relevant to the issues in the case and not privileged or hearsay. Definitions of relevance, privilege, and hearsay fill the law books and are explored more fully in the separate course on evidence. A brief description here will suffice.

The relevance of specific evidence is determined in relation to the scope of the issues in the case. Irrelevant evidence is excluded in order to aid the trier of fact in focusing on what actually is in issue. Privileged matter is excluded to protect the privacy of individuals in certain relationships (e.g., doctor-patient, lawyer-client). Persons in a privileged relationship need not reveal any communications that occurred between them. The law places a greater value on preserving the sanctity of those relationships than on the need to determine the truth in a particular case based on all the possible evidence.

Hearsay is defined as an out-of-court statement offered to prove the fact or truth of the matter stated. The rules defining hearsay are riddled with exceptions. In general, the prohibition against hearsay evidence exists because hearsay is deemed inherently unreliable since there is no opportunity to cross-examine the person who allegedly made the statement or saw the event in question. The exceptions that are recognized typically involve situations in which other circumstances appear to ensure that the evidence is reliable (such as the exception for the introduction of records created during the day-to-day operation of a business), or in which there does not appear to be other evidence that could be used to prove the matter at issue (such as statements by a person regarding his motives).

Counsel must raise evidentiary objections immediately when the evidence or testimony is about to be given or they will be waived. In addition, in the case of privileged information, the parties to the relationship can waive their right to claim privilege by conduct that indicates that they have not kept the information confidential. If an objection is sustained, the evidence will be stricken or the jury will be instructed not to take it into account in rendering the verdict. There often is a serious question, however, whether it is reasonable to expect jurors to disregard improper evidence that has been mentioned in their presence, even if instructed to do so, or whether the jury has been so prejudiced that a mistrial should be directed and the case retried before another jury. In contrast, a judge trial often is less rigid in adhering strictly to the evidentiary rules and fewer evidentiary objections are raised because it is assumed that the professionally trained and experienced judge will disregard improper evidence and consider only proper evidence in rendering a decision.

B. JURY TRIAL

1. IN GENERAL

§ 5–3. The Jury—Its History, Character, and Function

Jury trial is a fundamental part of the Anglo-American dispute resolution process. It was first formalized in the Twelfth Century in England during the reign of King Henry II and it fast became the hallmark of the common law courts. The historic jury was composed of twelve men from the community. Jurors were asked to determine what were the actual facts underlying a controversy and the judge then would apply the law. The jury's decision had to be unanimous. Although the form of the jury remained the same when it was transplanted to the American colonies, over time it has assumed additional significance. Jury trial became a symbol of American freedom or popular justice as opposed to the king's justice. Even though the need to establish an independent judicial system has long since passed, jury trial remains at the core of the civil trial system in the United States.

Several state and federal courts have modified the original character of the jury to allow juries composed of less than twelve members, as well as permitting non-unanimous verdicts. These changes are an effort to reduce the costliness of jury trials. Smaller juries theoretically can be selected more rapidly, and their deliberations should be shorter simply because there are fewer individual opinions to consider. Non-unanimous verdicts lessen the possibility of a deadlock, with its attendant need for a new trial. The United States Supreme Court upheld the use of six-member juries in civil cases in Colgrove v. Battin, 413 U.S. 149 (1973), and non-unanimous verdicts in criminal cases in Apodaca v. Oregon, 406 U.S. 404 (1972), against challenges that these changes violated the jury trial guarantee embodied in the Constitution. But in Ramos v. Louisiana, 590 U.S. 83 (2020), the Court changed course with respect to criminal juries, which are governed by the Sixth Amendment, holding that a unanimous verdict is required for felony convictions. It has not yet ruled on non-unanimous civil verdicts. Thus, the lower courts are left to decide for themselves whether to modify the twelve-person, unanimous jury, and the character of a state jury may vary depending on the rules in the court in which suit is brought.

The role of the jury remains unchanged, however. It is to decide questions of fact; the judge determines issues of law. This distribution of responsibility recognizes the special qualities of the jury and the judge. The jury is present to conform legal standards to current experience. For example, if a case involves the interpretation of a contract, a question of fact is presented and a jury decision on the meaning of certain contract language relies on community experience as to common practices when persons enter into a contract. The judge's role is to provide rules to bind litigants in the future so that the community can know how to conduct future dealings. In contract disputes the judge decides whether a legally binding or valid contract has been made. The jury decides all issues of credibility since those are questions of fact, but the judge determines if the law allows relief under the facts as determined by the jury.

The line between issues of fact and of law is not always easy to ascertain and the case reports are filled with instances in which judges improperly have removed issues from the jury. The appropriate delineation of the jury's role is clouded further because of the jury nullification process. Most often, the judge instructs the jury on the law applicable to a given set of facts, and the jury not only determines the facts but also applies the law to those facts. See § 5–10, below, on types of verdicts.

However, in contexts in which the law has been slow to adapt to changes in society or culture or commercial practice, the jury may decide to dispense what it believes is justice, ignoring the law as described by the judge. For example, historically there have been negligence cases in which it is quite clear that the jury ignored contributory negligence rules that would completely bar plaintiff's recovery and simply took the plaintiff's negligence into account in assessing the damages—utilizing a comparative negligence standard before it was adopted by the courts. Jury proponents argue that this is one of the special functions of the jury and is simply a means of modernizing the law in light of current community mores. However, allowing the jury to put aside the law presents potential dangers in situations, such as in the civil rights field, in which local community standards are inconsistent with more general, indeed constitutional, national standards. For these reasons, all judicial systems contain some devices by which the judge is given power to guide the jury and prevent it from acting in ways that are inconsistent with established legal principles. These devices are explored in later sections. See §§ 5–8—5–11, below.

2. SCOPE OF JURY TRIAL RIGHTS

§ 5-4. Sources of Jury Trial Rights

The right to a jury trial in a civil action may derive from one of three sources. The first, and broadest, is constitutional. Federal and state constitutions set the minimal standards for jury trial in their respective judicial systems. The legislature has the power to authorize jury trial in cases not within the constitutional guarantee. Thus, the second jury trial source is statutory and represents those situations in which the legislature in establishing a particular cause of action has granted a right to a jury trial in actions under the statute. Finally, the trial court always has the discretionary power to impanel a jury, although in those instances the jury will be advisory only and the judge may accept or disregard its findings.

The most significant problems in determining the scope of jury trial rights have been in the constitutional area. It should be noted that the federal constitutional jury provision for civil cases (the Seventh Amendment) is not binding on the states so that states have been free to develop their own scheme of civil jury trial rights for their courts. All but four states (Colorado, Utah, Louisiana, and Wyoming) have constitutional provisions similar to the federal and even in those four states statutory jury trial rights exist. Further, with the exception of four other states (Georgia, North Carolina, Tennessee, and Texas), which provide a jury trial in equity, all the states appear to interpret the applicability of their constitutional and statutory provisions similarly to the federal courts in that they determine the right to jury trial based on whether that right would have existed in a comparable case at the time the governing constitutional provision was adopted. Thus, the following discussion explores civil jury trial rights in the federal courts as that provides the most common model for study.

§ 5-5. Constitutional Juries in Nonstatutory Actions

The Seventh Amendment to the United States Constitution provides for a right to jury trial "in suits at common law" in which the amount in controversy exceeds twenty dollars. Thus, the test for determining whether the Seventh Amendment guarantees a jury trial requires an inquiry into history and whether the action was one that could have been brought at common law, rather than in an equity court. This inquiry can be very complex because separate equity and law courts no longer exist; the federal courts now are empowered to try all claims. Moreover, the availability of joinder of claims and parties under modern rules of procedure presents situations unknown at common law. Finally, much of contemporary substantive law simply did not exist "at common law."

To accommodate these realities to the historical orientation of the Constitution's language, the Supreme Court has developed the following approach to applying the Seventh Amendment in modern cases. The right to a jury trial depends on the nature of the *issue* on which a jury trial is demanded. If the underlying nature of the issue is legal, then it does not matter that the type of proceeding involved (i.e., class or derivative suits or interpleader proceedings) historically was recognized only in equity. A jury trial is required on that issue. Ross v. Bernhard, 396 U.S. 531 (1970). Further, it does not matter whether the legal issue is introduced by way of the plaintiff's claim or by the defendant's answer; a jury trial is required either way. In cases in which there is a factual issue common to both a legal and an equitable aspect of the same case, that issue must be tried first by the jury, before the judge can rule on the equitable claim, and its determination governs throughout the entire case. Beacon Theatres, Inc. v. Westover, 359 U.S. 500 (1959).

Focusing on the character of each issue rather than the action as a whole and ordering the trial court to permit a jury trial on any common factual issues prior to deciding the equitable claims represents a definite departure from history. Traditionally, the so-called equity clean-up doctrine provided that in suits first properly lodged in equity, the judge could determine any incidental legal issues. The Supreme Court has specifically rejected the clean-up doctrine, exhibiting a definite preference for jury trial given its constitutional status. Not all the states have followed this approach in interpreting their own jury trial provisions.

The basis for this movement away from a rigid historical test is the Court's belief that the availability of new legal remedies and procedures necessarily reduces the scope of equity jurisdiction, which historically was developed to apply only when there were no adequate legal remedies. Under the current standard, history alone does not reveal whether an action will be deemed a "suit at common law" for Seventh Amendment purposes. Rather, the court must determine whether changes in the availability of legal remedies and procedures have made it unnecessary to resort to equity so that the claim or issue involved now properly may be characterized as legal and within the scope of the constitutional jury trial guarantee.

This same flexible approach appears in the current standard for determining the legal nature of an issue. The historical treatment of an issue still is important. For example, in many contexts fraud remains equitable and no jury trial right attaches. Further, the remedy being sought aids in deciding whether a jury is required. As a consequence, suits seeking only injunctive relief, being traditionally equitable, should not require a jury. However, the form of relief is not always determinative and, once again, if new applicable legal remedies exist, the claim may be treated as legal. For example, a claim for an accounting was deemed legal for jury trial purposes because increases in juror literacy and the availability of masters to assist the jury removed the historical reason for referring those claims to equity and the judge. Dairy Queen, Inc. v. Wood, 369 U.S. 469 (1962).

In a footnote in one opinion, the Supreme Court also suggested that a proper consideration in deciding whether a jury trial should be used may be the "practical abilities and limitations of juries." Ross v. Bernhard, 396 U.S. 531 (1970). Relying on this footnote, it has been argued that there may be a complexity exception to the Seventh Amendment—if the court finds that certain litigation is so complex that a jury could not be expected to decide the issues by using a reasonable process, it may determine that there is no constitutional right to a jury trial. The lower courts are divided on the complexity question.

In a 1996 patent-infringement action, the Supreme Court appeared to support using complexity as a factor in that context, but only after a review of the historical treatment of the critical issue before it provided no clear answer as to whether it was traditionally one tried to a jury or to a judge. In Markman v. Westview Instruments, Inc., 517 U.S. 370 (1996) the Court concluded that judges, rather than jurors, are "better suited" to determine the meaning of terms in a patent claim document. And in Merck Sharp & Dohme Corp. v. Albrecht, 587 U.S. 299 (2019), the Court decided that a judge was better suited to decide whether a federal agency would accept or reject a proposed change in the labeling of a drug.

§ 5–6. Constitutional Juries in Statutory Actions

In most cases the fact that an action is statutory does not determine whether the Seventh Amendment applies. If Congress specifically provides for jury trial, then the constitutional question need not be reached. In the absence of a statutory jury trial right, the availability of jury trial will depend on whether the issues involved in presenting a claim under the statute are legal or equitable in nature. Since most federal liability statutes merely codify pre-existing common law rights, statutory actions often involve the same jury trial analysis as the Supreme Court has developed for nonstatutory actions. See § 5–5, above.

One important issue peculiar to statutory actions does arise, however. That is whether the Congress can effectively declare something equitable and outside the scope of the Seventh Amendment, even though historically the issue would have received a jury trial in an action at common law. Generally, if the statute involved provides for a statutory proceeding before an administrative board or a specialized court, rather than an action before a trial court with general jurisdiction, and if there is evidence supporting the need for non-jury treatment, the enactment will withstand constitutional attack. Atlas Roofing Co. v. Occupational Safety & Health Review Comm'n, 430 U.S. 442 (1977) (administrative tribunal); Katchen v. Landy, 382 U.S. 323 (1966) (bankruptcy court); and NLRB v. Jones & Laughlin Steel Corp., 301 U.S. 1 (1937) (administrative tribunal). The answer is not so clear when the statute provides for adjudicating disputes in the federal district courts.

In two Supreme Court cases in which an argument was raised that jury trial was inconsistent with congressional intent in the statutes on which the suits were based, the Court upheld the constitutional right to a jury trial, noting that the actions had common law analogs and the only arguments for non-jury trial were unsupported allegations that the jury would not function so as to do justice and that it was inconsistent with the policies underlying the enactments. Curtis v. Loether, 415 U.S. 189 (1974), (claim jury prejudice would undermine enforcement of civil rights act regulating housing discrimination), and Pernell v. Southall Realty, 416 U.S. 363 (1974) (claim congressional intent to provide speedy remedy in landlord-tenant area inconsistent with use of jury trial). In both of these cases the arguments against jury trial rested on implied legislative intent, and the Court was not persuaded.

In contrast, in Tull v. United States, 481 U.S. 412 (1987), the Court held that Congress could provide for a civil penalty to be assessed for violation of a statute and, although the jury would need to determine whether a penalty should be imposed, the amount of the penalty could be set by the judge in keeping with congressional intent.

Securities and Exchange Commission v. Jarkesy, 603 U.S. 109 (2024), provides more insight on this. In a 6–3 decision, the Court held that the Seventh Amendment guarantees a right to a jury trial when the Securities and Exchange Commission (SEC) seeks civil monetary penalties for securities fraud. Because of the similarities between securities fraud under the federal statutes and common law fraud, the Court concluded that the defendants were entitled to a jury trial in an Article III court. The decision effectively struck down a federal statute authorizing the SEC to initiate enforcement actions seeking civil penalties before an Administrative Law Judge without a jury.

In a subsequent case, Perttu v. Richards, 605 U.S. 460 (2025), the Court held that a party is entitled to a jury trial on the issue of exhaustion of administrative grievance procedures before filing suit in federal court alleging violations of his constitutional rights by a prison employee when the question of exhaustion is intertwined with the merits of a claim that would be jury triable under the Seventh Amendment. Four Justices dissented and rejected the "intertwinement with the merits" theory of jury triability. Notably, the Court did not address whether it would violate the Seventh Amendment for Congress to provide explicitly that there is no right to a jury trial on the exhaustion issue.

Thus, the Court has not yet ruled on the question whether clearly expressed congressional intent to create a statutory cause of action to be enforced in the courts without the availability of any jury trial is sufficient to place the action outside the scope of the Seventh Amendment. As discussed in the preceding section, the constitutional presumption for jury trial is clear, and there always will be a heavy burden of proof on the legislature if it attempts to overcome the guarantee requiring substantial and express reasons supporting the legislative preference for a non-jury trial.

§ 5–7. Demand Requirements

In a few state court systems, there will be a jury trial unless a non-jury trial is requested. In most states and in the federal system, the converse is true. Unless a jury trial is demanded within a prescribed period, the right to trial by jury is waived. Although the court has the discretion to allow an untimely demand, that discretion is exercised sparingly and in most instances there is no relief from the waiver.

Demand requirements have withstood constitutional challenge. They are not viewed as unduly burdensome to the parties and thus their impact on constitutional jury rights is thought to be minimal. That minimal effect is deemed justifiable because of the generally recognized need for the courts to be able to exercise some docket control. The ability to determine at an early stage whether an action requires a jury permits the courts to schedule their cases accordingly and in that way better administer their caseloads. Thus, it is important for counsel to check the specific demand requirements of the court in which suit is to be brought in order not to inadvertently fail to make a timely request.

3. MEANS OF CONTROLLING THE JURY

§ 5–8. In General

There are various methods or procedures designed to ensure that the jury performs its proper role. The evidentiary rules, for example, limit the jury to considering only legally relevant and generally reliable evidence in determining the facts. A judge who sustains objections to proposed evidence or testimony protects the jury from considering possibly irrelevant and prejudicial matters. See § 5–2, above. Similarly, the judge's instructions to the jury describe and define the proper scope of its inquiry, prescribing who has the burden of persuasion on the facts in issue. And the attorneys may ask the judge to poll the jury after a verdict has been announced to make certain that each of the jurors is in agreement with and understands the verdict. Alternatively, the judge has the power to select the type of verdict that should be rendered, which is designed to promote jurors' attention to the proceeding and may limit their ability to ignore the controlling law. See § 5–10, below. Of course, the effectiveness of any of these controls depends totally on whether the jury understands and honors the judge's charges. The following sections describe some of the means of jury control.

§ 5–9. Selection Process

Even though the details of the jury selection process varies from court to court, a few generalized statements can be made. The process begins by sending notices to community members drawn from various lists—such as voter registries, driver licenses, telephone directories—by the court clerk requesting them to appear and be placed in the jury pool (called the *array*). Potential jurors may exclude themselves if they qualify under statutory exceptions. Excuses from jury service usually are limited to vocational categories (e.g., firefighters or doctors), health reasons or incompetence. Jurors also may be excused if they can show that it would be an undue hardship to serve. Under the federal jury selection statutes, the procedures used to create the jury pool are designed to obtain a broad cross-section of the community. Although state jury systems are not required to develop processes fostering this cross-section concept, it is common to most systems. States are limited by the Fourteenth Amendment in designing their methods of jury selection, however. This means that no particular group can be systematically excluded, and that litigants must be afforded procedures within the selection process consistent with fundamental fairness.

Individual jurors from the array are selected to sit on a specific case (*panel*) after being examined before the court. That screening is called *voir dire*. In some courts the judge asks the potential jurors all questions; the attorneys submit in advance any questions they would like answered. In other courts the attorneys themselves conduct voir dire. The purpose under either approach is to determine if any prospective juror is likely to be so biased or prejudiced regarding the case that he or she could not reach an independent and unbiased verdict based on the evidence presented. If so, the attorney may *challenge for cause* and, if the judge agrees, that person will be disqualified. If the judge permits the juror to remain, the same challenge can be raised on appeal from the final judgment and the verdict will be overturned if the trial court's decision was an abuse of discretion.

Attorneys also are given a limited number of *peremptory challenges*, which permit them to reject a potential juror without stating the reason. This device allows the attorney to try to select those persons most likely to be sympathetic to the client or to the type of evidence that will be presented. The attorney can reject persons who do not reveal enough bias to merit a challenge for cause, but who the attorney feels will be prejudiced against the client or case. By careful use of their challenges, trial attorneys can shape the character of the jury to some degree. The only limitations on the use of peremptory challenges is that they cannot be used to exclude jurors on the basis of their race or gender because doing so violates the constitutional rights of the excluded jurors. Edmonson v. Leesville Concrete Co., 500 U.S. 614 (1991); J.E.B. v. Alabama ex rel. T.B., 511 U.S. 127 (1994).

§ 5-10. Types of Verdicts

In a case tried without a jury, the judge is required to make findings of fact and conclusions of law. When there is a jury, there are three types of verdicts that may be used. The type of verdict used may help ensure that the jury performs its assigned function of resolving issues of fact.

Most frequently a *general verdict* is requested. The judge instructs the jury on the law and the jury applies the law to the facts as it finds them, reporting to the court only which party wins and the relief, if any, to be awarded. Obviously, the general verdict provides little jury control because there is no way to determine on what the verdict is based. There is no way of knowing what the jurors thought about any of the issues or the credibility of any of the witnesses. Further, in the event of an appeal, the reviewing court may have to reverse if there has been an error involving any of the claims, theories, or defenses presented to the jury because it cannot be certain whether the jury rested its decision on findings supported by improper evidence or on some other ground.

The *special verdict* is at the opposite end of the spectrum. The court requests the jury to make specific findings of fact and the judge applies the law to those facts and renders judgment accordingly. The special verdict is designed to make the verdict rendition process more scientific and discourages the jury from acting on bias or ignoring the law. In this way, the number of appellate reversals should be reduced. The device has been criticized, however, because it makes the jury deliberation process more difficult and slow. Additionally, the exercise of such tight control over the jury has been challenged as inconsistent with the historic power of the jury to bring the community's standards to bear on a case, even when those standards differ from specific legal principles. Despite these objections, which generally have been rejected, any party may request the court to use a special verdict or the court may decide on its own to do so. It is totally within the discretion of the trial judge whether to utilize a special verdict or not.

As a middle ground between special and general verdicts, the court may use a *general verdict with answers to written questions.* The judge instructs the jury on the law and requests a general verdict as described above. Additionally, however, certain specific cross-check questions are submitted to enable the judge to determine whether the verdict rendered is consistent with the facts as found. The judge is not supposed to restrict the jury by including so many detailed questions that the jury has no discretion regarding the size or type of award it is obliged to render. Rather, the questions typically are designed to make certain that the liability determination is consistent with the facts and that the law as charged by the judge was applied properly. In addition to the difficulty in drafting clear and unambiguous questions to be sent to the jury, the use of a special verdict or a general verdict with written questions may present some problems for the court if the jury cannot or does not respond clearly or consistently to the inquiries presented to it.

The jury's findings generally must be unambiguous in order to allow the court to enter judgment on them, although the judge has a duty to try to harmonize any apparent inconsistencies when it is possible to do so. In the case of a general verdict with written questions, specific rules usually outline the options for a judge when the answers to the questions do not support the jury's verdict. If the answers are internally consistent, but simply cannot be reconciled with the verdict, the judge is authorized to return the case to the jury for further consideration, to enter a verdict consistent with the specific answers, or to set the case for a new trial. If some of the answers are not consistent internally, as well as contrary to the verdict, then the judge's options are to return the case to the jury or order a new trial. See Fed.Rule 49(b). The choice of which corrective option to use is within the court's discretion, and typically will depend on the judge's perception of whether the jury is so confused that further deliberations merely might mask jury error.

§ 5–11. Impeachment of the Verdict

Although a verdict may appear proper on its face, a variety of circumstances may have occurred suggesting that the jury did not function properly and the verdict should be set aside. For example, the jurors may have considered evidence not introduced at the trial and thus not subject to examination and cross-examination. They may have visited the scene of the accident on their own or one of the jurors may have "testified" to the others on the matters in question. A juror may have failed to reveal during voir dire a relationship with one of the parties or their attorneys. The jury may not have reached a unanimous verdict on liability and then determined damages. Instead, it may have used a "quotient verdict" with each member simply writing down the judgment felt to be fair and then dividing the total amount by the number of jury members. This could result in a verdict for the plaintiff even though one or more of the jurors had entered a verdict of $0 because they believed no liability had been proven. In any one of these or a number of other circumstances, the parties have been deprived of their right to a totally impartial, properly functioning jury that considers only admissible evidence and reaches a decision on the basis of that evidence alone.

A question that exists in any of the above situations is what evidence may be introduced to prove juror misconduct to the possible prejudice of the losing party and thus to impeach the verdict. There are serious systemic reasons supporting only a very limited opportunity to impeach. First, the sanctity and total privacy of jury deliberations has been seen as the best means of assuring a fair trial; it encourages the jurors to feel free to discuss and vote their conscience because they know that whatever takes place will not be revealed publicly. Thus, any evidence of juror misconduct that requires an inquiry into the deliberation process is suspect. Second, it is argued that there is no way to assure a completely impartial jury as each member necessarily brings to the trial certain individual feelings or predispositions; the jury process is designed to obtain the views of what is theoretically a cross-section of the community and the various prejudices will be counterbalanced in the ultimate verdict that is rendered. Finally, the consequence of overturning the verdict because the jury did not act properly is to require a second trial with no assurance of reaching a more appropriate result.

Given these considerations, it should not be surprising that the historic and most widely followed rule (the Mansfield rule) has been that juror affidavits regarding what occurred during their deliberations cannot be used to impeach the verdict. However, a verdict may be impeached on the basis of juror affidavits regarding misconduct prior to their deliberations, such as if it can be shown that one juror lied during voir dire regarding a prior relationship with one of the parties, or on the basis of evidence from other nonjury sources. For example, a person who observed the jury visiting the scene of the accident could testify to that effect in order to support an argument that the jury relied on evidence not presented at the trial. And the Supreme Court recently held that if a juror in a criminal case makes a clear statement indicating he relied on racial stereotypes or animus to convict a criminal defendant, the Sixth Amendment requires the trial court to consider that evidence if the verdict is challenged. Pena-Rodriguez v. Colorado, 580 U.S. 206 (2017). Whether that holding applies in the civil context remains to be seen.

Most jurisdictions today have attempted to ameliorate the restrictiveness of the Mansfield rule by allowing the verdict to be challenged on the basis of juror testimony concerning overt acts of other jury members that may have been prejudicial. The impeaching evidence cannot rest on the state of mind or feelings of individual jurors, however. Under this approach, a verdict can be impeached on the basis of a juror affidavit to the effect that one of the members told the jury that she had a family emergency and urged them to reach a quick decision and terminate their discussion so that she could return home. In contrast, an affidavit stating that one of the jurors had received news of a family emergency and had acted under great stress and hastily when reaching the verdict will not be allowed because it attempts to testify as to the motives and state of mind of that juror. Under the Mansfield rule, neither affidavit is permissible.

The federal courts have adopted a compromise position on this question. Federal Rule of Evidence 606 allows the introduction of juror testimony only to show that prejudicial outside evidence was brought into the jury room or extraneous influences were improperly brought to bear on any juror. The federal formulation thus avoids the problem of determining what constitutes an "act" and recognizes that a verdict can be tainted by any information. However, it too precludes the use of testimony concerning the effect that improper information had on the jurors. The likelihood of prejudice must be determined objectively by the court pursuant to a reasonable-person test.

C. TRIAL AND POST-TRIAL MOTIONS

§ 5–12. Directed Verdicts

Directed verdict motions (called motions for judgment as a matter of law in the federal system, see Federal Rule 50(a)) may be made by either party at the close of their opponent's evidence. The theory behind the motion is that there is insufficient evidence to warrant submitting the case to the jury or that the evidence is so compelling that only one result could follow, so that to save trial time the court should enter a judgment for the movant. Although the effect of a successful directed verdict motion is to take the case away from the jury, the Supreme Court has ruled that directed verdict motions do not violate the constitutional jury trial guarantee because comparable procedures—i.e., demurrers to the evidence—existed at common law. Galloway v. United States, 319 U.S. 372 (1943).

The issue before the trial court on a directed verdict motion is whether there is sufficient evidence to raise a fact issue at trial. If there is, the motion will be denied and the case left to the jury. In order to answer this question, the court will view the evidence in the light most favorable to the nonmovant. In a few jurisdictions this means that the judge will not consider the moving party's evidence. But this rule of construction makes it almost impossible to obtain a directed verdict. Thus, more commonly, the court will review all the evidence, deciding any credibility issues in favor of the nonmovant.

There are two different formulations of the standard for granting a directed verdict: the scintilla test and the substantial evidence test. Under the scintilla test the court will deny the motion and leave the case to the jury if there is a scintilla, or *any*, evidence on which the jury might possibly render a verdict for the nonmovant. Under the substantial evidence test, the court will grant the motion unless there is sufficient or substantial evidence suggesting that the jury might decide for the nonmovant. The difference between these two tests reflects the different attitudes that courts have with regard to the importance of jury trial and the amount of control that properly may be exercised by the judge over the jury. The modern trend has been toward the use of the substantial evidence test.

The application of either the scintilla or substantial evidence test involves a complex analysis of what evidence is necessary to prove a particular claim or defense, what are the permissible inferences to draw if there are gaps in the evidence, who has the burden of proof on the issues presented, and, in some cases, whether questions concerning the credibility of some of the witnesses require denial of the motion or may be evaluated against the background of the other evidence that was introduced. A discussion of these factors may be found in J. Friedenthal, M. Kane, A. Miller & A. Steinman, *Civil Procedure* § 12.3 (6th ed.2021).

§ 5-13. Judgments Notwithstanding the Verdict

The major difference between a motion for judgment notwithstanding the verdict (JNOV) and a directed verdict motion is the timing. Indeed, since 1991, the federal system refers to both as motions for judgment as a matter of law, underscoring their common identity. As discussed in the previous section, Federal Rule 50(a) permits a motion prior to the jury deliberating. Rule 50(b) allows a party to renew that motion after the jury renders a verdict. A JNOV motion must be made to the trial judge after verdict (in the federal system within 28 days of the entry of judgment) and seeks a judgment contrary to the verdict on the ground that there was insufficient evidence for the jury to find as it did. In effect it argues that the case never should have gone to the jury. The motion's primary use is when there is some overriding issue of law that indicates that the jury verdict is erroneous. The court deciding a JNOV motion does not weigh the evidence any more than it does on a directed verdict motion. Rather, it considers whether there was any evidence supporting the jury's verdict in light of the law governing the case.

Arguably, the JNOV motion has certain advantages. First, its availability encourages the judge to be more restrained at the directed verdict motion stage. At the time of that earlier motion the judge may not be ready to decide whether the evidence is sufficient to warrant a judgment, although he or she might be inclined to do so. The judge can submit the case to the jury, and in many cases the verdict will be the same as would have occurred on the directed verdict motion. When the judge's inclination and the jury's disposition agree, quarrels (and appeals) about directed verdicts cannot arise. When they disagree, the court still can follow its original view that the case should not have been submitted to the jury by granting the post-verdict JNOV motion. The JNOV may also be more efficient than a directed verdict in the event of an appeal. If a JNOV is reversed, a judgment on the jury's verdict can be entered. But if a directed verdict was entered initially and that is reversed, a new trial is necessary so that the case can be sent to a second jury. This ultimate savings in trial time on JNOV may be offset, however, by the fact that more appeals may be taken from JNOV rulings than from directed verdicts because the difference between the judge and jury is only speculative in the directed verdict context.

In the federal courts, a motion for judgment as a matter of law can be made after the jury's verdict is rendered only if it is conceptualized as a renewal of the same motion made at the close of evidence and before the case was submitted to the jury. According to the Supreme Court, this is because there is no historic common law analog for the post-verdict JNOV motion. Those motions have withstood the challenge that they violate federal constitutional jury trial rights solely on the theory that they are renewed directed verdict motions and directed verdicts were authorized in common law actions. See § 5–12, above. Since the states are not bound by the Supreme Court's interpretation of the Seventh Amendment, they are free to treat these two motions differently and several states allow JNOV motions to be made even though no directed verdict motion was interposed before the case was given to the jury.

§ 5–14. New Trial

Judicial systems typically provide some means by which a party dissatisfied with the initial proceeding may request a new trial. In this way, the trial judge is given an opportunity to correct any errors that may have occurred during the first trial. Under some rules, specific grounds, such as misconduct of the jury, newly discovered material evidence, or errors of law, are set out in court rules and automatically authorize the right to grant a new trial. See, e.g., Minn. Rules of Proc. 59.01. Under others, the trial court is allowed more discretion and is given the power to grant a new trial motion based on any ground on which a new trial had "heretofore been granted." See, e.g., Fed.Rule 59(a)(1). In either case, the discretion granted the judge to set aside the verdict and order a new trial is much greater than on a JNOV motion. In short, the trial judge can consider any error of law in the trial that may have prejudiced the movant. The court may take into account prejudicial errors in rulings on the evidence or in the instructions to the jury, evidence of jury or attorney misconduct, newly discovered evidence, or the fact that the verdict is against the weight of the evidence. This last ground may merit relief even though the legal insufficiency of the evidence falls short of that required to support a directed verdict or JNOV motion.

The contrast between new trial and JNOV rulings sometimes appears shadowy, especially when the ground for a new trial relates to the sufficiency of the evidence. But the difference is real. The evidence may be such that reasonable people could find as the jury found, precluding a JNOV, but the judge still may conclude that the verdict may be against the weight of the evidence, meriting a new trial. The resulting impact of an order granting a JNOV also differs sharply from the grant of a new trial. The losing party on a JNOV is denied the benefit of a favorable jury verdict; the losing party on a new trial motion complains that there is too much jury trial, not too little.

The only real limitation imposed on a person moving for a new trial is time. Generally, new trial motions are governed by strict and short timing provisions (e.g., 10–28 days after the judgment is entered or the verdict is returned). The failure to move within that period is fatal to a new trial motion.

The trial judge's decision on a motion for new trial most frequently is controlling. In most judicial systems an immediate appeal cannot be taken from an order granting a new trial as it is interlocutory. This delays appellate review of the new trial order until after the second trial and its verdict, thereby decreasing substantially the likelihood of reversal. If the second proceeding lacks prejudicial errors, there typically is no justification for disregarding the judgment entered in it simply because the second trial was not necessary. It is difficult to determine which of two reasonable juries was most reasonable.

On an appeal from a ruling denying a new trial, the appellate court can reverse only if it finds an abuse of discretion. Gasperini v. Center for Humanities, Inc., 518 U.S. 415 (1996). This seldom occurs on sufficiency of evidence grounds. Typically, the appellate court will find that the trial court abused its discretion when it determined that the evidence was sufficient to support the jury's verdict only when the trial judge was wrong as a matter of law as to the reasons that would support the grant or denial of the motion. In general, the deference to the trial court shown by the appellate court stems from the fact that the trial judge was present at the initial proceedings and thus is likely to be in the best position to assess whether any reasons exist to justify a second trial in the court below. A few courts have suggested, however, that a broader review of the trial judge's action may be appropriate when a new trial is granted on the ground that the weight of the evidence was against the verdict. These cases reflect the concern that allowing the trial judge too much discretion to reject the verdict could result in improper intrusions on the jury's decision-making authority.

§ 5–15. Partial and Conditional New Trials

In order to avoid the expense of an entire new trial, the judge may decide to order a new trial only on those issues tainted with error. Although a partial new trial may result in considerable savings, it also presents some potential problems. The court must make certain that the issues not retried are truly separable from those resubmitted. Otherwise, the second judgment will remain tainted by the error in the first trial. Indeed, the court generally should not order a partial new trial on liability alone. Jurors' attitudes toward liability frequently are reflected in the amount of damages they award and the issues are so intertwined that if there has been some error concerning the evidence directed toward liability, a new jury should consider both aspects of the case. Thus, most commonly partial new trials are ordered on the amount of damages, not on liability. A minority of courts have argued that partial new trials always are defective because the parties are entitled to a properly instructed and informed jury and, if any prejudicial defect is discovered, the entire first trial is tainted incurably.

Another alternative to ordering a full new trial is to grant the order conditionally. This occurs when the challenge to the first proceeding is that the damages awarded by the jury are either excessive or inadequate as a matter of law. If the court agrees with that assertion, it may try to avoid the cost of a new trial by ruling that it will grant the motion unless the opposing party agrees to a specified reduction or increase in the verdict. Strong arguments against conditional new trial orders have been made on the ground that the judge effectively is supplanting the jury's determination in violation of the parties' rights to a jury decision on the question of damages. By and large these arguments have been unsuccessful. The power to reduce damages (remittitur) is recognized by virtually all judicial systems and has been resistant to constitutional attack. The court cannot simply reduce damages without allowing the plaintiff the option of a new trial, however. Hetzel v. Prince William County, Virginia, 523 U.S. 208 (1998).

The power to increase damages (additur), even conditionally, does not exist in the federal courts because it has been held to violate the Seventh Amendment. However, additur is allowed in some state courts.

The different treatment accorded remittitur and additur in the federal system does not rest on policy, but rather on the fact that remittitur existed at common law and thus is within the scope of the

Seventh Amendment. Additur is a more modern device and since it does have an impact on the jury's decision, it is not constitutionally permissible. Dimick v. Schiedt, 293 U.S. 474 (1935). The continued vitality of this distinction is doubted by many today.

There are no specific rules governing the amount to be remitted or added. Different states follow different verbal standards. However, there are three basic formulations that can be identified. The judge may reduce or increase the award to the legally sufficient minimum the jury could have awarded or to the maximum that would have been permissible. Alternatively, the judge may set the figure between those two extremes at the amount the judge believes is justified by the evidence. Once the judge applies one of these standards and sets the figure, the opposing party's decision is simply whether to accept that figure or to proceed to a new trial. If the judge's figure is acceptable to the opposing party, the party who originally requested a new trial will find the new trial motion denied and the only option if the party is unhappy with the new damage award is to appeal, alleging that even the new figure is improper as a matter of law.

§ 5–16. Combined Motions for New Trial and Judgment Notwithstanding the Verdict

In some judicial systems a party may move simultaneously for a JNOV and for a new trial and the judge must rule on both motions. The theory behind requiring concurrent alternative rulings is that it will save time on appeal and will provide further guidance to the appellate court as to why the trial judge believes the verdict must be supplanted. If the motions were bifurcated with the movant seeking and obtaining first a ruling on the JNOV and then a ruling on new trial, a separate appeal would be required from each of those rulings resulting in a lengthy delay before a final decision was reached or a new trial actually begun. To avoid this result, the trial judge is instructed to rule on both motions simultaneously.

One effect of the joint rulings is to alter some of the normal appealability rules. As is described elsewhere, see § 7-1, below, most judicial systems authorize appeals only from final judgments. A grant or denial of a JNOV, alone, results in a final judgment being entered. The denial of a new trial motion, alone, also is final as the jury's verdict then is incorporated into a judgment. The grant of a new trial motion is interlocutory, however, as it requires that the trial court begin anew and thus it normally is not immediately appealable. The losing party must wait to appeal that ruling until after the second trial concludes. The combination of these rules would mean that when joint rulings are involved and a new trial is granted, there would be no effective appellate review because it would be difficult to show that even if the denial of the JNOV were erroneous, it had a prejudicial effect in the second trial. The rules governing joint JNOV-new trial motions address this problem by providing that if the court grants both the JNOV and the new trial motions, that ruling is appealable immediately. The new trial order is viewed as an alternative to be used only if the JNOV is reversed. If on the initial motion the JNOV is denied and a new trial granted, no immediate appeal lies, however. See Fed.Rule 50(c), (e).

CHAPTER 6

JUDGMENTS AND THEIR EFFECTS

A. RELIEF FROM JUDGMENTS

§ 6–1. Principles Governing

The entry of a judgment marks the final act in the trial-court adjudication of a dispute. Errors in the judgment that are the result of clerical mistakes or some omission or oversight when the judgment was entered may be corrected by a motion to correct or alter the judgment. This can be done by any of the parties or by the court sua sponte. Although correction may relieve a party from an erroneous judgment, it is a ministerial procedure and does not require the judgment to be formally reopened or retrial of the case. In most systems the ability to correct a judgment for clerical mistakes exists at any time. In federal court, the alteration of a judgment because of the omission of some element is limited to 28 days. But the use of a motion to alter the judgment is strictly limited to clerical errors, not questions involving the right to additional recovery or a reduction in an award. Attempts to reopen the judgment or to alter it for some nontechnical reason or outside the time period provided must be made by a motion for new trial or by appeal.

All judicial systems, however, provide some limited means by which a party may seek to set aside a judgment and obtain a new trial after the time for moving for a new trial or appealing has passed. There are essentially four methods for seeking relief from a trial court judgment: (1) special statutes may authorize specific procedures for seeking relief from certain types of judgments; (2) contemporary rules of procedure usually provide that a party may make a motion in the original trial court for relief based on certain listed grounds; (3) a party may be allowed to bring an independent action challenging a judgment on grounds long recognized in equity; and (4) a party may apply to set a judgment aside for fraud, appealing to the court's inherent equity powers.

These provisions are attempts to accommodate the need for finality with the desire to make certain that the result reached in the original trial is sound. Most commonly, relief must be sought only within certain time periods, varying between six months and one year from the entry of the judgment. More rarely, relief is limited only by a reasonable time requirement. Timing restrictions on post-judgment relief operate to promote finality; the certainty produced by finality is merely postponed. The only exception to these rigid time restraints is when the defect in the first proceeding is one going to the very power of the court to try the controversy, as when the court lacked subject-matter or personal jurisdiction.

The most common example of cases in which relief is granted is when there is a default judgment. The due process notion of giving litigants an effective opportunity to be heard favors adjudications after an adversarial presentation. Thus, the courts treat default relief motions liberally and will deny relief from those judgments only when it is clear the defendant has no defense to the action or when the defendant has delayed so long that the plaintiff now would be prejudiced by being required to proceed to trial.

The most common procedure for setting aside a judgment is to make a motion for relief from the judgment under the appropriate rule. It typically is totally within the trial court's discretion whether to grant or deny relief. The court, in addition to considering whether the reasons alleged for setting aside the judgment are permissible grounds for relief under the applicable procedural rule, see § 6–2, below, usually will take into account other equitable considerations. These may include the prejudice to the opposing party—who may have acted in reliance on the judgment—if the motion is granted, whether the movant has proceeded with due diligence in making the motion, or any other matter that might bear on the fairness of reconsidering the judgment. The court will not determine whether the first judgment is erroneous, although it may take into account whether opening the judgment and ordering a new trial is likely to produce a different result.

Another method by which a party may seek relief is to bring an independent action to set aside the judgment on any ground historically recognized in equity. Additionally, regardless of the specific bases for relief listed in the procedural rules, most systems recognize the right of a party to move to set aside a judgment for a "fraud on the court." Both of these methods are historically grounded and may provide an extra safety valve when restrictions in the rules (usually timing constraints) otherwise would preclude relief. However, these provisions are encumbered with their own historic restrictions, which most often severely limit their usefulness.

§ 6–2. Grounds for Relief

Federal Rule 60(b) sets out the most widely recognized grounds for seeking relief from a judgment. Relief may be granted if the party moves within one year and shows that the judgment was entered due to a mistake, surprise, or excusable neglect, or that some material evidence exists that could not have been discovered earlier, or that the judgment was obtained fraudulently. The courts have not interpreted these grounds very broadly. If mistake or neglect is alleged, but gross neglect on the part of the movant is found, relief will be denied. In this context, "mistake" includes a judge's error of law. Accordingly, a motion for relief from judgment based on such an error is subject to a one-year limitations period. Kemp v. United States, 596 U.S. 528 (2022). Newly discovered evidence may be the subject of a motion for relief only if the evidence was available during the original proceeding. For example, the development of new medical treatments after a damage verdict has been entered in a personal-injury suit does not qualify as newly discovered evidence justifying the reopening of the judgment. The applicability of this ground is further limited because the liberal discovery rules present in most jurisdictions, see §§ 3–21—3–30, above, make it difficult to show that evidence that existed at the time of the trial could not have been discovered earlier. In several state systems, a party moving on the basis of fraud is limited to extrinsic fraud on the theory that the trial itself is designed to weed out intrinsic fraud, such as perjury. This judicial reluctance to grant relief is designed to protect the judgment winner from being constantly harassed by motions for relief from judgment.

A party also may seek relief on the ground that the judgment is void, that it has been satisfied, or, in the case of an equitable decree, that the circumstances have changed and the decree is no longer needed, or that the law on which the court relied has been materially changed. In these situations the motion must be made "within a reasonable time." The less rigid time restraints applicable to these bases for relief reflect the seriousness of the defect involved and, in some instances, the fact that it would not be possible to discover the ground for relief until more than one year had passed. It is within the court's discretion to decide whether the motion is so untimely that its grant would prejudice the opposing party unduly. Again, however, the grounds listed are rather specific and are interpreted narrowly.

An additional ground for relief that also is subject only to the "reasonable time" limitation is the rule's catch-all clause: "any other reason that justifies relief." Although its wording seems all inclusive, the courts have applied the clause sparingly to only those "extraordinary circumstances" demanding redress. Illustratively, the provision has been invoked successfully when a party has failed to comply with a settlement after a dismissal was entered, and when a party failed to appeal a denaturalization order or move for relief within a year because he or she was jailed and denied counsel. The courts have not used the clause as an open-ended loophole to circumvent the other time restrictions.

B. SECURING AND ENFORCING JUDGMENTS

§ 6–3. How a Judgment Is Enforced

Many judgments are self-enforcing. Judgments declaring the law or quieting title to property are good examples. Other judgments may require the losing party to pay money or to complete some act. In many of these cases a judgment winner need not use any enforcement method because the loser simply will pay the judgment or otherwise comply with the decree. If that does not occur, however, the method of enforcing the judgment varies depending on whether the judgment is local, that of a sister state, or international in character.

Enforcement of a local judgment is a purely administrative matter. The judgment winner (creditor) presents a copy of the judgment to the sheriff or other appropriate officer who issues a writ of execution on the loser's (debtor's) property designated by the judgment creditor. The writ orders any person or corporation in control of the property to turn it over to that officer for the purpose of satisfying the judgment winner. Illustratively, the sheriff may issue a writ garnishing the judgment loser's wages until the judgment has been satisfied. A writ of execution also can be directed at the debtor's automobile, which then would be seized and sold at a judicial sale with the proceeds used to pay the judgment. Any sale proceeds that exceed the judgment amount would be returned to the judgment loser. In cases in which the judgment involves an injunction, the judgment winner can move to hold the loser in contempt of court for failing to comply with the injunction. If the contemnor fails to comply he or she may be fined or jailed, or both, depending on the court's exercise of discretion regarding the nature of the contemptuous conduct.

When an out-of-state judgment is involved, it becomes necessary to convert the judgment into a local one before execution. This requires the judgment creditor to bring an action on the judgment in the enforcement court, serving process on the debtor and providing an opportunity to respond. In virtually all instances the requested judgment will be entered and enforcement will proceed as described above. This is because full faith and credit must be given to sister state judgments under the United States Constitution, Article IV, § 1. Therefore, except for a very limited number of possible objections, the enforcement court cannot look behind the judgment to reexamine the earlier proceedings. The rationale for requiring the creditor to bring an action on the out-of-state judgment rather than allowing immediate execution is based on notions of sovereignty. Each state is an independent, sovereign power and cannot directly invade another state's authority over its own residents or property by attempting to enforce its judgment there. Thus, the procedure defers to the sovereignty of the enforcement state by requiring the judgment winner to bring an action asking a court in that state to recognize the judgment so that execution may follow.

International judgments are treated similarly—an action to enforce must be brought. However, there is no constitutional full-faith-and-credit requirement applicable to judgments from a foreign country and no federal statute governs the matter. In some states, statutes provide criteria for determining when a foreign country money judgment should be enforced. In the absence of such a statute, and in the federal courts, it is left to the court's discretion to decide whether as a matter of comity enforcement should take place.

The process of bringing an action on a judgment is often a burdensome formality. Thus, several states have adopted uniform legislation authorizing a foreign judgment holder to file the judgment with the local court and mail a notice to that effect to the judgment debtor. After a short period of time, typically thirty days, during which the debtor can move to vacate, but only on grounds consistent with full faith and credit, the out-of-state judgment may be executed upon in the same manner as any local court judgment. See Uniform Enforcement of Foreign Judgments Act of 1964, 9A Uniform Laws Ann. 488 (1965). The process for enforcing a federal judgment from one state in a federal court in another state is similar, but even simpler. As provided by special statute, 28 U.S.C.A. § 1963, a federal judgment may be registered in another federal court by filing a copy there and, once that is done, it will be treated as a local judgment.

§ 6-4. Securing a Judgment—Constitutional Limitations

In some cases the plaintiff may fear that the defendant will transfer all his property to others or send it to someone outside of the jurisdiction in order to make the enforcement of any judgment, should the defendant lose, very difficult and costly or even impossible. In order to safeguard any potential judgment against this possibility, the plaintiff may request the court to order a provisional remedy issued against some of the defendant's assets immediately upon the filing of the action. In this way the plaintiff ensures that any judgment obtained will be easily enforceable should the losing defendant refuse to pay.

The process of securing a potential judgment with a provisional remedy is governed by state statutes and is accomplished by seeking one of a variety of writs, such as writs of replevin, attachment, garnishment, or sequestration. Under most statutes, the plaintiff is required to post a bond, which will be forfeited to the defendant if the suit is found to be frivolous or if the provisional remedy is shown to be solely a means of harassment. Historically, the clerk of the court or the judge simply entered the order ex parte and the sheriff seized the property. The defendant received notice only when the seizure took place; the defendant then could appear before the court to ask for relief or to post a counterbond and regain possession of or control over the property.

Prejudgment provisional remedies such as those just described have been successfully challenged as violating the constitutional due process rights of the defendant since no hearing or notice was provided prior to the creditor's assertion of control over the property. See Sniadach v. Family Finance Corp., 395 U.S. 337 (1969). The Supreme Court in a series of cases in the 1970s developed a balancing test by which to assess the constitutional validity of any prejudgment attachment, garnishment, or similar provisional remedy. See Fuentes v. Shevin, 407 U.S. 67 (1972). The test takes into account the public or governmental interest that would justify the deprivation of a property right or postponing the opportunity to be heard—for example, if attachment depends upon a showing that immediate action is necessary because the defendant is likely to transfer or hide the property. Further, the decision to issue an order for a provisional remedy must be committed to the discretion of a judicial officer, not merely the clerk of the court or a sheriff. Finally, the debtor must be provided an opportunity to dissolve the writ immediately, with the burden placed on the plaintiff to show why the attachment or other remedy was justified. See Mitchell v. W.T. Grant Co., 416 U.S. 600 (1974).

Further refinements were added by the Supreme Court in Connecticut v. Doehr, 501 U.S. 1 (1991), which found that the prejudgment attachment of real estate violated due process when the plaintiff had no prior interest in the property, the lawsuit involved a tort claim unrelated to the property, the merits of the plaintiff's claim hinged on credibility issues that could not be resolved based on documents alone, and the attachment statute did not require the plaintiff either to show extraordinary circumstances or to post a bond. The Court suggested that the appropriate due process analysis is to weigh the private defendant's interests affected by the seizure against the risk of a possible erroneous deprivation in light of the procedure involved and the safeguards, such as a bond, that apply, and the need for expeditious handling because of exigent circumstances. Thus, it is now clear that the ability of states to provide prejudgment provisional remedies has been severely limited.

One of the open questions raised by this line of cases is to what extent they affect the ability of a court to assert quasi-in-rem jurisdiction, which necessarily is based on a prejudgment attachment. See § 2–18, above. Is the desire to assert jurisdiction over the property a sufficient governmental interest to justify delaying the defendant's due process rights to a hearing? The Supreme Court has not yet ruled on this question and the lower courts that have considered it are divided.

C. THE BINDING EFFECT OF JUDGMENTS

1. IN GENERAL

§ 6–5. The Nomenclature

A complete vocabulary has been developed in connection with the law on the binding effect of judgments. Unfortunately, both courts and lawyers sometimes misuse terms. It therefore is important to learn the proper terminology in order to understand the results that may be reached in certain cases.

Res judicata or *claim preclusion* refers to the effect that a final adjudication on the merits of a cause of action (or claim) has on an attempt to relitigate the same cause of action within the same judicial system. The doctrine prevents the relitigation of causes of action, regardless of what issues actually were litigated in the first suit. When res judicata is asserted against a person who was victorious in the first action, the cause of action is said to have been merged into the judgment in that action. *Merger* prevents the second action from going forward. When res judicata is asserted against a person who lost the first suit, the second assertion of the claim is said to be barred by the first judgment. *Bar* prevents the second suit from proceeding. *Collateral estoppel* or *issue preclusion* can be invoked even when different causes of action are presented in the first and second suits. The doctrine provides that any issue that was actually litigated and necessarily decided in an action cannot be relitigated in a subsequent suit.

When res judicata or collateral estoppel is asserted on the basis of a judgment that was entered in a different court system than the second suit, namely another state, or a federal court if the first action was in a state court, or vice-versa, the judgment is given binding effect because of *Full Faith and Credit.* The Constitution, Art. IV, § 1, and its enabling legislation, 28 U.S.C.A. § 1738, require the second court—the enforcing court—to give the first judgment the same effect it would have been given in the forum where it was rendered. Thus, the law of res judicata as developed in the originating court will govern the binding effect of that judgment in the second court.

Claim preclusion and issue preclusion should be distinguished from three other doctrines. *Stare decisis* refers to the policy of the courts to adhere to precedent. Adherence to precedent is the foundation underlying the common law system; it provides the certainty necessary for persons to plan their activities knowing what the governing law is. Stare decisis effect is given only to actual determinations, not dicta. Further, a court has discretion to depart from precedent if it feels the circumstances have changed or that the prior case was decided wrongly. The doctrine of *law of the case* provides that the opinion or judgment of an appellate court on an appeal or writ of error is binding on the trial court when the case is remanded for further action. The doctrine arises out of the rule that a final judgment in the higher court is the final determination of the parties' rights. Finally, *election of remedies* is an historic, common law doctrine developed when parties were not allowed to plead alternatively or inconsistently. It provided that a party who chose between two or more theories of recovery had elected a remedy and, should the action fail, the party could not then sue on any other theory. A few states still invoke the doctrine to bar inconsistent theories of recovery. Under this approach, for example, to seek reformation of a contract, which is premised on the existence of a contract, will preclude a later action for quasi-contract, which assumes no contract exists. However, most modern courts have abandoned election doctrine as inconsistent with today's liberal pleading and joinder.

§ 6–6. General Principles Governing Binding Effect

Res judicata and collateral estoppel both operate with almost total disregard for what the truth or right result is. They are premised on the beliefs that the judicial system cannot tolerate repeated relitigation or it will be overburdened; that judgments must be stable and final so that litigants will be able to rely on them and plan for the future; and that the judicial system must prevent itself from being used as a tool of harassment. Thus, collateral estoppel precludes the relitigation of the same issue on the assumption that even if the issue was wrongly decided in the first action, the parties had a full and fair opportunity to present their case on that issue and systemic concerns must prevail. Res judicata takes this reasoning one step further. It provides that once the parties have been given a hearing on a claim, there can be no relitigation even though there may be some issues that were never introduced or considered in the first action that could have had a substantial impact on the outcome. Both doctrines are extremely important tools for planning litigation. The cautious attorney must be aware of these doctrines and their consequences and take care to frame the client's case so as not to be unexpectedly precluded in a later action, should subsequent litigation materialize.

Res judicata and collateral estoppel are judicial doctrines and their scope varies from jurisdiction to jurisdiction. Consequently, it is necessary to examine the precedents in the jurisdiction where suit is to be brought to determine exactly what binding effect is likely to attach to a particular judgment or issue. Because there is considerable variation in the way binding effect doctrines are applied, what follows is only a general description of them. The reader is advised for more comprehensive treatment to refer to J. Friedenthal, M. Kane, A. Miller & A. Steinman, Civil Procedure §§ 14.1–14.16 (6th ed.2021).

2. RES JUDICATA

§ 6-7. Requirements for Applying

A party asserting res judicata or claim preclusion must show that the *same cause of action* or *same claim* is involved in both suits, that there was a *valid* and *final judgment* on that matter, and, in most jurisdictions, that the prior judgment was *on the merits.* The problem of defining what constitutes a single claim or cause of action is discussed in the next section. This section takes a brief look at the other requirements.

The validity of a judgment is determined solely in terms of whether the first court had authority to decide the case, not whether there was error in the first proceeding. Only judgments entered by a court having proper subject-matter jurisdiction, see §§ 2–1—2–6, above, as well as proper personal jurisdiction over the defendant, see §§ 2–9—2–22, above, are entitled to full res judicata effect. However, as was discussed earlier, a judgment may be subject to collateral attack and the court may refuse to give it claim preclusive effect because of a lack of jurisdiction only under certain conditions, such as when the defect never was raised in the first proceeding and defendant defaulted at that time. See § 2–31, above. Further, if a state court had jurisdiction, then its judgment may have preclusive effect on claims that otherwise were within the federal courts' jurisdiction—even their exclusive jurisdiction—if those claims are within the cause of action asserted in the state court action. Matsushita Elec. Indus. Co. v. Epstein, 516 U.S. 367 (1996).

Finality, for res judicata purposes, "represents the completion of all steps in the adjudication of a claim by the court, short of execution." American Law Institute, *Restatement Second of Judgments* § 13 (1982). Thus, finality occurs when the trial court enters a judgment and is not affected by the taking of an appeal, unless the appellate court vacates the judgment and orders a trial de novo. Nonetheless, the court in which the initial judgment is being asserted as binding may stay the action before it until the appeal from the first judgment is completed. Although that is the sounder practice because it avoids the risk that binding effect will be given to what ultimately may be found to be an invalid or erroneous judgment, the court has discretion simply to apply res judicata and dismiss the second suit based on the first trial court's judgment.

Even when a judgment involving a cause of action is final, claim prelusion will not prevent a second action on the same matter if that judgment was not on the merits. For example, a dismissal for lack of subject-matter or personal jurisdiction will not bar the identical action from being brought in a court having proper jurisdiction. The requirement of a judgment on the merits has created several problems with pretrial dismissals that bear closely on the merits. For example, courts do not agree on how to treat demurrers or dismissals for failure to state a claim for relief for res judicata purposes. It is clear that if the pleader merely restates the same grievance in a second action, res judicata will apply. But some courts have overruled res judicata challenges when the second complaint alleges facts or theories that were not in the first complaint, concluding that the merits never were actually considered in the first action when it was dismissed because of a pleading defect. Other courts handle this problem by granting the plaintiff a right to amend at the time of the first dismissal. If the plaintiff fails to do so or fails to appeal, claim preclusion will apply. This approach is particularly prevalent in systems that have pleading rules that permit pretrial dismissals on the pleadings leading to the entry of a judgment only when there is no plausible theory on which the plaintiff could base a viable case. See § 3–4, above.

Another problem in determining when a judgment is on the merits is presented by involuntary dismissals entered for failure to prosecute or for failure to comply with a court rule or order. The rules governing these dismissals typically provide that they will be with prejudice unless otherwise ordered. See, e.g., Fed.Rule 41(b). Thus, the question presented is whether they should be given res judicata effect even though it is clear by the very nature of the dismissal that the merits of the case never were reached. Most courts apply res judicata, noting that the availability of motions for relief from a judgment following an involuntary dismissal and of an appeal from that type of judgment ameliorates the harshness of applying res judicata to an involuntary dismissal in these circumstances. Some courts, however, do not give preclusive effect on the ground that the dismissal was not on the merits.

In order to avoid the kinds of problems just discussed, the American Law Institute, *Restatement Second of Judgments* § 19, Comment a (1982), omits entirely the phrase "on the merits" from its definition of bar. Instead, the question whether preclusive effect should be given to a pretrial dismissal is determined as a matter of sound judicial administration on the basis of the circumstances and by considering the fairness to the defendant if a second action is allowed. To that end, the ALI approach states a general rule that a judgment will bar other actions on the same claim, but lists several exceptions—such as when the judgment is a dismissal for lack of jurisdiction or improper venue, or when the plaintiff was unable to rely on a certain theory or to seek a certain remedy in the first action because of limits on the court's jurisdiction or authority. *Restatement* §§ 20, 26. Unless a specific exception applies, preclusion operates to terminate litigation on the matter once and for all after the first dismissal and the question whether the court's decision involved "the merits" is irrelevant under the ALI's approach.

§ 6–8. Defining a Cause of Action or Claim

The particular test that a court adopts to define a cause of action (or claim) for res judicata purposes may be influenced by several outside considerations. Some courts utilize a very broad test in keeping with the policies of their judicial systems to encourage the broadest possible joinder of claims and defenses in the first suit and thereby to avoid multiple suits. Others invoke a narrower conception because they are concerned about the harsh effect of claim preclusion and prefer to rely on collateral estoppel to prevent duplicative litigation. Yet others may be influenced by the merits of the claim of the party opposing the assertion of res judicata and thus define the cause of action narrowly to allow the presentation of the case. A few courts appear to take into account whether the cause of action was split intentionally to enable the bringing of two suits. What follows is a description of the various tests utilized by different courts. However, whichever test is used in the forum court, the court asked to apply res judicata also may be swayed to apply its own standards by the larger policy factors just mentioned.

There are essentially four different tests that have been used to define what constitutes a cause of action for binding effect purposes. The first, which may be called the *destruction-of-prior-judgment* test, focuses on whether a decision in the second action would have the effect of undoing or contradicting what is embraced in the first judgment. This test can be applied in different ways depending on what the court considers as being within the scope of the first judgment. Thus, res judicata may be invoked successfully under this standard if the court considers the initial judgment to include not only the relief awarded but all the explicit and implicit findings that supported the award of relief; if the court focuses merely on the desire to avoid providing an inconsistent remedy, then the test is very narrow and no preclusive effect will be given.

A second conception of cause of action looks to the legal rights and wrongs involved in the first suit and seeks to prevent multiple lawsuits based on any of the grounds for the same right or wrong. This is sometimes referred to as the *primary rights* test. Under it, separate causes of action are involved when more than one right is claimed to have been infringed, even though the several rights involved were impinged upon by a single act. For example, personal injury and car damages arising from the same accident present different causes of action under this standard because one involves trespass to the person, the other trespass to a chattel. Back injuries and neurological damage resulting from a single event, however, constitute the violation of one right—trespass to the person—and constitute a single cause of action. Actions involving injuries to separate pieces of property also involve different rights. Res judicata will be applied in contract disputes depending on whether the contract is deemed indivisible or divisible, providing for separate rights. In a somewhat similar vein, if the legal rights in two actions rest on different statutes, then multiple causes of action will be found if both are claimed to have been violated.

The "primary rights" definition of cause of action is a product of the common-law writ system, a time when cases could consist only of a single issue. Thus, most courts do not adhere to it today. Although it was necessary historically to protect parties from preclusion because they could not have raised the multiple claims they might have in one suit, more recent claim joinder systems afford that opportunity, which suggests that a broader res judicata test be utilized. See § 3–19, above. In order to modernize the test, a variant has evolved in some states that define rights, not in terms of historic distinctions, but in terms of the wrongs that were committed. Focus under this approach is on the defendant's acts, rather than the plaintiff's injuries. One tortious act constitutes one cause of action even though it may have produced a series of injuries to both person and property. In actions based on violations of property or contract rights, the focus will be on the acts of the defendant that produced injury or served to breach the contract.

The third approach to defining cause of action for binding effect purposes attempts to avoid duplicative litigation by determining whether the *same evidence* would be used in both actions. The difficulty with this standard—and the probable reason why it has not gained wide acceptance—is that there is no clear measuring rod as to how much evidence needs to be the same before it is proper to find that a single cause of action was presented in the initial action.

The fourth test for the assertion of res judicata is the *transaction* test, described in American Law Institute, *Restatement Second of Judgments* § 24(1) (1982). Under that standard any acts, transactions, or closely related series of occurrences that may have produced an injury or several injuries should be presented in a single suit or be barred in subsequent actions. The obvious practical effect of this approach is to encourage the joinder of all related claims in the first action. Thus, there has been some resistance to this "transaction or occurrence" standard on the ground that if the pleading and joinder rules are permissive only, see § 3–19, above, then it is unfair and improper for the courts to create a compulsory joinder system indirectly through the expansion of res judicata. However, as more and more judicial systems have adopted procedural rules encouraging the broadest possible joinder of claims, utilization of the transaction-or-occurrence test to determine what claims must be joined in the first proceeding has received growing acceptance.

The application of the various standards just described to the assertion of claims in a second action by the person who was the defendant in the first suit must be considered separately. Both the "rights" and the "wrongs" test for cause of action necessitate not only that the same parties or their privies be involved in both suits, see § 6–9, below, but also that the parties remain in essentially the same offensive-defensive posture in both actions. In an action between A and B, those tests look to how many of A's rights were violated or how many wrongful acts were committed by B. If B also has a potential claim against A arising out of the same series of events, that will constitute a separate cause of action because it will require an inquiry into B's rights and A's wrongful acts. The transaction test does not recognize this distinction and res judicata theoretically could apply to both A's and B's claims if it were applied.

Defining cause of action in terms of whose rights or wrongs are involved has caused some problems in situations in which the same facts may be asserted by B both as an affirmative defense and as a counterclaim. The judicial economy and harassment rationales underlying the doctrine of claim preclusion suggest that B should be compelled to raise both the defense and the counterclaim in the first suit. Although this result may be readily achieved in jurisdictions that have a compulsory counterclaim rule, see § 3–20, above, in states without such a provision the result rests on the application of res judicata principles. Indeed, a broad application of those principles might suggest that even if B defaults, res judicata should bar another action by B against A. This would be based on the fact that B had the opportunity to raise the defense, and the counterclaim was merged into the defense.

But most courts faced with this problem have not gone so far. A distinction often is drawn between omitted and litigated defenses, with res judicata being applied in a subsequent suit by B against A only if B asserted the affirmative defense but failed to include the counterclaim. The focus in determining whether B has improperly split the cause of action is whether the same facts are in issue and the same evidence would be utilized for both the defense and the omitted counterclaim. Some courts have refused to go even that far. They have applied the same evidence test in such a way that res judicata cannot ever be invoked successfully in this situation by pointing to new evidence on damages for the counterclaim—that are not germane to the defense—to substantiate the conclusion that different causes of action are involved.

§ 6–9. Who Will Be Bound

Res judicata or claim preclusion is applicable only when the second action is between persons who were parties or who are in privity with persons who were parties in the first action. When there are new parties in the second action, a separate or different cause of action is presented. If any preclusive effect is to attach to the first judgment, it will be through the application of collateral estoppel, not res judicata. See § 6–13, below. The sole exception to this is when a proper class action judgment is involved, in which case all absent class members will be bound by that judgment. See § 8–4, below. Thus, the question of who will be bound by res judicata depends on the definition of who is in privity with the named parties in the first action.

Historically, a person in privity with a party was someone who acquired an interest in the subject matter of the suit after it had been instituted. Successors in interest, whether they obtained their interests by virtue of an assignment, by inheritance or by law were treated as parties for res judicata purposes and were bound by any judgment entered against or for their predecessors. Modern courts have extended privity concepts to additional circumstances. For example, a person who actually controls the first suit will be found to be in privity with the named parties to that suit. This would occur, for example, when an insurance company controlled the defense of its insured. Appointed or legal representatives, such as guardians or administrators, are in privity with the person whom they are representing. Additionally, privity has been found in a wide range of commercial relationships, such as those involving employer-employee and indemnitor-indemnitee relationships. The decision to expand privity to those relationships depends heavily on the substantive law regulating the relationship. Thus, generalizations about the binding effect of judgments in those areas are dangerous to make because of the complicated nature of the rules used to determine both who is in privity, as well as when applying privity is appropriate.

Suffice it to note that the modern trend has been to expand the scope of res judicata—for example, by extending claim preclusion to the entire transaction or occurrence at issue in the first lawsuit, as discussed in § 6–8, above. In general, however, courts have been reluctant to extend privity to embrace persons having similar, or even identical, interests if there is no special relationship existing between them. Thus, for example, the fact that the same lawyer is representing the parties in the first and second action will not, standing alone, establish privity. And the Supreme Court rejected the opportunity to adopt for the federal courts a "virtual representation" theory of claim preclusion in a case in which the claims in the two actions were basically identical. The Court noted that there are only discrete and limited exceptions to the rule against nonparty preclusion. A good discussion of this appears in Taylor v. Sturgell, 553 U.S. 880 (2008).

§ 6–10. Policies Outweighing Res Judicata

There are some circumstances in which preclusion will not be applied even though the standard for applying res judicata has been met. These situations arise when the judicial economy policies fostered by claim preclusion are outweighed by some other public policy underlying the type of action that is involved. Illustratively, in a suit involving the sale of land in which both the buyer and the seller were claiming title, a court overruled all res judicata objections because to hold otherwise would be inequitable and would result in an unclear title to the land. The policies underlying the transfer of property required that some judicial determination regarding ownership be given the parties. Adams v. Pearson, 104 N.E.2d 267 (Ill.1952). In another action res judicata was outweighed by the policies underlying the worker's compensation laws so that a prior common law negligence action did not preclude seeking a statutory remedy; it only reduced the amount of the judgment previously awarded. Varsity Amusement Co. v. Butters, 394 P.2d 603 (Colo.1964). Necessarily, these exceptions to the normal application of claim preclusion principles are quite limited. They depend on a court finding that a specific and important public policy requires the decision not to apply res judicata.

3. COLLATERAL ESTOPPEL

§ 6-11. Requirements for Applying

In order for collateral estoppel to be invoked successfully, the party asserting it must show that the same or *identical issue* is presented in action-2 that was decided in action-1, and that the issue was *actually litigated* and *necessarily decided* in action-1. The presence of each element of this test assures that preclusion will result only after a party has had a full opportunity to litigate the particular issue. When this assurance exists, the economy and efficiency of the civil justice system becomes paramount.

The requirement of identical issues is met easily when the plaintiff is asserting several claims based on a single act or transaction entered into by the defendant. The question whether the defendant acted negligently in driving an automobile will be the same in a suit claiming damages for personal injuries to the driver of the other car as in a later suit by the injured driver's spouse for loss of consortium. However, in actions arising out of acts that occurred at different times or places, the issues, even though very similar, necessarily are not identical. For example, a suit to establish the taxability of income earned in 2025 by an organization claiming a tax exemption as a religious group will have no preclusive effect on a similar action in 2026 involving precisely the same kind of activities. A finding that the defendant did or did not function as a religious organization in 2025 will not be given issue preclusive effect because the character of the defendant's activities or objective in 2026 may have changed—the issue is not identical. Similarly, collateral estoppel will not be available in successive actions on separate bonds or negotiable instruments in which the same defense—whether the plaintiff purchased the bonds for value—is raised. The issues are not identical; the proof that the plaintiff was or was not a bona fide purchaser of one bond does not serve to prove how any of the other bonds or negotiable instruments were obtained by him.

Differences between the burden of proof in the first and second action also may result in a finding that the issues presented in the two actions are not identical. This is because if the burden of proof differs, there is no assurance that the result would be the same in both actions and the requirements of collateral estoppel are designed to provide that assurance. The question arises most often when one proceeding is criminal and the other civil. This is because in criminal proceedings the prosecution must prove each element beyond a reasonable doubt, but in civil actions the plaintiff need only establish the matter by a preponderance of the evidence. If an issue is established first under the stricter criminal standard, then it may be given collateral estoppel effect in the later civil proceeding, but the converse is not true.

The requirement that the issues actually be litigated prevents collateral estoppel effect from being given to default judgments or consent judgments in which a judgment on the merits is reached, but a full adversary presentation on the underlying issues has not occurred. The requirement is more difficult to apply, however, in cases in which a review of the pleadings fails to reveal whether the issues framed in them actually were litigated at the trial and thus are embraced by the judgment. This problem occurs, for example, when a general verdict is rendered by the jury but the judgment could be based on findings on alternative issues in the case. The minority view is that the court in the second action should treat all issues as actually litigated, giving a broad collateral estoppel effect to the judgment. The majority view, however, is that when the judgment in the first action may have been based on different findings on more than one issue, no collateral estoppel effect will be given to any issue in the case unless evidence is introduced showing which issues actually were litigated and decided, as might be possible when the jury has responded to specific interrogatories propounded by the court. See § 5–10, above.

As a further limitation, only extrinsic evidence that supports the verdict is allowed; the evidence cannot contradict the verdict. For example, consider an action in which A sues B for injuries caused by B's negligence. B alleges as a defense that A was contributorily negligent. At the trial the jury returns a general verdict for B. That verdict could be based on a finding that A was contributorily negligent, that B was free from negligence, or both. B can assert collateral estoppel in a subsequent suit against A only if B can show the basis on which the jury rested its verdict in the first action. However, under no circumstances can A introduce evidence to the effect that the alleged contributory negligence was not actually litigated or considered by the jury because that would contradict the verdict.

The third requirement for applying collateral estoppel—whether the issue was necessary to the first proceeding—has posed some difficulty for the courts. This requirement is designed to assure that the parties vigorously litigated the issue so that it is fair to prevent its relitigation in a second action because there is little likelihood that the results will be different the second time around. Accordingly, facts found against the prevailing party in the first action are deemed unnecessary. The prevailing party has no incentive to appeal and thus the issue will not be given collateral estoppel effect because vigorous prosecution on that issue is not assured.

Courts are divided on whether to give alternative holdings—either of which are sufficient to support the judgment—full collateral estoppel effect. Some do, reasoning that one holding is no less necessary than the other. For example, in the negligence hypothetical above, if a special verdict had been rendered specifically finding A contributorily negligent and B free from negligence, B could assert collateral estoppel against A on both issues. The specific findings give some assurance that the jury took both issues seriously.

Other courts, however, do not give alternative holdings issue-preclusive effect, on the theory that neither one is strictly necessary to the judgment. Interestingly, the American Law Institute, *Restatement Second of Judgments* § 27 (1982), advocates that no collateral estoppel effect be given to alternative holdings because of a concern that this broad preclusion approach will encourage appeals. However, if the parties have appealed and the appellate court affirms the alternative findings, then the *Restatement* would apply collateral estoppel to both issues.

§ 6-12. Mediate and Ultimate Facts

Another method utilized in the past by courts to determine when to uphold the assertion of collateral estoppel was to distinguish between mediate and ultimate facts, giving preclusive effect only to the latter. Ultimate facts were those on which the case actually was based—e.g., does plaintiff have title. Mediate facts were those that provided the means by which the court could reach a conclusion on the ultimate facts—e.g., did plaintiff obtain title through a fraudulent scheme. Concerns over how to establish whether a mediate fact actually was litigated led to a rule that mediate facts in the first action should not be given collateral estoppel effect.

Another concern prompting the use of the mediate/ultimate fact distinction was the problem of foreseeability. This concern was particularly prevalent when a fact found in the first action, whether mediate or ultimate in that context, was only a mediate fact in the second action. Courts refused collateral estoppel effect under those circumstances in order to prevent surprise to the losing litigant in the first action, who, it was assumed, could not have foreseen all the possible future contexts in which mediate facts might be associated with a given issue and thus may not have litigated that issue fully in the first action.

Today the mediate/ultimate fact distinction is largely of historic significance. The policies it addressed are now satisfied in other ways without relying on pleading distinctions that have lost much of their meaning. Further, the availability of devices such as special verdicts and general verdicts with answers to questions has eroded the need for this rule. See § 5–10, above. The American Law Institute, *Restatement Second of Judgments* § 27 (1982), states that the modern approach is to determine whether the fact issue on which collateral estoppel is being asserted was necessary and important, rather than merely evidentiary, in the first suit. If so, and if the issue was actually litigated, then it is fair to give the issue preclusive effect in another action. There is no need to be concerned with foreseeability because the parties had incentive to litigate the issue vigorously in the first proceeding.

§ 6-13. Who Will Be Bound

Historically, the question of who could benefit from or who would be bound by collateral estoppel was treated the same way as when res judicata was involved: only parties and their privies could invoke or be precluded by collateral estoppel. See § 6-9, above. Even though an issue was identical in two different actions and judicial economy concerns would support preventing its relitigation in a second action, collateral estoppel effect was denied. The reasoning supporting this restriction was twofold. In cases in which collateral estoppel is asserted against someone who was not a party to the first action, due process considerations prevent its application because the nonparty must be given an opportunity to be heard—the right to day-in-court principle. Second, the doctrine of mutuality prevented the successful assertion of collateral estoppel by a non-party against someone who did litigate the issue unsuccessfully in the first suit. Mutuality was premised on the notion that everyone should be treated equally. Since a party to an action cannot assert collateral estoppel against someone who was not a party to that suit, neither should the nonparty be allowed to assert estoppel against the party. In this way mutuality operated in favor of someone who had been heard, giving that person a second chance to succeed on the issue.

Due process continues to prevent the assertion of collateral estoppel against someone who was not a party to the first suit. This was reaffirmed by the Supreme Court when it held that an unnamed class member cannot be considered a "party" before the class is certified and thus cannot be bound by a court's decision to deny class certification. Smith v. Bayer Corp., 564 U.S. 299 (2011).

The question whether mutuality is a necessary limitation on the application of collateral estoppel, however, always was debatable. Thus, perhaps not surprisingly, adherence to the mutuality doctrine has steadily eroded, following the lead of the California Supreme Court in Bernhard v. Bank of America Nat. Trust & Sav. Ass'n, 122 P.2d 892 (Cal.1942). Those courts that have abandoned the doctrine have concluded that a person should not be allowed to litigate a fruitless claim continuously, particularly when relitigation is unlikely to change the result. Instead of automatically denying preclusive effect to a nonparty asserting estoppel against a prior party, they focus on whether the prior party had a full and fair opportunity to litigate the issue in the first action. If so, then collateral estoppel may be applied. Of course, the issues also must be identical in both suits.

Over the years courts have abandoned the mutuality principle in varying degrees. The most commonly recognized situation is when the person asserting issue preclusion is doing so defensively. In those cases judicial economy concerns are great because it appears that the unsuccessful party in the first suit simply may be suing different defendants seriatim. There is a natural desire to protect the new defendant from such harassing litigation.

The problem becomes more difficult when collateral estoppel is being asserted offensively—when a nonparty to the first action is attempting in a second action to take advantage of a judgment that was adverse to a party in the earlier suit. One concern is whether the defendant should have foreseen this second suit at the time of the first action so that there was an incentive to litigate the first suit fully. If not, it would be unfair to preclude the issue from being litigated in the second action. Another concern centers on the new party who is trying to take advantage of the judgment even though he or she was not a party in the first action and therefore would not have been at any risk if an adverse judgment resulted.

Accordingly, some courts have simply refused to allow collateral estoppel to be asserted offensively by a nonparty. Others have allowed its assertion when it is against someone who was the aggressor in the first suit, but not when it is against someone who was a defendant in the first suit. This distinction is based on the belief that the defending party to the first action necessarily was at a disadvantage by not having the right to pick the time and place to litigate; to make certain that he or she has a fair opportunity to be heard, collateral estoppel should not be applied. A few courts have refused to reject collateral estoppel merely because of the posture of the parties in the first action. Instead, they focus on whether the party to both actions had an incentive to litigate the first action fully and could have foreseen the second suit. If so, the burden shifts to that party to show that the issue was not fully litigated in the first action. If that is not shown, issue preclusion will be applied.

The United States Supreme Court has endorsed the abandonment of mutuality in the federal courts and has set out guidelines for those courts to aid in evaluating the propriety of the assertion of collateral estoppel by nonparties. In Parklane Hosiery Co. v. Shore, 439 U.S. 322 (1979), the Court ruled that the trial court has broad discretion to determine this question and that collateral estoppel should be applied even when it is being asserted by a plaintiff against someone who was a defendant in the first action, unless the court finds that the plaintiff easily could have joined in the first action or that the application of collateral estoppel would be unfair to the defendant. The federal standard thus looks not only to the foreseeability of a subsequent action, but also to other potential unfairness, and seeks to avoid rewarding a plaintiff who chose not to join in the first suit in order not to be bound by the result if it proved to be in favor of the defendant in the first action. Fairness also may take into account whether there is any reason to fear that the first judgment is patently unreliable and whether there are procedural opportunities available in the second action that did not exist in the first, suggesting that the possibility of a different result might result if the issue were retried. However, the Parklane Court (over a strong dissent) specifically stated that the availability of a jury trial in the second suit when there was none in the first is not such a procedural opportunity.

State courts are not obliged to follow the lead of the Supreme Court because they may define for themselves the scope of their own state court judgments, and many continue to define categories of cases in which mutuality applies. Thus, it is most important to examine the law of the judgment-rendering court to determine who may use collateral estoppel or be bound by it because variations among jurisdictions in their adherence to or rejection of mutuality are great.

§ 6–14. Limitations on Collateral Estoppel

The availability of collateral estoppel may be limited by other policies outweighing the desire for judicial economy and certainty, although, as will be seen, there are few limitations. For example, it was argued that the doctrine could not be invoked when to do so would effectively deny the opposing party a right to a jury trial on an issue because the first suit was tried without a jury. However, as noted in the preceding section, the Supreme Court rejected this argument for the federal courts, ruling that an equitable determination by a judge sitting without a jury can have issue preclusive effect in a subsequent jury triable legal action without violating the Seventh Amendment. Parklane Hosiery Co. v. Shore, 439 U.S. 322 (1979).

A limitation on the application of collateral estoppel that is generally recognized is when the first action was heard before a court of limited jurisdiction. The courts are divided on the question whether to give collateral estoppel effect to issues when the claims raised in the second action to which those issues pertain were outside the subject-matter jurisdiction of the first court. For example, judgments of small-claims courts typically are not given issue-preclusive effect.

The question becomes more difficult when the first action was in state court, the second is in federal court, and the claims in the second action are ones over which the federal court has exclusive subject matter jurisdiction. Illustratively, this question has arisen in federal court antitrust and patent cases when there have been prior state proceedings in which those courts have ruled on issues pertaining to antitrust violations or patent validity in the course of deciding whether a contract was illegal or whether royalties were due under a patent licensing agreement.

An early Supreme Court decision in a patent case recognized that issue preclusion was proper as to any of the underlying facts decided in the state court; federal courts might refrain from giving collateral estoppel effect only to the "congerie of facts" establishing the ultimate issue of patent validity or infringement. Becher v. Contoure Laboratories, Inc., 279 U.S. 388 (1929). In this way the federal courts could avoid duplicative relitigation but protect their exclusive right to rule on the patent itself. More recently, however, this distinction has lost its vitality. Full faith and credit now requires that the federal courts give the same binding effect to a judgment that would be given by the rendering court. If the state court would not bar the relitigation of the issues (as, for example, if it still adhered to mutuality), then the state court judgment will not preclude federal relitigation of those issues. Marrese v. American Academy of Orthopaedic Surgeons, 470 U.S. 373 (1985). If the state court would preclude the relitigation of the issues decided in the first action, then the federal court must extend full faith and credit to that judgment, even though those matters otherwise would have been within exclusive federal jurisdiction. Matsushita Elec. Indus. Co. v. Epstein, 516 U.S. 367 (1996). Other Supreme Court decisions have concluded that, absent some evidence that Congress intended to provide an unrestricted opportunity to relitigate in federal court issues already decided in state court, a state court decision could be given collateral estoppel effect. Allen v. McCurry, 449 U.S. 90 (1980).

The final limitation on the application of collateral estoppel arises because of changes in the law that occur between the first and second lawsuits. If the law is altered to change the operative facts necessary to obtain a favorable ruling, then issue preclusion will not apply. To hold otherwise would result in unequal treatment being afforded persons under the law simply because of the fortuity of a person obtaining a prior ruling. For example, A brings a tax refund action on the theory that an assignment of royalties under a 1998 patent licensing agreement to his wife B was valid so that income under that agreement during the years 1999–2001 was not taxable to him. The court finds the assignment valid and thus A is not liable for tax on those royalties, but is due a refund. The law changes as to what must be shown to constitute a valid assignment between husband and wife. Collateral estoppel will not be available to A in a refund suit for taxes collected on royalties earned from 2019–2022 on the issue of whether there has been a valid assignment; new additional evidence must be introduced to justify the refund for the years 2019–2022. Commissioner v. Sunnen, 333 U.S. 591 (1948) (addressing a similar fact pattern). The need for tax equality outweighs the judicial economy policies underlying collateral estoppel.

It is worth noting that concern over changes in relevant law led some courts to suggest that issue preclusion never is appropriate for issues of pure law. Consequently, several decisions can be found in which the courts have struggled to determine what constitutes an issue of law rather than one of fact or one of mixed fact and law, to which estoppel can be applied. More recent decisions have abandoned this approach, however, focusing instead on whether those changes in the law suggest that estoppel would be inappropriate.

§ 6–15. Administrative and Arbitral Decisions

The decisions of nonjudicial bodies—namely, administrative agencies and arbitral tribunals—also may foreclose judicial proceedings as a result of either claim preclusion or issue preclusion. Although the general principles of former adjudication apply to administrative and arbitral decisions, there are important differences in the analysis. Starting with governmental agencies, there are four settings in which administrative decisions can have preclusive effect: in successive proceedings before the same agency; successive proceedings before different agencies; between an earlier court decision and a later agency proceeding; or between an earlier agency decision and a later court proceeding.

In successive proceedings before the same agency, courts generally have adopted a somewhat flexible approach to preclusion. The general approach is that courts will apply the traditional rules of preclusion but remain willing to allow agencies to avoid preclusion in order to accommodate policies embodied in their organic or authorizing statutes. For example, in Hicks v. Commissioner of Social Security, 909 F.3d 786 (6th Cir.2018), the court found that plaintiffs' eligibility for benefits was not subject to preclusion, even though the Social Security Administration had previously administratively determined that they were eligible. By contrast, when a proceeding in one agency is followed by a proceeding in a different agency, the decision of the first agency is less likely to be given preclusive effect.

When an agency proceeding follows a judicial determination, the general rule is that the agency must recognize the preclusive effect of the court's judgment with respect to common issues. A contrary rule could permit a party to make a direct attack on an unfavorable federal judicial judgment in an administrative proceeding. An agency is not required, however, to give preclusive effect to a court's determination in situations in which a subsequent court would not be required to find preclusive effect.

When judicial proceedings follow an agency decision, the general rule now is that a court will recognize the preclusive effect of administrative adjudications subject to two qualifications. First, the administrative decisions must result from a procedure that is an adequate substitute for the procedure one would expect in a court. The agency must act in a judicial capacity to resolve factual issues and provide the parties with an adequate opportunity to litigate them. Second, particular regulatory schemes, unique to each agency, may intend that administrative decisions have more or less preclusive effect in federal courts.

The analysis is different when there is a federal judicial proceeding and a prior administrative decision rendered by a state agency. The rule is clear in cases in which a federal administrator was not a party to the state agency proceeding: the federal administrator is not bound by the state agency determination in a subsequent federal judicial proceeding. Courts now commonly apply issue preclusion, however, when a party in the federal judicial proceeding was also a party to the state administrative proceeding, unless Congress intended that federal courts provide an independent determination of the facts with respect to certain federal rights. University of Tennessee v. Elliott, 478 U.S. 788 (1986). By contrast, the rule in diversity-of-citizenship actions is that forum state law governs the preclusive effect of state administrative determinations. This principle applies equally to state claims brought in a federal court under its supplemental subject-matter jurisdiction.

Similar to administrative agencies, arbitral tribunals often serve as nonjudicial forums for certain kinds of legal disputes. Arbitration, however, raises additional complications. First, administrative adjudication falls on a court-like procedural spectrum between highly informal proceedings and formal hearings. Arbitration, by contrast, is much more likely to depart from the procedures one sees in an ordinary court.

What preclusive effect must a court give to an arbitral decision? A common approach courts have taken is to remit preclusion defenses to arbitration if the original arbitration agreement appears to cover the new dispute. Some courts have taken a more active role, however. Since arbitration is not considered a judicial proceeding within the meaning of the Constitution's full faith and credit clause, courts are not obligated by that document to recognize arbitral awards. But if a court recognizes an arbitral award, then courts of another state must give that judicial judgment full faith and credit.

With respect to claim preclusion, most courts are willing to infer that an arbitration agreement presupposes that the award will be enforceable and preclusive. A contrary rule allowing a party to make precisely the same claim subsequently in court as previously made in the arbitration would defeat the purpose of agreeing to arbitration in the first place. The nature of the arbitration and the agreement to arbitrate will often determine the claim-preclusive effect of the arbitral decision. For instance, if the agreement does not include a particular issue that is advanced in later litigation or if the arbitrators exceeded their authority by deciding an issue advanced in later litigation, a court will not give those arbitral decisions claim preclusive effect.

Certain aspects of arbitration can create obstacles to preclusion. For instance, issue preclusion will require a court to determine whether the arbitrator dealt with the same issue that has come before the court. But arbitrators tend to produce short opinions without extensive reasoning, or sometimes provide no opinion at all. Moreover, a court may not consider arbitration to have provided a "full and fair opportunity" to litigate a matter for which preclusion is invoked. In general, however, that deviation from the ordinary procedure of a judicial proceeding is not sufficient by itself to deny giving issue-preclusive effect to an arbitral decision.

Courts also may be reluctant to accord preclusive effect to an arbitral decision when a relevant statute indicates that independent judicial review is necessary to protect or further the statute's purpose. In Alexander v. Gardner-Denver Company, 415 U.S. 36 (1974), for example, the Supreme Court held that a grievance arbitration agreement under a collective bargaining contract did not preclude employment discrimination claims under Title VII of the Civil Rights Act of 1964. Courts have extended this logic to cases under the Civil Rights Act of 1866, the Age Discrimination in Employment Act, securities laws, antitrust laws, and the Fair Labor Standards Act.

The Supreme Court severely limited the Gardner-Denver holding and its progeny in 14 Penn Plaza Limited Liability Company v. Pyett, 556 U.S. 247 (2009). In that case, the employer sought to compel arbitration of employee age discrimination claims under the arbitration agreement in their collective bargaining agreement. The agreement prohibited age discrimination that violated the Age Discrimination in Employment Act, but provided that arbitration was the exclusive remedy. The Court applied federal law and compelled arbitration, distinguishing Gardner-Denver and the cases that followed it on the ground that the arbitration agreements in those cases required arbitration only of contract claims and failed to include statutory claims. The Court also indicated in dicta that the Gardner-Denver court was inappropriately skeptical of arbitration. Although 14 Penn Plaza did not involve preclusion, it strongly indicates that an arbitral determination regarding a statutory claim may be entitled to preclusive effect only if the arbitration agreement expressly covers it.

CHAPTER 7
APPEALS

A. TIME FOR BRINGING AN APPEAL

1. THE FINAL JUDGMENT RULE

§ 7–1. Final Judgment Rule

Most jurisdictions authorize an appeal only from the entry of a final judgment in the action. The final judgment is defined as that order that leaves nothing to be done in the action except to execute on the judgment. It concludes all the rights that were subject to litigation. For example, an order dismissing a juror for cause, though conclusive on that question, is not a final judgment because the rights that are the subject of the underlying lawsuit have not been decided. If the attorney objects to the ruling, that objection may be raised on appeal, but the attorney must wait to take an appeal until a judgment on the merits is entered. This type of order commonly is described as reviewable, but not appealable. The only exceptions to the final judgment rule are incorporated in specific statutes, see § 7–3, below, or in a few well-recognized judicial doctrines, see § 7–4, below.

The rationales supporting the final judgment rule are severalfold. In part the rule stems from a desire to obtain judicial economy—a single appeal in which all objections to the trial court's rulings are raised should be more efficient than several appeals, each requiring its own set of briefs, records, oral argument, and opinions. Indeed, the need for an appeal on a given ruling may be avoided totally if the losing party on that issue ultimately prevails in the trial court. Appeals from final judgments also avoid the problem of delaying the trial in order to decide interlocutory matters. In this way, the final judgment rule protects against the possibility that an appeal may be used to harass the opposing party.

A few jurisdictions, such as New York, have not been persuaded by these arguments and are more permissive about allowing immediate appeals from trial court orders. These jurisdictions focus on the fact that an immediate appeal may avoid an unnecessary trial if the question is one that will decide whether the suit should proceed. Alternatively, an immediate appeal may result in a better trial as all preliminary issues will be resolved fully. Further, the final judgment rule effectively prevents some orders from ever being reviewed because they do not affect the merits and will not be deemed sufficiently prejudicial to warrant review after the trial is completed. The absence of appellate guidance on these matters can result in inconsistent treatment by the lower courts. Allowing interlocutory appeals on all preliminary orders assures the appellate courts the opportunity to fulfill their function of establishing uniform law.

Thus, there are persuasive arguments both supporting and criticizing the final judgment rule. The important thing to note is whether the jurisdiction in which suit is filed adheres to the rule. In addition, differences exist among jurisdictions following the final judgment rule in interpreting what is "final" and in the exceptions that are recognized. The question of what constitutes finality is one that has posed significant difficulties for the courts. Thus, it is most critical to consult the law in the jurisdiction where the initial proceeding is filed to determine whether an immediate appeal is allowed because the failure to take an immediate appeal, if it is permitted, may waive the right to raise that issue on an appeal from the final judgment.

§ 7–2. Specialized Rules for Multi-Claim, Multi-Party Cases

The application of the final judgment rule in multi-claim, multi-party litigation has posed some problems when the trial court reaches a final decision on some of the claims before it is ready to render judgment on the entire action. Postponing an appeal until all the claims have been decided may result in an unnecessary delay on a claim that has been fully and finally determined. Thus, special rules have been developed for identifying those orders in multi-claim, multi-party disputes that determine finally the action as it pertains to a given party or claim in order to allow an immediate appeal in those situations. These provisions are not exceptions to the final judgment rule. Rather, they represent standards for applying that rule in those multi-claim, multi-party contexts.

A good example is Federal Rule 54(b). Under that rule, in an action having multiple claims or parties, the trial court identifies its order as appealable by directing the entry of a judgment on the claim involved and by expressly certifying that there is no just reason to delay the appeal. In the absence of this certification, the appellate court will dismiss the appeal as violative of the final judgment rule.

If the trial court makes a Rule 54(b) certification, the appellate court will review the decision of the trial court that there was no just reason to delay the appeal, utilizing an abuse of discretion standard. It will consider de novo (1) whether in fact more than one claim is present in the suit or whether the court merely ruled on one of the alternative theories on which the plaintiff's single claim was based, and (2) whether a final determination has been made on that claim. The standard exercised is that multiple claims are present if the theories of recovery that are presented could have been separately and concurrently enforced; the fact that the claims are related or rest on overlapping facts does not prevent a finding that multiple claims exist.

In general, courts are agreed that only the infrequent, harsh case merits a finding that there is no just reason for delay. The court must balance whether an immediate appeal could simplify the trial or whether it would result in a repetitive review of many of the same issues after a judgment is reached on the remaining claims. Similarly, it may weigh the immediate benefit of a recovery to the winning party on an earlier appeal against the possibility that the judgment on one claim should be stayed because it may be set-off by a judgment for the opposing party on the remaining claims.

Note that when applying the final judgment rule, multiple cases that are consolidated retain their separate identities. Thus, if one entire case reaches a final judgment, that judgment may be appealed immediately even if the other consolidated cases remain pending. Hall v. Hall, 584 U.S. 59 (2018). In that situation, it is not necessary to obtain Rule 54(b) certification. Gelboim v. Bank of America Corp., 574 U.S. 405 (2015).

2. EXCEPTIONS TO THE FINAL JUDGMENT RULE

§ 7-3. Statutory Interlocutory Appeals Routes

A brief examination of the federal interlocutory appeals statutes provides a good illustration of the types of exceptions that typically are recognized in systems observing the final judgment rule. For a more extended discussion, see J. Friedenthal, M. Kane, A. Miller & A. Steinman, *Civil Procedure* § 13.3 (6th ed.2021), or 15A & 15B C. Wright, A. Miller & E. Cooper, *Federal Practice and Procedure* §§ 3905–3917.

One statute, 28 U.S.C.A. § 1292(b), provides a general procedure for discretionary interlocutory appeals that requires both the trial court and the appellate court to certify that the order can be appealed immediately. The standard for certification is that the issue involves a "controlling question of law," that there is "substantial ground for difference of opinion" on that issue, and that an immediate appeal may "materially advance the ultimate termination of the litigation." The purpose of this appeals route is to allow immediate review of important questions. By requiring certification at both levels, the trial court, which is most familiar with the entire proceeding, can assess whether the appellant raises a crucial issue or is appealing as a dilatory tactic. The appellate court can then estimate its own burdens and make its decision on appealability relatively free from pressures by the litigants. The standard rests heavily on the discretion of both courts, and there may be considerable differences of opinion as to whether any given issue is controlling or what will aid the early termination of the suit.

Another statutory appeals measure is embodied in 28 U.S.C.A. § 1292(a). That provision sets out specific categories of orders or types of proceedings from which an interlocutory appeal is permissible. It lists three categories: (1) orders "granting, continuing, modifying, refusing or dissolving injunctions, or refusing to dissolve or modify injunctions"; (2) orders involving receiverships; and (3) interlocutory decrees in admiralty cases. Each one of these exceptions is quite concrete and represents a decision based on concerns that immediacy is particularly important in these areas. Analogous state provisions delineate other orders that are perceived as demanding immediate appellate review. For example, Minnesota includes a right of appeal from an order vacating or sustaining an attachment. Minn.R.Civ.App.Proc. § 103.03(c). Other states specifically authorize appeals from orders granting new trial motions. Cal.Civ.Proc.Code § 904.1(a)(4).

Finally, a 1992 statute, 28 U.S.C.A. § 1292(e), authorized the Supreme Court to prescribe rules that provide for interlocutory appeals in categories of cases not already covered by Section 1292. The Court utilized this authority in 1998 to amend the federal class action rule to allow discretionary appeals from orders granting or denying class certification. See Fed.Rule 23(f).

§ 7-4. Judicial Interlocutory Appeals Routes

There are a few well-recognized judicial exceptions to the final judgment rule by which courts will allow an appeal even though portions of the case remain undecided. The best known of these is the *collateral order doctrine*. Under the collateral order doctrine an immediate appeal may be taken from an order that is final and unrelated to the merits (collateral) and that, if it is not appealed immediately, may result in irreparable harm to the appellant. Cohen v. Beneficial Industrial Loan Corp., 337 U.S. 541 (1949). The appellate court determines whether this standard has been met when the appeal is filed.

Determining whether an order is collateral has not posed too much difficulty for the courts. Many orders are clearly unrelated to the merits. Orders that are separate, but more closely intertwined, also may meet the standard. In those cases, however, the courts place greater emphasis on the irreparable harm portion of the standard. What constitutes irreparable harm is within the court's discretion. In large measure the court will focus on the severity of the potential injury, the probability of harm occurring, and the likelihood that review would be ineffective if it were delayed. Examples of some orders that have been held within the collateral order doctrine are: the denial of a motion to impose security for costs on plaintiffs in a shareholder derivative suit; the denial of a motion to proceed in forma pauperis; the denial of claims of immunity from suit; the grant of an order that a state prisoner be transported to a hospital for medical testing that could support his claim for federal habeas relief; and the grant of a motion to require the plaintiff in a class action to send individual notice to all the unnamed class members.

In the federal class action area, some courts had developed an off-shoot of the collateral order doctrine called the *death knell doctrine.* Orders denying class certification are not truly collateral because the certification process often requires some inquiry into the merits of the underlying claims, if only to examine what common questions are involved. Also, they are not final since the court is directed by rule to consider their revision throughout the trial. However, in many class suits the individual members each have only very small claims and it would not be feasible to bring the action except on a class basis, so that denial of class certification may result as a practical matter in ending the litigation. In response to this possibility, the Second Circuit developed the death knell doctrine, allowing an immediate appeal under these circumstances on the theory that the refusal to certify the class was effectively a final order collateral to the merits that if not appealable would result in the death of the action, irreparably harming the plaintiffs. Eisen v. Carlisle & Jacquelin, 370 F.2d 119 (2d Cir.1966). A party could also appeal an order granting class certification on what was termed an "inverse death knell theory." Herbst v. International Tel. & Tel. Corp., 495 F.2d 1308 (2d Cir.1974). The Supreme Court, however, ultimately rejected the death knell doctrine (and by implication the inverse death knell doctrine). It ruled that the doctrine violated the final judgment rule and, insofar as it rested on the peculiar nature of class actions, the decision whether to allow an appeal should be a legislative one. Coopers & Lybrand v. Livesay, 437 U.S. 463 (1978). Subsequent amendments to the federal class action rule, Fed.Rule 23(f), now authorize interlocutory appeals of class certification decisions at the appellate court's discretion. See § 7–3, above.

Another judicial interlocutory appeals route involves nonfinal decisions having *irremediable consequences*. This very limited approach was first invoked by the Supreme Court in Forgay v. Conrad, 47 U.S. 201 (1848). In that case, the district court made a partial adjudication of a claim but ordered the losing party to deliver immediately the physical property at issue. The appellate court allowed the appeal of the partial ruling to avoid the potentially irreparable harm that would occur to the losing party in the absence of immediate review. This theory applies only in exceptional circumstances, however, and it does not support a rule that a party can appeal any interlocutory district court order that threatens irreparable injury.

§ 7–5. Extraordinary Routes of Appeal

There are two extraordinary routes of appeal that must be mentioned, though they are of limited use. The first is an application to the appellate court for a *writ of mandamus* ordering the trial court to reverse its ruling. As a formal matter, this method is not an appeal, but rather an original proceeding in the appellate court seeking an order directing the trial judge to enter or vacate a particular order.

Mandamus is based on the theory that the trial court has abused its discretion to such a degree that the appellate court must consider the question immediately. It typically is successful only in extreme cases because it represents a deliberate and direct interference with the lower court during the course of a trial. For example, mandamus was held proper when the appellate court found that the trial judge had totally abdicated his judicial function by essentially allowing a case to be tried by a master. La Buy v. Howes Leather Co., 352 U.S. 249 (1957). It also was used to review Judge Sirica's ruling on the discoverability of the presidential tapes during the Watergate controversy because of the great public interest in ending the controversy over that issue as soon as possible. Nixon v. Sirica, 487 F.2d 700 (D.C.Cir.1973).

Although mandamus typically is utilized only in extraordinary circumstances, a few states have made greater use of that appeals route to provide for immediate review of certain issues. Illustratively, in California rulings denying motions to quash service of process on the ground of lack of personal jurisdiction must be appealed immediately by an application for mandamus. Cal.Civ.Proc.Code § 418.10(c). This use of mandamus is so deeply rooted that failure to seek it results in a waiver of the objection; personal jurisdiction cannot be raised on a later appeal from the final judgment.

Another extraordinary route of appeal that should be noted is *contempt*. This method most commonly is available when discovery orders are involved. Failure to obey the court's order may result in the disobedient party being held in contempt. A contempt judgment is a final judgment and may be appealed immediately. This method of appeal is very risky because if the appellate court affirms the lower court's discovery order, the contempt judgment will stand. Further, only criminal contempt is immediately appealable; if the court determines that the party was adjudged in civil contempt, an appeal may not be allowed. The difference between civil and criminal contempt depends on the nature of the proceeding and the type of sentence imposed. See D. Dobbs & C. Roberts, *Law of Remedies* 140–147 (3d ed.2018). Despite these risks, in some cases litigants have used this method to avoid the delay that otherwise would result in obtaining review because of adherence to the final judgment rule in the main action. See, e.g., Hickman v. Taylor, 329 U.S. 495 (1947).

B. THE MECHANICS OF APPEAL

§ 7–6. Appealable Issues

Although it might seem obvious that the losing party can appeal adverse findings, the rules concerning what issues can be raised on appeal or cross-appeal are somewhat more complex. To begin with, only rulings that were objected to in the trial court may be presented by the appellant. Losing parties may appeal all adverse rulings to which they objected. However, winning parties may not appeal from findings deemed erroneous if those findings are not necessary to the judgment. The rationale for this restriction is that unnecessary findings will not be the basis for collateral estoppel. See § 6–11, above. Thus, there is no need for the appeal because no prejudice will result to the winning party by denying it.

On the other hand, if the losing party appeals, the appellee may raise in response any issue that would sustain the judgment, whether or not it was decided below. The basic question in deciding whether the appellee can raise new grounds sustaining the judgment is one of fairness: is the case in the same basic posture it would have been had the issue been introduced below?

The appellee cannot attack the judgment with a view to enlarging its own rights or lessening the rights of its adversary, unless the appellee files a cross-appeal. This is particularly important in the third-party context. Assume A sues B for personal injuries and B joins C, the insurer, as a third-party defendant based on an indemnity theory. A loses and the claim against C is dismissed as no right to indemnity arose. A appeals. If B wants to preserve the right to indemnity in the event of a reversal on the main claim, B must cross-appeal against C. B cannot merely raise that issue by way of its responsive brief.

§ 7-7. Standard of Review

The scope and standard of review that will be used by the appellate court will depend on the nature of the alleged error—whether it involved an issue of fact or one of law—as well as whether the trial was before a jury or not. The fullest scope of review is for errors of law: appellate courts may decide such questions de novo. Rulings that are committed to the trial judge's discretion are reviewed under an abuse of discretion standard, which allows reversal only if the trial judge was clearly wrong.

Findings of fact receive greater deference than issues of law. In a case tried to a judge, they may be overturned only if they are clearly erroneous. Fed.Rule 52(a)(6). This means that they will be reversed only if the trial judge's findings are based on a misunderstanding of the law or are totally without evidentiary support. See Cooper v. Harris, 581 U.S. 285 (2017). When a jury trial is involved, the appellate court will give even greater deference to the findings because constitutional jury trial rights protect the jurors' factual determinations from review except to the extent allowed at common law. For mixed questions of fact and law, the standard of review varies; whether review is deferential or de novo depends on, among other things, the nature of the mixed question and whether a trial court or an appellate court is better suited to resolve it. U.S. Bank Nat'l Ass'n ex rel. CW Cap. Asset Mgmt. LLC v. Village at Lakeridge, LLC, 583 U.S. 387 (2018).

CHAPTER 8

SPECIALIZED MULTI-PARTY—MULTI-CLAIM PROCEEDINGS

A. CLASS ACTIONS

§ 8–1. General Purpose and Utility of Class Actions

The class action allows one or more persons to sue or be sued on behalf of themselves and other individuals who allegedly possess similar grievances or have been harmed in a similar way. The action is permitted to be brought in a representative fashion in order to allow the determination of legal rights in situations in which the number of people involved and, in some instances, the small individual amounts involved, otherwise effectively would prevent the vindication of those rights. The procedure also is an efficient and economical means for the courts and the parties to try a case in which there are common substantive objectives, rather than having to resort to multiple, duplicative lawsuits. Thus, class suits serve several important objectives.

Current opinion is divided as to the actual utility of class actions. Critics point to the fact that many of the suits filed over the years have been burdensome, costly, and time-consuming, and only a few have reached an adjudication on the merits. Further, during the early 1970s class action filings increased to such an extent that it was argued that many had become strike suits, filed by attorneys seeking large fees but producing few real benefits for class members. Although class action filings decreased in the 1980s, in the 1990s an upsurge in nationwide consumer and product-liability class actions occurred. In many instances competing class actions were filed in the state and federal courts as lawyers sought to find a judge sympathetic to class certification. This resulted in wasteful duplication and critics again charged that class suits had become unmanageable, filed only to force early settlements including large attorneys' fees.

Critics have also argued that the large, complex modern class suit alters our concept of the adversary system. This can be shown, it is said, in two ways. First, the judge's role changes from a passive one to a very active one. This is necessitated by the fact that the judge must oversee the proceedings very carefully to make certain that the rights of the absent class members are being protected. The judge cannot rely on the named representative or counsel because at various points, such as during the settlement stage, their interests may diverge from those of the absent class members. Additionally, the complexity of the action requires the judge to act in many instances as an administrator or manager, devising or monitoring notice schemes, evaluating proposed settlements, and appraising methods of computing and distributing damages and attorneys' fees. The second major change produced by class actions, it is claimed, is that they often thrust the courts into the policy arena. In the traditional two-party suit, the court has little overt concern for the creation of law and the focus is on the specific problem in the case before it. Class suits often oblige judges to deal with public policy questions, rather than leaving those issues to the executive or the legislature. The very number of persons involved may reflect the fact that the policy or law on which the suit is based is a matter of significant public interest. Further, class action litigants and their counsel often function as private attorneys' general pressing for adherence to or changes in the law by the very impact of their lawsuits.

In response to some of the criticisms and concerns that have been raised, several class action reforms have been instituted since 2000. Stated generally, these efforts attempt to provide some protections to curtail the asserted practice abuses and to streamline class action procedures while preserving the class remedy as an important tool to vindicate various rights. Thus, 2003 and 2018 amendments to the federal class action rule were designed to provide guidance to the courts in their review and management of class proceedings, the judicial appraisal of settlements, and district judge appointment of class counsel and the award of class attorney fees. See Fed.Rule 23(e), (g), and (h). And in 2005, Congress enacted the Class Action Fairness Act, imposing additional settlement requirements and creating a new form of minimal diversity jurisdiction for many interstate class actions, 28 U.S.C.A. § 1332(d), as well as authorizing removal of those actions from state to federal courts, 28 U.S.C.A. § 1453(b). These jurisdictional changes were made to address the problem of overlapping federal and state class actions by requiring more of them to be brought in the federal courts. The statute's effect has been to federalize most sizeable class actions. See § 8–3, below.

The debate on whether the benefits of the class action outweigh its burdens and complications undoubtedly will continue and additional procedural amendments to deal with some of the problems can be expected. Thus, it is important to realize that an individual court's application of the class action rule's requirements (either narrowly or liberally) or its willingness to adopt new management procedures often may be influenced by feelings as to whether class action critics or advocates present the more accurate picture of the class action environment.

§ 8–2. Types of Class Action Rules and Statutes

There are basically five types of class action provisions in the United States. A brief look at those provisions illustrates some of the issues relevant under each approach.

Historically, many states modeled their class action rules on the original equity rules inherited from the English Court of Chancery. Class suits were permitted when joinder of all the members was not feasible and there was adequate representation of the absentees' interests. No further guidance was given to the courts. The major limitation on the availability of class action relief was that the device was authorized only in equity, which meant it was not available when damages were being sought. Today, with the merger of law and equity, states generally have abandoned this approach in favor of one of those that are described below.

Similar to the equity approach is that followed by those states that adopted the nineteenth-century New York Field Code as their procedural rules. E.g., Cal.Civ.Proc.Code § 382. In those states the same minimum requirements of impracticable joinder and adequacy of representation apply, but class actions are available in both law and equity. Further, common questions must be raised by the class members. Courts frequently also interpret the code requirements as necessitating that there be an ascertainable class and that the class possess a community of interest. In looking at those requirements the judge essentially will consider whether the individual class members will be identifiable, at least at the damage stage, the number of common questions that exist as compared to the individual issues that will have to be litigated, and, at least to some degree, the social utility of the action. The test is a balancing one, with the court weighing the economies to be gained by allowing a representative action to proceed against concerns about the adequacy of representation and cohesiveness of interest among the class members.

Another type of class action rule is the 1938 federal provision, which, although it no longer is used in the federal courts, is followed in some states. Under that approach the same requirements of impracticable joinder, common questions and adequacy of representation are present. Additionally, the suit must fall into one of three categories, labeled by the courts as "true," "hybrid," and "spurious." In a "true" action the class members share a common and undivided interest. This means that under law they are recognized as united in interest—for example, the partners in a limited partnership or a husband and wife in a community property state suing to protect their common interests. In a "hybrid" suit the members share an interest in the property that is the subject of the suit. Their interests need not be joint; rather the focus is on the property (typically a limited fund from which they are seeking relief). In a "spurious" action the presence of common questions authorizes the class suit. The classification of a given lawsuit into one of these three categories in effect determines the binding effect of the judgment. Because of the loose connection among class members existing in spurious suits, only those class members who opt into the action will be bound by the judgment. In practice this means that an unsuccessful spurious class suit will bind only the named parties. If a judgment on liability is reached in favor of the class, then the absent members may take advantage of it and enter the action to seek damages. Judgments in true or hybrid class suits will be binding on all the absent class members whether they are successful or not.

The most widely used class action procedure today is the 1966 version of Federal Rule 23. That rule governs in the federal courts, and it has been adopted in several states as well. The rule sets out requirements in its first two subdivisions, and then in the remaining subdivisions provides guidance to the courts on how to manage class actions. These last provisions have been amended several times to improve the guidance given, but those amendments have not been adopted by most of the states that continue to use the 1966 version of Rule 23. The management sections of the rule include: notice provisions, setting forth when notice is required and what should be included (Rule 23(c)(2) and (d)(1)(B)); authority for certifying a class with respect to particular issues (Rule 23(c)(4)), dividing a class into subclasses (Rule 23(c)(5)), and allowing absent members to intervene (Rule 23(d)(1)(C)); and provisions for approving and controlling settlements (Rule 23(e)), for appointing class counsel (Rule 23(g)) and for awarding attorney's fees (Rule 23(h)). The focus of these amendments is to encourage the development of flexible management devices and to provide lawyers and judges with more guidance in that area than existed in the text of the rule originally promulgated in 1938.

The class requirements under Federal Rule 23 are stated pragmatically and are discussed in some detail in J. Friedenthal, M. Kane, A. Miller & A. Steinman, Civil Procedure §§ 16.2–16.3 (6th ed.2021). The party seeking class certification must show that the action meets all of the requirements set out in Rule 23(a)—numerosity, commonality, typicality, and adequate representation—and falls within at least one of the three categories of Rule 23(b). At the class certification stage, merits questions are considered only to determine if the class certification requirements are satisfied. The two usually are intertwined, however. In addition, courts have recognized two implied prerequisites—there must be a defined class with ascertainable members and the proposed class representatives must be members of that class. Moreover, every class member must have standing under Article III of the Constitution to recover individual damages. TransUnion LLC v. Ramirez, 594 U.S. 413 (2021).

Today, the basic requirements of Rule 23 are the same as those just described under the 1966 version of the Rule. One of the most frequently litigated is that the class members share common questions of law or fact. Fed.Rule 23(a)(2). In 2011, the Supreme Court gave new content to that requirement, holding that it was not sufficient merely to find that some common questions existed. Rather, the inquiry must be into whether the class claims share a common question that will result in a common answer that will be critical to resolving the dispute. Wal-Mart Stores, Inc. v. Dukes, 564 U.S. 338, 350 (2011).

Similar to these requirements, one justice of the Supreme Court has argued that a federal court may not certify a damages class that includes both injured and uninjured class members. Laboratory Corp. of America Holdings v. Davis, 605 U.S. 327, 328 (2025). (Kavanaugh, J., dissenting). The Supreme Court has yet to resolve this question, however; it dismissed the Laboratory Corp. case without deciding the merits.

The subdivision (b) categories adopted in 1966 provide more guidance, with the intention that all class action judgments will be binding, regardless of which type of suit has been certified. Rule 23(b)(1) focuses on the possible adverse impact of a non-class judgment on the opposing party, who might be placed in an impossible position if faced with conflicting individual judgments, or on the absent class members, whose interests might be practically impaired if class action treatment were denied. Rule 23(b)(2) authorizes class suits in which injunctive or declaratory relief is appropriate on a class-wide basis. Rule 23(b)(3) allows class treatment if common questions predominate and if a class suit is deemed the superior means of handling the controversy. This last provision is in the nature of a catchall and gives the judge considerable discretion to determine superiority. Among other things, the court may take into account whether the action appears to pose severe management problems, what other possible modes of adjudication exist, and whether the suit is deemed important as a policy matter.

Because the only connection between the class members in a Rule 23(b)(3) suit is the presence of predominant common questions, various procedures exist in the other portions of the rule to ensure that the interests of the absent class members are adequately protected. Notice is mandatory in these suits and individual notice must be mailed to all identifiable class members, Fed.Rule 23(c)(2); Eisen v. Carlisle & Jacquelin, 417 U.S. 156 (1974). Absent class members may opt out of the action, Fed.Rule 23(c)(3). If they do opt out, they will not be bound by the judgment; conversely, however, they cannot later take advantage of the judgment.

Because these added protections—predominance, superiority, individual notice, and the right to exclude oneself from the class—often are costly and burdensome, it is common for class counsel to try to fit the action within one of the first two categories of Rule 23(b) so as to avoid them. However, in an employment discrimination case, the Supreme Court ruled that actions seeking both equitable relief and damages (back pay, for example) cannot be certified solely under Rule 23(b)(2) and thereby avoid the additional requirements of Rule 23(b)(3), unless the damages claims are merely incidental to the equitable relief claim. Wal-Mart Stores, Inc. v. Dukes, 564 U.S. 338 (2011). What types of damage claims might be found incidental was left to the lower courts to develop.

In the federal courts, class actions can only be brought through the procedure set out in Rule 23. A member of a class may sue on behalf of the representative class only if all of the Rule 23 requirements are met. The Supreme Court recently held that so-called universal injunctions cannot serve as a shortcut that allows federal courts to circumvent the procedural requirements and safeguards of Rule 23 by creating de facto class actions. Trump v. CASA, Inc., 606 U.S. 831 (2025).

The final type of class action statute is represented by the New York statute, adopted in 1975, N.Y.C.P.L.R. 901–908, and by the 1976 proposed Uniform Class Action Statute, drafted by the Commissioners on Uniform State Laws and adopted in North Dakota and Iowa. Both of these share a common approach—they are lengthy and complex and attempt to deal specifically with most of the many issues that have arisen under prior class action rules. They provide much more detailed guidance on how to handle class actions and attempt to provide some solutions to problems with which the federal courts have struggled.

The desire to provide more guidance to the federal courts on how to manage class actions also has motivated several amendments to the 1966 federal rule. In 1998, a new Rule 23(f) was added authorizing discretionary interlocutory appeals from class certification decisions, thereby facilitating an increase of appellate guidance to the district courts on certification issues. Amendments to Rule 23 in 2003 further provide direct guidance to the district courts concerning how to manage class action settlements, the appointment of class counsel, and the award of attorney fees to class counsel. And the 2018 amendments added new provisions to Rule 23 governing objections to class action settlements.

§ 8-3. Jurisdiction Requirements

Class action rules are merely procedural and do not themselves confer jurisdiction on the courts. The question of how to apply the traditional rules regarding the establishment of subject-matter and personal jurisdiction in this complex setting raises special problems.

First, in federal courts, when the basis for jurisdiction is diversity, whose citizenship controls and how is the amount in controversy to be calculated? Until recently, the first question was answered easily—only the citizenship of the named representative parties would be considered for purposes of determining whether diversity existed.

With regard to the amount involved, the Supreme Court ruled that the claims of the class members cannot be aggregated to meet the more than $75,000 requirement unless the class members were asserting a common and undivided interest in a single title or right. Zahn v. International Paper Co., 414 U.S. 291 (1973). What constitutes a joint and common interest is described earlier, see § 2–4, above. Failure to show a joint or common interest meant that each class member had to possess a claim exceeding the jurisdictional minimum. In practice, this rule severely restricted the ability to bring a common question damage suit in the federal courts when jurisdiction was based on diversity and individual claims were small—as, for example, in much consumer and environmental litigation.

Much changed in 2005. First, the Supreme Court ruled that the supplemental jurisdiction statute adopted in 1990, see § 2–5, above, had the effect of overruling Zahn, at least when at least one claimant seeks more than the jurisdictional minimum. Exxon Mobil Corp. v. Allapattah Servs., Inc., 545 U.S. 546 (2005). Additionally, in the same year, Congress enacted the Class Action Fairness Act, which created a new form of minimal diversity jurisdiction allowing jurisdiction in class actions in which more than $5,000,000 in the aggregate is being claimed by all of the class members and diversity exists between "any" plaintiff class member and "any" defendant. 28 U.S.C.A. § 1332(d)(2). These two changes enlarged the scope of federal subject matter jurisdiction in class actions significantly. And the Supreme Court has also ruled that a class representative cannot avoid removal under those provisions by stipulating not to seek more than $5,000,000 because the representative cannot bind the absent class members before the class is certified. Standard Fire Ins. Co. v. Knowles, 568 U.S. 588 (2013). Relatedly, a defendant cannot remove a class action to federal court by asserting a speculative counter-estimate of damages that exceeds the $5,000,000 amount-in-controversy requirement. Lizama v. Victoria's Secret Stores, LLC, 36 F.4th 762, 765 (8th Cir. 2022).

The question involving the applicability of personal jurisdiction requirements in the class setting was addressed by the Supreme Court in Phillips Petroleum Co. v. Shutts, 472 U.S. 797 (1985). The problem is important because if traditional jurisdiction requirements apply, then both the notice and the contact elements of due process would have to be satisfied for all absent class members. A court would have to find that every absent class member had sufficient minimum contacts with the forum state that it would be consistent with notions of fair play and substantial justice for the court to enter a binding judgment on that member's claims. See generally §§ 2–9—2–20, above. This effectively would preclude any nationwide or multistate plaintiff class actions since it would be rare that all the nonresident class members (the "victims") had sufficient contacts with the forum state. Class action protagonists thus argued that class actions should be treated differently. They noted that the focus on forum contacts typically is designed to ensure that it is fair to require a defendant to defend "away from home," whereas there is no intention in the class setting of having the absentees appear and litigate in the forum. The purpose of the class suit is to allow the members' representative to proceed on their behalf. Thus, relying predominantly on Hansberry v. Lee, 311 U.S. 32 (1940), it was argued that the binding effect of class action judgments should not be determined by personal jurisdiction principles, but by general due process notions, which require only that the representative adequately represent the nonresident members and that adequate notice be given. Application of these two criteria is discussed in the next section.

The Supreme Court resolved the debate in Phillips Petroleum Co. v. Shutts, 472 U.S. 797 (1985), ruling that it was not necessary for the court to obtain personal jurisdiction over each of the absent class members. Due process was satisfied because the class members in that case had been adequately represented and they had been sent individual notice with an opportunity to opt out. The failure to opt out acted almost as a form of implied consent. On its facts, the Shutts class action easily satisfied due process concerns because sufficient protections for the absentee's rights existed. As is discussed in the next section, it is unclear in actions not "wholly or predominately" for monetary relief whether individual notice and the opportunity to exclude oneself from the class are necessary constitutional requirements for binding nonresident class members who also are adequately represented.

Even if a court has jurisdiction over the members of a class action, they may be unable to pursue it if they have contractually waived their right to do so. The Fourth Circuit recently upheld a class-action waiver that barred the plaintiffs from proceeding as a damages class and found that the Federal Rules of Civil Procedure do not prohibit contractual class-action waivers. Maldini v. Marriott Int'l, Inc., 140 F.4th 123, 126 (4th Cir. 2025). That is quite typical of today's consumer and commercial contracts restricting the resolution of disputes to individual arbitration. See § 9–7, below.

§ 8–4. Procedural Fairness: Adequacy of Representation, Notice, and Binding Effect

A major problem in class action practice has been how to accord class judgments total binding effect consistent with due process concerns of providing each person to be bound an opportunity to be heard. It is absolutely necessary for class judgments to bind the unnamed class members in order to achieve the desired judicial economy. Thus, the Supreme Court has recognized class judgments as an exception to the traditional rule that only named parties to a suit are bound by a judgment therein. Taylor v. Sturgell, 553 U.S. 880 (2008); Supreme Tribe of Ben Hur v. Cauble, 255 U.S. 356 (1921). There will be a failure of due process only when the procedures utilized do not ensure the adequate protection of the absent members. Hansberry v. Lee, 311 U.S. 32 (1940).

Two procedures designed to meet due process requirements are an appropriate system for notifying the absent members and a careful inquiry by the court into the named representative's ability to protect those interests adequately. It is not clear whether these requirements are both necessary or if the satisfaction of one may cure a deficiency in the other. The lower courts have divided on the question whether some form of notice is constitutionally compelled in all class suits. The Supreme Court's only decision in this area rested on a rule interpretation, mandating individual notice in actions under Federal Rule 23(b)(3), but not addressing actions under the other provisions in that subdivision of the Rule. Eisen v. Carlisle & Jacquelin, 417 U.S. 156 (1974). Similarly, the Court has not answered the question whether actual notice might result in the waiver of a class member's right later to object to inadequate representation. In Phillips Petroleum Co. v. Shutts, 472 U.S. 797 (1985), a purely monetary action discussed in the preceding section, both adequate representation and individual notice were present and class members were provided an opportunity to opt out, as well, so the Court did not need to rule on whether due process could be satisfied in the absence of one of those three protections. But the Court indicated that at least in class actions seeking predominately money damages, they are constitutional requirements. Thus, careful counsel should not overlook any of these requirements in order to ensure that a class action judgment will not be subject to collateral attack.

Adequacy of representation is a flexible concept embracing any matter that might influence how vigorously the named party or parties will prosecute or defend the action on behalf of the class. Most central is that the interests of the absent class members and those of the class representatives not be conflicting or antagonistic. The court also may inquire as to the competence of the lawyers who are proposed to represent the class or the ability of the representatives to pursue the litigation to its end, whether by settlement or adjudication. Because adequacy of representation is so important, the court is obliged to consider its sufficiency throughout the course of the suit, not just at the certification stage.

Adequacy problems need not always result in a dismissal of the action or denial of certification, however. The court can add additional representatives, redefine or subclass the action to avoid or eliminate conflicts, or appoint new representatives or counsel if that will permit the action to proceed with adequate protection for the absent members. But if it is shown that the absentees were not adequately represented, the judgment in the action can be attacked collaterally.

A serious question regarding notice is whether, in the absence of a mandatory statutory or rule requirement that all class members be given notice, due process demands some form of actual or individual notice, when feasible, or if alternative constructive or substitute notice schemes may suffice. The constitutional standards for notice spring from a non-class suit, Mullane v. Central Hanover Bank & Trust Co., 339 U.S. 306 (1950). Although that case required mailed notice to all persons whose addresses were readily available, that conclusion rested on a finding that individual notice was feasible—not too costly or burdensome—and the

Court seemed more generally to be adopting a "reasonableness" and contextual test for notice in future actions. See § 2–21, above. Further, there is the practical problem of what to include in the notice to make it meaningful to the recipient. Amendments to Rule 23 in 2003 added a list of items that should be included in any notice and require that the notice "must clearly and concisely state [those matters] in plain, easily understood language." Fed.Rule 23(c)(2)(B). In short, what notice is appropriate must be decided on a case-by-case basis, taking into account Mullane, the essence of which is captured in the Federal Rule, and the desire to reach as many absent class members as possible.

Finally, it seems clear that, at least in damage class actions, due process requires that nonresident absentee class members be provided an opportunity to opt out. This argument rests on the fact that when the Supreme Court upheld the Kansas judgment in Phillips Petroleum Co. v. Shutts, 472 U.S. 797 (1985), it noted that one of the protections provided the class members was the opportunity to opt out of the action. However, as is true with regard to the notice and adequate representation requirements, it remains unclear whether all of the safeguards existing in Shutts must be available in a nonmonetary class action to ensure the constitutionality of the judgment's binding effect or whether a more flexible approach might be taken in an injunctive action or one in which all the class members must be treated in the same fashion to make relief effective.

A judgment in a properly certified and adjudicated class action will be given preclusive effect. See §§ 6-01—6-14, above. That applies to both named and unnamed class members. Cooper v. Federal Reserve Bank of Richmond, 467 U.S. 867 (1984). However, a class action that has not been certified will bar only the named representative parties regarding the failure to certify. Smith v. Bayer Corp., 364 U.S. 299 (2011).

§ 8-5. Two Problems: Damage Assessment and Attorney's Fees

A wide variety of other procedural problems have surfaced in the class action field. Two of the more important issues will be mentioned here: damage assessment and attorney's fees.

One of the biggest difficulties in many damage class actions is how to assess and distribute the remedy the class may recover when the individual class members' claims are very small or the class is extremely large or it is potentially difficult to identify all of the individual members. Different approaches have been tried, although all of them are controversial and not widely adopted. In some cases the courts have assessed lump sum damages based on the defendants' records, which reveal illegal profits or overcharges. This alleviates the need for individual damage trials and distribution can be done through a less costly and burdensome method—perhaps even administered by the attorneys.

A few courts have gone further and have utilized what is called "fluid" or "cy pres" recovery for cases in which it would be extremely costly and probably futile to try to identify and send small sums to individual class members. Under that approach, after lump sum damages are proven, the court does not attempt to distribute the damages to the class members. Instead, recognizing that class suits are in the public interest, the court devises a means by which the damages can be distributed to benefit a comparable segment of the public and yet require little court supervision. For example, in a case in which a taxicab company was found to have overcharged riders, it was realized that it would be impossible to identify and compensate those actually victimized. Instead, the defendant was ordered to reduce fares for a certain period of time until it had disgorged the illegal profits. Daar v. Yellow Cab Co., 433 P.2d 732 (Cal.1967). The beneficiaries of the fare reductions could be thought of as "the next best" class. The Second Circuit has rejected this approach on the ground that it is unauthorized by the rules and violates the defendant's due process right to be confronted by its accusers. Eisen v. Carlisle & Jacquelin, 479 F.2d 1005 (2d Cir.1973). Most federal courts have agreed, however, that a fluid recovery may be approved as part of a negotiated settlement when consistent with the requirements of Rule 23(e) (discussed in § 8–6, below). E.g., Hyland v. Navlent Corp., 48 F.4th 110, 122 (2d Cir. 2022). In state courts, the fluid recovery device remains viable even in litigated actions.

Additional problems of assessing damages exist when they cannot be calculated with reference to the defendant's records, but require inquiry into the individual class member's losses. Such individual inquiries in large class suits could result in thousands of minitrials, undercutting the judicial economy and efficiency of the class action, creating management difficulties, and perhaps preventing class certification in the first instance. In response, a few courts have experimented with allowing proof of damages based on statistical sampling and other similar procedures. But these approaches have been challenged, sometimes successfully, as violating the defendant's jury trial rights. The Supreme Court, in an overtime wage dispute, has upheld the use of representative proof of damages from a sample with expert testimony showing that the methodology was reliable and sufficient. Tyson Foods, Inc. v. Bouaphakeo, 577 U.S. 442 (2016). Whether this approach can be used in other contexts in which sampling may be more or less difficult to apply remains an open question that has important implications for the future viability of damage class actions.

Another serious source of dispute in the class action field is determining attorney's fees for successful class counsel. Class opponents have argued that class suits often are brought not to vindicate the public interest or to obtain meaningful compensation for class members, but to generate large fees. Thus, many courts have devoted considerable attention to developing and refining standards for assessing attorney's fees in order to keep them within reasonable limits. Further, judges are particularly sensitive when reviewing proposed class action settlements that include attorney's fees to ensure that the fee award is appropriate in light of what has been recovered for the class. The objective is to set a fee award that will act as an incentive to attorneys and fairly compensate them, but not result in a windfall at the expense of the class members. Many courts award a percentage of the benefits provided to the class that is thought to be reasonable compensation. A few of these courts have established a "benchmark" percentage; in some federal courts that is 25%. Other courts believe that the amount of time an attorney spent on a case multiplied by that attorney's normal billing rate is the "lodestar" on which fees are to be based, although the courts are requiring much more detailed records reflecting the time spent on each aspect of representing the class. This base amount then may be enhanced depending on the novel character and complexity of the case and the perceived benefit produced by it, how long it took to resolve, and, when the work was done on a contingency basis, how risky the undertaking was. The court may reduce the amount if it finds that the attorneys proceeded inefficiently or to eliminate time spent on issues on which the class did not prevail. The inquiry on attorney fees thus is necessarily a detailed and complex one.

§ 8–6. Settlement, Dismissal, and Compromise

To provide additional protection for absent class members, most class action rules specifically require court approval of any termination of the class claims arranged by the parties. These provisions are designed to prevent an unjust or unfair settlement resulting either from the class representatives becoming faint-hearted or having been bought off by the class's opponent, possibly with an inflated attorney fee award. Thus, the judge in deciding whether to approve a class settlement must consider whether the agreement's proposed terms are "fair, reasonable, and adequate." Fed.Rule 23(e)(2). Provisions for judicial involvement in the class action settlement arena are unique in American law because they are inconsistent with the general principle that litigants are free to settle, terminate, or discontinue a lawsuit as they see fit.

A 2018 amendment to Federal Rule 23 identified several factors that a court must consider in deciding whether to approve a proposed settlement: (1) whether the representatives and counsel have adequately represented the class members; (2) whether the proposal was negotiated at arm's length; (3) the adequacy of the class relief taking account of the costs, risks, and delay of proceeding to a possible trial and appeal, the effectiveness of any proposed method of distributing relief, the terms and timing of any proposed attorney's fees, and any side agreements made in connection with the proposal; and (4) whether the proposal treats class members equitably.

An issue that has caused particular concern in evaluating a class settlement is when the proposal includes provisions that any unclaimed funds may be directed to a third person or entity not connected to the case, typically a charitable or governmental organization, to ensure that the defendant does not avoid payment of the agreed-upon losses—a kind of "cy pres" distribution. See § 8–5, above. The difficulty is in ensuring that the non-party recipient is aligned appropriately with the interests of the class members so that the funds will be used to foster the substantive policies that underlay the lawsuit or remediate the losses sustained by the class. The propriety of judges making these awards has been challenged, but not definitively resolved, which probably will take a decision by the Supreme Court.

§ 8–7. Mass-Tort Class Actions

The use of class actions in mass-tort cases has been extremely controversial ever since the 1966 amendments to Federal Rule 23. The certification of a mass-tort class action would typically depend on an application of Rule 23(b)(3), which requires that questions of law or fact common to the class will predominate over individualized questions, and that a class action is superior to other available methods to adjudicate the controversy.

Although many courts have been reluctant to certify mass-tort class actions, others have approved them (typically for settlement purposes) and found that they satisfy the basic prerequisites of the Federal Rule. In Amchem Products, Inc. v. Windsor, 521 U.S. 591 (1997), the Supreme Court refused to adopt a bright-line rule forbidding mass-tort class actions. Justice Ginsburg's majority opinion emphasized that "the text of the Rule does not categorically exclude mass tort cases from class certification." She recognized, however, the need for "caution when individual stakes are high and disparities among class members great."

Amchem itself involved an unusually ambitious use of the class action device that posed unique challenges. The parties sought certification for settlement purposes of a proposed nationwide class of people who had been exposed to asbestos. The Court held that the common issues concerning the health consequences of asbestos exposure were outweighed by the individual questions concerning class members with varying levels of exposure, from different products, over different time periods, as well as those who had suffered varying injuries or no injuries at all but simply had been exposed to the substance. The fact that different state laws applied to various class members further exacerbated the problem. Justice Breyer dissented, arguing that whatever the shortcomings of the settlement, the class action was the only practical pathway for providing any possibility of relief for those suffering from asbestos-related diseases.

The Amchem decision also illustrates how some mass-tort class actions can raise adequacy-of-representation concerns under Rule 23(a)(4). Justice Ginsburg observed that there was a potential misalignment of interests between class members who had current injuries and illnesses and class members who had been exposed to asbestos but had not yet developed injuries or even symptoms. Without subclasses to address these distinct interests, she wrote, there was no "structural assurance of fair and adequate representation for the diverse groups and individuals affected." Similar issues regarding adequacy of representation may present themselves in consumer cases in which class members have claims containing significantly different elements requiring different types and amounts of awards. E.g., Murray v. Grocery Delivery E-Servs. USA Inc., 55 F.4th 340, 351 (1st Cir. 2022).

A noteworthy mass-tort class action was In re National Football League Players Concussion Injury Litigation, 821 F.3d 410 (3d Cir.2016). The Third Circuit affirmed the district court's certification and settlement of a class of 20,000 retired NFL players, in a suit against the NFL for its failure to inform its players of and protect them from the risk of concussions. Among other things, the court rejected the argument that the class representatives failed Rule 23(a)(3)'s typicality requirement because of differences between them and other class members in the number of seasons played and the particular injuries suffered. The court explained that "class members need not share identical claims" as long as the same unlawful conduct affects both the named representatives and the class members. In this case, "the NFL's alleged fraudulent concealment of the risks of head injuries is the same."

The Third Circuit also found that the named plaintiffs were adequate representatives under Rule 23(a)(4) and that there was no risk of conflict, because the district court certified two subclasses—one for players with current injuries and one for players whose injuries might only manifest in the future. As for Rule 23(b)(3)'s predominance requirement, the Third Circuit found that common "factual questions regarding the NFL's knowledge and conduct as well as common scientific questions regarding causation" predominated over individualized issues. The Supreme Court denied certiorari. Gilchrist v. National Football League, 580 U.S. 1030 (2016).

B. MULTIDISTRICT LITIGATION

§ 8-8. Modern Techniques for Handling

The modern societal trends that have led to increased use of class actions has created another kind of challenge—multiple separate lawsuits filed all over the country, by separate plaintiffs, based on the same or related claims against the same defendant or defendants. The nationwide distribution of a single defective product may harm countless users; the single act of a nationwide business may affect hundreds or thousands of consumers; a potential securities irregularity may impact hundreds of thousands of investors; or an air crash will injure, often kill, hundreds of passengers. The result of these mass injuries frequently has been the filing of many individual lawsuits in courts—state and federal—where the injured parties reside. Thus, considerable attention has been given to ways in which to manage these separate suits to achieve judicial economy while promoting fairness to all concerned.

It is beyond the scope of this Nutshell to explore in detail the various techniques that have been utilized.

However, two major developments bear mention. The first is the Manual for Complex Litigation, Fourth (2004), produced by the Federal Judicial Center and designed to analyze several problem areas in complex litigation and to suggest some practices as possible solutions. It contains important guidance regarding case management and the scheduling of discovery and the pretrial process, discussions of some major issues that have occurred in class actions and other forms of aggregate litigation, citations to cases dealing with these issues, and many other useful aids for the courts and attorneys involved in those suits. As of this writing, the Federal Judicial Center is in the process of preparing the Fifth Edition of the Manual.

The second development of note is statutory. A 1968 amendment to the Judicial Code established the Judicial Panel on Multidistrict Litigation. 28 U.S.C.A. § 1407. Comprised of seven judges, the Panel is authorized upon application of any party to transfer to one district for coordinated pretrial proceedings all related actions filed in the federal courts. To obtain a transfer the movant must show that the cases share common questions of fact and that transfer will serve the "convenience of parties and witnesses" thereby promoting "the just and efficient conduct" of the actions. By this pretrial management device, duplicative discovery and motion practice can be eliminated. Further, the careful selection of the transferee court can produce efficiency by relieving heavily crowded court dockets in other federal courts of these cases, as well as assuring the parties relatively prompt (and sometimes very inventive) action in the transferee court. According to at least one court of appeals, Section 1407 grants the Judicial Panel on Multidistrict Litigation broad powers such that the court does not have to enforce collective action waivers when the centralization of litigation is appropriate. Uber Techs., Inc. v. United States Jud. Panel on Multidistrict Litig., 131 F.4th 661, 676 (9th Cir. 2025).

The Multidistrict Litigation statute explicitly requires that the actions must be returned to their original forums for trial and cannot be retained in the transferee court for trial there. Lexecon Inc. v. Milberg Weiss Bershad Hynes & Lerach, 523 U.S. 26 (1998). However, experience indicates that the vast majority of these coordinated actions will never return to the courts in which they were initiated because they will be dismissed or settled by the parties, or decided on motion before reaching trial. In 2025, the Supreme Court adopted a new Federal Rule 16.1 that will govern some aspects of practice in cases transferred under Section 1407. See § 3-36, above.

In the years since it was enacted, practice under Section 1407 has become very extensive and quite important as the number of large-scale and complex multidistrict litigations have increased quite substantially in many substantive areas. In some respects, Section 1407 has replaced class actions as the centerpiece of aggregate civil litigation in today's federal courts.

C. INTERPLEADER

§ 8–9. History and General Requirements

Interpleader is an equitable device by which a person who is in possession of something of value (the stakeholder) that he or she typically is not claiming ownership of but is unsure to whom it is owed deposits the money or property with the court and serves notice on the possible claimants that they can dispute ownership among themselves. The action proceeds in two stages. First, the court determines if the use of interpleader is proper. If so, the stakeholder is dismissed from the suit. Second, the court will determine the respective rights to the property. Those persons served with fair notice and given an opportunity to litigate are bound both against the stakeholder and among themselves. In this way, the procedure acts to reduce multiple litigation and to protect the stakeholder from double or multiple liability regarding the stake or even the threat of it.

Historically, in order to utilize interpleader the stakeholder had to show a legitimate fear of multiple vexation by two or more claimants. The claimants need not have been asserting ownership based on the same right, but they had to be claiming exactly the same property. Further, the stakeholder had to allege that it was not independently liable to any of the claimants on some other claims and that it was disinterested in the stake and did not assert any claim or defense with regard to the stake. Modern interpleader provisions have largely abandoned these last two requirements and only a threat of multiple vexation still needs to be shown.

Other equitable restrictions may prevent interpleader, however. For example, if the stakeholder has been guilty of undue delay or contributed to the development of the adverse claims, the court may exercise its discretion to deny the procedure. Another limitation that may prevent the use of interpleader in the state courts is that the Supreme Court has ruled that an interpleader action is in personam and that it is necessary for the court to obtain personal jurisdiction over each of the claimants in order to bind them to the decree. New York Life Ins. Co. v. Dunlevy, 241 U.S. 518 (1916). Most states have not adopted long-arm interpleader statutes to meet this requirement. See §§ 2–9—2–10, above. Thus, the procedure is predominantly a federal phenomenon.

§ 8–10. Federal Statutory and Rule Interpleader Compared

There are two different means of invoking interpleader in the federal courts: one is Federal Rule 22; the other is by statute, 28 U.S.C.A. § 1335. Both procedures have similarities. There are no requirements that the stakeholder be disinterested or not be subject to independent liability. Under the rule, there must be a showing that the stakeholder may be subject to "multiple liability." The statute refers to "[t]wo or more adverse claimants." The courts have interpreted both phrases in the same way so that a showing of the threat of multiple suits will suffice under either provision. Further, the stakeholder may invoke either procedure based on the possibility that future claims will be made against the property; the stakeholder need not wait until two or more claims have been asserted before bringing suit.

Some major differences between rule and statutory interpleader do exist, however. To begin with, different jurisdiction and venue requirements are applicable to each method. Federal Rule 22 functions like all other federal joinder rules—actions utilizing it must meet normal subject matter jurisdiction and venue requirements. Statutory interpleader has special jurisdiction and venue provisions that apply. Thus, in a Rule 22 case, a stake of more than $75,000 must be at issue and there must be complete diversity—no claimant may share the same citizenship with the stakeholder. But minimal diversity applies in statutory interpleader cases and the stakeholder's citizenship is irrelevant. The only prerequisite is that diversity exist between at least two of the claimants to the stake. State Farm Fire & Cas. Co. v. Tashire, 386 U.S. 523 (1967). Further, only $500 need be involved in cases under the statute. 28 U.S.C.A. § 1335.

Personal jurisdiction over the claimants in a Rule 22 case is typically restricted to that which is authorized under the law of the state in which the court is located. Although Federal Rule 4 authorizes the federal courts to use state long-arm statutes to assert jurisdiction outside the forum court's borders, most such statutes do not fit the interpleader situation because they are premised on the nonresident defendant conducting some activity in the state, not simply being a claimant to property in the state or a local stakeholder. Thus, a Rule 22 action often is territorially restricted—all the claimants must reside in the forum state. In contrast, nationwide service of process is available in statutory interpleader actions. 28 U.S.C.A. § 2361.

Finally, venue in Rule 22 actions is proper under the general venue statute—where any claimant resides (but only if all claimants reside in the same state), where a substantial part of the events or omissions giving rise to the claim occurred (potentially difficult places to identify in this context), where a substantial part of the property that is the subject of the action is situated, or where any claimant is subject to personal jurisdiction (but only if no other district exists where suit may be brought). 28 U.S.C.A. § 1391(b). In actions under the interpleader statute, venue may be laid where any claimant resides. 28 U.S.C.A. § 1397.

Two other differences also bear mention. In statutory interpleader actions the stakeholder must deposit the property in issue with the court or post a bond for its value when suit is filed. 28 U.S.C.A. § 1335. There is no deposit requirement in Federal Rule 22, although the court may allow the stakeholder to do so if the stakeholder so desires. Fed.Rule 67. Thus, in cases in which the stakeholder would prefer to maintain control over the property as long as possible, rule interpleader provides the better alternative. On the other hand, the court is given specific authority in the statutory proceeding to enjoin the claimants from suits elsewhere. 28 U.S.C.A. § 2361. Although this power cannot be used indiscriminately to enjoin all related litigation, it does provide a potent weapon to protect the stakeholder from the harassment of multiple suits. The injunctive power of the federal court in actions under Federal Rule 22 is less clear, because the federal anti-injunction statute, 28 U.S.C.A. § 2283, generally prohibits the federal courts from enjoining state proceedings in the absence of specific statutory authority, such as the interpleader statute. The only possible applicable exception in Rule 22 interpleader actions would be if the interpleader court would consider an injunction in this context as "in aid of its jurisdiction." This possibility is far from certain, however, which means that the court's injunction power may be narrower in a Federal Rule 22 interpleader than in a statutory action.

§ 8–11. Assertion of Additional Claims

One troublesome question that has arisen in interpleader suits is whether, once it is clear that interpleader is proper, the claimants may assert additional claims against one another or against the stakeholder. For example, if an automobile insurer interpleads its insured and several persons allegedly harmed by the insured, can those persons then assert their tort claims against one another in that action? Clearly, any additional claims would need to satisfy independent bases of subject-matter and personal jurisdiction. This is particularly so if the claimants are properly before the court only because of the availability of nationwide service of process or minimal diversity. To hold otherwise would create an incredible burden on the claimants and is unjustified by notions of judicial economy alone. Indeed, even if there are no jurisdictional problems regarding the additional claims, a court may consider whether allowing those claims would unduly complicate or delay resolution of the interpleader proceeding and thus whether it is appropriate to inject them into the action. Courts decide that question on a case-by-case basis.

CHAPTER 9

OTHER SPECIAL PROBLEMS IN FEDERAL LITIGATION

A. ACCESS BARRIERS

§ 9–1. Standing, Mootness, and Justiciability

The constitutional provision authorizing the establishment of the system of federal courts specifically extends their judicial power only to "cases" or "controversies." Art. III, § 2, U.S. Constitution. Federal courts cannot render purely advisory opinions. The problem of ascertaining what constitutes a valid case or controversy is highly complex and is studied in more detail in courses and books on federal courts or federal jurisdiction. 13A C. Wright, A. Miller & E. Cooper, *Federal Practice and Procedure* §§ 3531–3535 (3d 2008). The primary doctrines that have been developed to apply the Article III, § 2 requirements are those of standing, mootness, and justiciability. A brief introduction follows.

To bring a properly cognizable action in the federal courts, the plaintiff must have standing. The Supreme Court has developed a three-part test for standing. First, standing requires the claimant to have suffered an "injury in fact" that is "concrete and particularized." TransUnion LLC v. Ramirez, 594 U.S. 413 (2021). Questions regarding standing often arise when a plaintiff attempts to challenge the constitutionality of a statute or seeks judicial review of some administrative or other governmental action.

The presence of an actual injury ensures that the questions raised in the suit are not merely hypothetical and that they are being presented in an adversarial context comprising a "case." Further, requiring an actual injury ensures that the plaintiff has a sufficient stake in the outcome to pursue the action to the fullest. Plaintiffs aggrieved by some aspect of public spending cannot file suit against the government solely on the ground that they are taxpayers and are affected thereby. There is no direct injury and standing is not satisfied.

The second and third elements of standing are causation and redressability. For causation, the plaintiff must establish that its injury likely was caused or likely will be caused by the defendant's conduct. The "line of causation between the illegal conduct and injury" cannot be "too speculative or too attenuated." FDA v. Alliance for Hippocratic Medicine, 602 U.S. 367 (2024). The redressability element requires that the plaintiff's injury is likely to be redressed by a remedy given by the court.

Although standing restrictions spring from the constitutional requirement that federal courts entertain only cases or controversies, decisions in particular cases have also involved policy considerations that are sometimes referred to as the "prudential" aspects of standing. Traditionally, prudential standing has required that the interest sought to be protected is within the zone of interests to be protected or regulated by the statutory or constitutional guarantee in question. Prudential standing also limits a litigant's ability to raise another person's legal rights and bars the adjudication of "generalized grievances" more appropriately addressed in the representative branches. In some more recent decisions, however, the Supreme Court has questioned such prudential constraints. Lexmark International, Inc. v. Static Control Components, 572 U.S. 118 (2014).

Mootness addresses the same basic question as standing: does the plaintiff have a live or real case? The main difference is the time at which mootness issues are raised. Standing is addressed at the outset of the action. But the plaintiff must continue to suffer actual injury throughout the course of the litigation in order to meet the case-or-controversy requirement. If the plaintiff does not, the action is said to be moot and will be dismissed. For example, a prisoner suing to challenge visitation regulations may have standing at the outset. However, if the prisoner is paroled or if the regulations are changed before the case reaches judgment, the claim is no longer live and the action may be dismissed for mootness. In this way the federal courts are protected from rendering advisory opinions on hypothetical questions. In some states the courts are not limited in this fashion.

There are, however, important mootness exceptions. If a case becomes moot simply because the defendant has voluntarily ceased the challenged conduct, the case may proceed unless the defendant can show that there is no reasonable expectation the challenged conduct will resume. Also, conduct that is "capable of repetition, yet evading review"—for example, because of its inherently short duration—

may be challenged even if the case becomes moot before judicial review is complete.

Justiciability focuses on the issues being raised, rather than the claimant. An issue may be held non-justiciable because it is not yet ripe for review. Or it may involve a so-called "political question," such as one that lacks "judicially discoverable and manageable standards for resolving it." Rucho v. Common Cause, 588 U.S. 684 (2019). The rationale utilized is that those issues do not comprise a controversy of the type envisioned by the drafters of the Constitution to be decided in the courts, but rather must be left to the other branches of government to resolve.

B. WHAT LAW GOVERNS

§ 9–2. The Erie Doctrine

The question of what law governs in a federal court sitting in a case that is not based on a specific federal law (most commonly, when federal jurisdiction is based on diversity of citizenship) has posed one of the most difficult problems in federal court litigation. It goes to the heart of the relationship between the federal and state governments. It is a problem studied intensively in advanced courses in conflicts or federal jurisdiction. A more detailed treatment may be found in J. Friedenthal, M. Kane, A. Miller & A. Steinman, *Civil Procedure* Ch. 4 (6th ed.2021).

Until 1938, the balance was tipped in favor of applying federal law in diversity cases as federal courts asserted the power to create general federal common law. This position derived from the Supreme Court's interpretation of the Rules of Decision Act, 28 U.S.C.A. § 1652, in Swift v. Tyson, 41 U.S. 1 (1842). The Act requires that except when the Constitution, a treaty, or an Act of Congress otherwise provides, the federal courts shall apply the "laws of the several states" as the rules of decision. The Swift Court interpreted the reference to "laws" in the Act as being limited to state constitutions, statutes, and state common law on issues peculiarly "local" in character.

Ninety-six years later, in Erie R. Co. v. Tompkins, 304 U.S. 64 (1938), the Court overruled Swift, holding that "laws" in the Rules of Decision Act includes judge-made law and in a controversial passage of the opinion went so far as to state that the Constitution did not give the federal courts the power to create common law on substantive matters in diversity cases. Thus, the Erie decision requires federal courts to apply the common law of the state in which they are sitting. In a series of decisions since 1938 the Supreme Court has carefully elucidated the kind of analysis necessary to decide whether federal or state law should govern on particular issues when a federal court is sitting in diversity jurisdiction. This entire line of cases is referred to as the Erie doctrine.

§ 9–3. The Doctrine Applied

There are two situations that should be distinguished. The first is when the federal court is deciding whether it has the authority to create federal common law on a particular issue. The second requires the federal court to decide whether it must follow state law even though there is a federal rule of civil procedure or statute or important federal interest that appears applicable. In the first, Erie makes it clear that federal courts have no power to create a body of general federal common law to govern substantive rights; that is a power reserved to the states under the Tenth Amendment. The only correct interpretation of the Rules of Decision Act is that state law, whether in statutory or common law form, governs on substantive matters in diversity of citizenship cases.

When a federal procedural rule is involved, however, the federal government has a legitimate interest in having federal law govern because part of the process of establishing the federal court system authorized by the United States Constitution, Art. III, § 2, includes prescribing procedural rules to regulate the processing of cases in those courts. Congress recognized this need and, utilizing its authority under the Necessary and Proper Clause (Art. I, § 8), enacted the Rules Enabling Act, 28 U.S.C.A. § 2072, which authorizes the Supreme Court to promulgate rules of procedure for the federal courts. The Supreme Court has used this authority to develop the current Federal Rules of Civil Procedure. They represent federal law. Thus, if a court is confronted with a question whether state law must be applied when a seemingly applicable and contradictory Federal Rule exists, the Rules of Decision Act is no longer controlling. The proper question is whether the rule is within the scope of the Rules Enabling Act. That statute expressly states that the rulemaking power it gives the Supreme

Court cannot abridge, enlarge, or modify any substantive right. This limitation requires an inquiry into whether the rule actually is designed to regulate the practice and procedure of the federal courts or whether it will alter the rules of decision by which the court will adjudicate the substantive merits of a dispute. If the former is so, the statutory and constitutional standards are met and the federal rule should control under the Constitution's Supremacy Clause in Article VI. Hanna v. Plumer, 380 U.S. 460 (1965).

This description presents the two ends of the substance-procedure spectrum. In many instances the state law or issue involved cannot be classified as purely substantive or the federal rule in question does not speak directly to the issue covered by the state provision. The proper analysis to determine whether the federal court is bound to apply state law under these circumstances was suggested in the Hanna case, cited above. It requires a federal court to proceed as follows.

The first step is to ascertain whether there is a federal rule or statute applicable to the issue. If not, then consider the following four factors. One: is the issue one which is tightly or loosely bound up with the creation of the state rights being sued upon? Stated alternatively, how substantive is the state's law? Two: would the application of a different law by the federal court be outcome determinative in the sense that it would result in forum shopping in favor of the federal courts or it would result in the unequal administration of the law in the federal and state courts? For example, the application of different limitations periods in federal and state courts regarding the same claim would be very outcome determinative. Guaranty Trust Co. v. York, 326 U.S. 99 (1945). Three: what federal interest will be furthered by not applying the state law or, stated differently, what federal policy will be fostered by applying federal law? Four: would the use of a federal standard have an adverse impact on federalism (would it intrude on the state's ability to regulate a legitimate matter of state interest)? In balancing these four factors, the court in close cases will take into account that the thrust of the Erie doctrine is to accommodate the state interest unless some important federal interest is involved or the application of federal law to the issue presented will interfere with the forum state's regulatory concern. Byrd v. Blue Ridge Rural Elec. Cooperative, Inc., 356 U.S. 525 (1958).

If there is a federal procedural rule that addresses the same issue that is before the court, then the second step is to decide whether there is a direct conflict between the state and that federal rule. If no conflict exists, then the inquiry is the same as just described above—is the federal court required to consider applying state law under the Rules of Decision Act in addition to federal law—and the same four-part balancing test outlined above applies. For example, if the federal rule does not speak specifically to the issue posed, but only generally regulates the area, and the state rule presents a very specific requirement that is not inconsistent with that regulation, then there is no conflict because the court could apply the state law without ignoring the federal provision. Cohen v. Beneficial Indus. Loan Corp., 337 U.S. 541 (1949). Similarly, even if the two rules appear to conflict on their face, if the federal and state rules are designed for different purposes, it may be possible to apply both if, after balancing the four factors, it appears that the federal court ought to try to accommodate state law. Walker v. Armco Steel Corp., 446 U.S. 740 (1980).

However, if the federal rule conflicts with the state law, then the inquiry becomes whether the federal rule is valid. For a federal rule adopted pursuant to the Rules Enabling Act, as described above, it must control as long as it is truly a rule of procedure and does not abridge, enlarge, or modify a substantive right. A conflict may be found, for example, if the federal rule is discretionary but the state rule sets out mandatory requirements, because the notion of mandatory requisites would be inconsistent with the federal court's ability to exercise its discretion and to decide each case on the basis of its facts. Burlington Northern R. Co. v. Woods, 480 U.S. 1 (1987). If the court determines that a particular federal rule is not within the permitted scope of the Rules Enabling Act, then it again must refer to the four-part analysis described above to determine whether it must follow the state law under the Rules of Decision Act. To date, no federal rule of civil procedure has been found to violate the Rules Enabling Act; therefore, as a practical matter, once a rule is found to be in conflict with a state rule, the federal rule will very likely govern.

Consistent with the general policy of deference to state law underlying Erie, the federal courts traditionally have strained to find that the state and federal rules are not in conflict so as to be able to defer to the state provision when no strong federal interest is involved. But the required analysis often is difficult and distinctions hard to perceive. See, for example, Gasperini v. Center for Humanities, Inc., 518 U.S. 415 (1996), upholding the application of state law establishing standards for judicial review of jury awards for excessiveness, but rejecting the application of state law regarding the standard of appellate review of the jury award as intruding on federal jury trial principles prescribed by the Seventh Amendment . In contrast, the Court in a 5–4 decision held that Federal Rule 23 authorizing class actions should govern in a federal diversity class action despite a state statute prohibiting class suits seeking penalties or statutory minimum damages. The majority found the provisions to be in conflict because Rule 23 authorizes class actions that meet its requirements and, therefore, in a diversity action in federal court any additional state law limitations need not be applied. The majority did not attempt to reconcile the laws' different purposes as it had in Gasperini. Shady Grove Orthopedic Assocs., P.A. v. Allstate Ins. Co., 559 U.S. 393 (2011). The impact of the Shady Grove decision on future Erie analysis remains to be seen.

When the question presented is whether a federal statute, rather than a federal rule of civil procedure, should displace state law on a particular issue, the federal court will also apply an Erie analysis. It will look to see whether the federal statute was designed to address the issue presented and whether the statute is in conflict with the way in which state law handles the matter. If the answer to those two questions is yes, the federal statute governs under the Supremacy Clause. Stewart Organization, Inc. v. Ricoh Corp., 487 U.S. 22 (1988). If the federal statute does not cover the issue, or is not in conflict with state law, or is unconstitutional, then the federal court must ascertain whether it must defer to state law under the Rules of Decision Act by balancing the four factors described above.

Throughout this discussion the assumption has been that the federal court easily can ascertain the existing state law on a given issue in order to do the kind of sensitive balancing of policies described. Unfortunately, this is not always so. It is not uncommon for the federal court to be faced with a situation in which state law is in flux with no recent ruling by the state supreme court or insufficient guidance from lower state courts. In those circumstances the federal judge must attempt to determine the law that the judge believes the state's highest court would follow if it were ruling on the issue; the federal court cannot simply apply the law the judge decides is "best." An "Erie guess" must be made.

§ 9-4. Choosing Which State's Law Controls

The question whether a federal court is bound by forum state law is only one of the questions of choice of law confronting a federal diversity court. In cases in which parties and events cross state lines, the court also must determine which state's law should control. The principles governing state-to-state choice of law decisions are taught in courses in Conflict of Laws and are outside the scope of this volume. Suffice it to note that no single set of choice of law principles prevails in the United States; instead various theories exist, and the states have adopted different approaches to this problem.

Because of the lack of coherence in choice of law doctrine among the states, a significant issue is posed in federal diversity cases as to whether the federal court can decide to apply a federal set of conflict of laws rules or must look to the forum state's choice of law rules for guidance. The Supreme Court answered this question in Klaxon Co. v. Stentor Elec. Manufacturing Co., 313 U.S. 487 (1941), ruling that the principle of vertical uniformity between the federal and state courts within the same state promoted by Erie R. Co. v. Tompkins (see § 9–2, above) requires the federal courts to apply the forum state's choice of law rules in order to determine which state's law controls. Although this result reduces the potential for forum shopping between federal and state courts in the same state, it necessarily encourages forum shopping between federal courts in order to bring suit in a court in the state whose conflict of laws principles will best serve the interests of the plaintiff. Nonetheless, the Klaxon rule has been reaffirmed by the Supreme Court and remains controlling today.

Forum shopping between federal courts in different states is encouraged further because of the rules applicable to choosing between competing state laws when cases are transferred from one federal court to another. See § 2–30, above. The Supreme Court has decided that the transferee court must apply the choice of law rules of the original transferor forum. Van Dusen v. Barrack, 376 U.S. 612 (1964). It is said that a transfer changes the courtroom, but not the law. The plaintiff's original forum selection must be proper and not arbitrary, however. If the case is transferred because the original court was not a proper venue, then the transferee court can apply the choice of law rules of its own state. The Klaxon rule applies even if it results in the application of a foreign sovereign's law; for example, in Garcia v. Chiquita Brands Int'l, Inc., 48 F.4th 1202 (11th Cir. 2022), Colombian law was applied to a multidistrict litigation pending in a Florida court that had originally been filed in New Jersey.

§ 9-5. Federal Common Law

Erie R. Co. v. Tompkins did not remove all authority from the federal courts to create common law. It restricted that power primarily in circumstances in which the court is sitting in diversity jurisdiction and no clear federal statutory or constitutional interest is present so that the Rules of Decision Act mandates that state law governs. The creation of federal common law remains appropriate in certain areas of substantial national concern that fall within the powers given the federal government by the Constitution, or when justified by history, tradition, necessity, or an explicit or implicit statutory grant of authority. There is no consistent or persistent practice regarding when federal common law will be generated, but the Supreme Court's recent decisions have urged restraint. For instance, in Rodriguez v. Federal Deposit Insurance Corp., 589 U.S. 132 (2020), a case involving a tax allocation dispute, Justice Gorsuch remarked that "The cases in which federal courts may engage in common lawmaking are few and far between." Plainly, federal common law should be limited to cases of unique federal interest.

A few examples show when the authority to declare federal common law may be exercised. Federal Rule of Evidence 501 instructs federal courts to apply "[t]he common law—as interpreted by United States courts in the light of reason and experience" to decide claims of privilege in federal question cases. Similarly, the Supreme Court found an implied congressional directive in the labor field, ruling that when Congress placed special labor law jurisdiction in the federal courts it impliedly authorized them to develop a uniform, national law of collective bargaining, unfettered by what the states might do. Textile Workers Union v. Lincoln Mills, 353 U.S. 448 (1957). The Supreme Court has also recognized federal authority to create common law in the international relations field, Banco Nacional de Cuba v. Sabbatino, 376 U.S. 398 (1964), on questions of apportioning interstate waters, Hinderlider v. La Plata River & Cherry Creek Ditch Co., 304 U.S. 92 (1938), in admiralty and maritime cases, Southern Pacific Company v. Jensen, 244 U.S.

205 (1917), on matters of military procurement, Boyle v. United Technologies Corp., 487 U.S. 500 (1988), and in cases defining the obligations of the United States government on federal commercial paper. Clearfield Trust Co. v. United States, 318 U.S. 363 (1943).

The distinction between these cases upholding federal common law authority and the Erie case itself hinges on the significance of the relevant federal interest. The grant of diversity jurisdiction in Article III, § 2, does not by itself establish a federal regulatory interest. Rather, it simply reflects a desire to provide an impartial forum for out-of-state residents who might feel prejudiced in the local forum. When there is a direct federal interest involved, such as those described in the preceding paragraph, the Tenth Amendment no longer controls and the federal courts may feel free in certain situations to create common law in order to implement or protect that interest. But the federal courts have taken a cautious approach toward establishing federal common law and have done so only in a few contexts. E.g., Semtek International Inc. v. Lockheed Martin Corp., 531 U.S. 497 (2001) (preclusion governed by federal common law in diversity actions). Once a decision has been made that it is appropriate to create federal common law on a particular issue or in a particular field, that law displaces state statutory as well as decisional law by virtue of the Constitution's Supremacy Clause, can provide a basis for federal question subject matter jurisdiction, and, as is discussed in the next section, is binding on and must be applied by both federal and state courts.

§ 9–6. Federal Law in State Courts

When an action based on a federal statute is brought in state court, the Supremacy Clause of the Constitution requires that court to follow federal law—no careful balancing of interests is necessary. The state court not only is bound by the federal law but also is faced with a governing law question for any matter that is not explicitly provided for in the federal statute. Can the state court utilize its own procedures and develop common law on the issue, or must it be bound by the approach or law developed in the federal courts? Although the statement of the problem appears the same as that confronting a federal diversity court, its resolution is somewhat different. The rationale supporting the Erie doctrine is based on the Tenth Amendment's reservation of power not delegated to the federal government to the states. That requires the difficult analysis of whether there is some federal interest that occasionally would place the matter outside the reservation of power clause and puts it within the Supremacy Clause.

In order not to place too great a burden on state courts having concurrent jurisdiction over a federal question, such as liability for an interstate railroad worker's on-the-job injury, the Supreme Court has ruled that the state court may generally utilize its own procedures for adjudicating the case. The key is that those procedures must be applied nondiscriminatorily to state and federal cases, Testa

v. Katt, 330 U.S. 386 (1947), and they cannot impinge on the federal substantive rights being asserted, such as jury trial. Dice v. Akron, Canton & Youngstown R. Co., 342 U.S. 359 (1952). The state courts are not required to adopt an entire new procedural superstructure that corresponds to the federal system in order to adjudicate actions involving federal law.

§ 9–7. Arbitration

Arbitration is said to solve some of the cost and delay problems of the judicial system. But the procedure is purely a matter of contract. The question of which parties (if any) other than the initial signatories are bound by arbitration agreements is often litigated. Recently, the Seventh Circuit declined to extend an arbitration agreement to the children of parents who assented to online Terms and Conditions on their behalf. Coatney v. Ancestry.com DNA, LLC, 93 F.4th 1014 (7th Cir. 2024). If a dispute proceeds through arbitration, the parties engage in a private process that is not bound by strict rules of law and is outside the view of the courts and the public. The parties present their respective arguments to an agreed-upon arbitrator or possibly a panel of three, who may have greater leeway to admit evidence than a judge who must abide by federal and state evidentiary and testimonial rules. The arbitrator's decision is typically binding on the contracting parties. The arbitrator need not explain his or her decision (although may be instructed or choose to do so), there is no appellate process, the records remain private, and the decision has no precedential value.

In today's world, to obtain standard services and products, such as internet, online streaming services, or a cell phone, or to accept employment, Americans often must enter into take-it-or-leave-it adhesion contracts with major corporations. These contracts may demand that any dispute that might arise related to the agreement must be arbitrated, obliging people to forego access to the courts. Compelled private adjudication essentially is now competing with the public adjudicatory system and replacing the proverbial day in court, the possibility of jury trial, appellate review, and any process transparency. It has enabled business entities to capture control over the manner and means for resolving disputes with their customers or employees. Many people believe that business entities have a built-in adjudicatory and tactical advantage in arbitration as they are better resourced, have more experience with arbitration, and are typically repeat players in that arena.

A federal court occasionally will stay an arbitration or grant other relief when it believes that the arbitration is going beyond the scope of the parties' agreement. In Coinbase, Inc. v. Bielski, 599 U.S. 736 (2023), the Supreme Court reversed the Ninth Circuit's refusal to stay an arbitration proceeding during an interlocutory appeal, with the Court's majority reasoning that such an appeal should have divested the district court of authority over the case and triggered an automatic stay.

However, footnote 2 of the majority opinion acknowledged that "matters that are not involved in the appeal," such as awarding costs and attorney's fees, could proceed. The Supreme Court again required a stay in Smith v. Spizzirri, 601 U.S. 472 (2024), unanimously holding that staying proceedings rather than dismissing them when all claims were subject to arbitration preserves some desirable supervisory role for federal courts in ongoing arbitration disputes.

The most significant legal development of the last few decades in the arbitration arena has been under the Federal Arbitration Act (FAA). Enacted in 1925, the FAA was designed to overcome what then was a "judicial hostility" to the arbitration of contract disputes between businesses, most commonly in diversity-of-citizenship cases. In recent years, the Supreme Court has consistently cited the FAA to uphold the validity of arbitration clauses requiring arbitration and forbidding any form of aggregation, especially class actions or class arbitration.

The FAA has been transformed by the Supreme Court through constant expansions describing it as an expression of a "federal policy" favoring arbitration, which is to be applied whether a bilateral business dispute between commercial entities is involved or not. Indeed, the Court has repeatedly said that the Act "reflects an emphatic federal policy in favor of arbitral dispute resolution." Even though the FAA includes a saving clause providing that an arbitration clause can be overridden "upon such grounds as exist . . . for the revocation of any contract," the Court has had an exceedingly accepting attitude toward enforcing arbitration clauses even when they violate state contract law. Most significantly, a quartet of decisions has upheld the use of arbitration clauses, helping to shape the modern dispute resolution landscape.

In AT&T Mobility LLC v. Concepcion, 563 U.S. 333 (2011), the single issue was the legitimacy of a $30.22 sales tax fee for a phone advertised as being free, making class treatment desirable and efficient. In an opinion by Justice Scalia, the Court upheld a clause in the telephone contract calling for the arbitration of disputes but barring arbitration on a class basis. In a striking preemption of state contract law, the five-to-four decision overrode the California Supreme Court's conclusion that the clause was unconscionable under that state's law. In partial justification, the Court expressed a concern that class arbitration poses risks for defendants by noting that "when damages allegedly owed to tens of thousands of potential claimants are aggregated and decided at once, the risk of an error will often become unacceptable."

The Concepcion decision has not eliminated entirely the ability to challenge arbitration provisions on state unconscionability grounds. In Heckman v. Live Nation Entertainment, Inc., 120 F.4th 670 (9th Cir. 2024), the Ninth Circuit held that the delegation and arbitration clauses at issue were unconscionable and thus unenforceable, and that the FAA does not preempt California's prohibition of class action waivers in these contracts. See also

Ponkey v. LLR, Inc., 2023 WL 4863296 (9th Cir. 2023) (finding that aspects of an arbitration clause were unconscionable under California law).

In another important Supreme Court decision, American Express Company v. Italian Colors Restaurant, 570 U.S. 228 (2013), the Court enforced adhesive no-aggregate-arbitration clauses to disputes involving claims that were uneconomical to be arbitrated individually. When a merchant brought a federal class action against American Express, asserting violations of the federal antitrust laws and seeking recovery of a relatively small amount for each class member, Justice Scalia again wrote the Court's opinion and explained that the supposed policy of the FAA superseded the objectives embedded in the private enforcement provisions of federal antitrust law.

Relying on Concepcion and Italian Colors, the Court in 2018 decided in favor of corporate entities seeking to compel individual arbitration of employment contract disputes in a case involving the relationship between the FAA and the National Labor Relations Act (NLRA). In Epic Systems Corp. v. Lewis, 584 U.S. 497 (2018), the Court refused to "read a right to class actions into the NLRA" in the face of mandatory arbitration clauses in employment contracts. In another five-to-four decision, the Court upheld employment agreements compelling individual arbitration and class and collective action waivers despite protections otherwise afforded by the NLRA. In effect, the Epic Systems Court not only determined that the saving clause of the FAA did not allow for an exception to the enforcement of the arbitration clauses, but it pushed the NLRA aside in favor of the FAA.

The Court continued to express its expansive view of the FAA in Lamps Plus, Inc. v. Varela, 587 U.S. 176 (2019), when it was faced with an employment contract that was silent as to the employee's right to class arbitration. Once again, in a five-to-four decision, the Court determined that the FAA required resolving ambiguities "in favor of arbitration," despite a strong argument that ambiguous language should be read against the employer. The majority concluded that a court "may not infer from an ambiguous agreement that parties have consented to arbitrate on a classwide basis."

Thus, people are being obliged to arbitrate even though virtually none of them realize the significance of arbitration clauses or have the ability to negotiate them or the experience or resources that are needed to arbitrate effectively. Nor are they likely to find attorneys to represent them because the stakes are typically too small to justify contingent compensation arrangements.

Two things should be mentioned that somewhat ameliorate the effects of the Supreme Court decisions. First, in certain contexts a significant percentage of mandatory, no-aggregation arbitration clauses have a carve-out that allow the signatories to sue in small claims courts, which generally are thought to be consumer friendly. Many of those courts, however, do not have class action or aggregate procedures, and some are not empowered to grant equitable relief. Second, the two most significant providers of arbitrator services have protocols that assure a modicum of procedural regularity.

A significant exception to the FAA exists for "contracts of employment of . . . any . . . class of workers engaged in foreign or interstate commerce," 9 U.S.C.A § 1, which has yet to be defined with clarity. The Court in Southwest Airlines Co. v. Saxon, 596 U.S. 450 (2022), defined this provision as embracing those workers who play a "necessary role" in the transport of interstate goods and affirmed that airline ramp supervisors fit this exception. However, Postmates delivery couriers were excluded from the exception in Bissonnette v. LePage Bakeries Park St., LLC, 601 U.S. 246 (2024), because their transportation of goods constituted "part of separate intrastate transactions that are not themselves within interstate commerce." Moreover, some courts have permitted individuals bound by arbitration clauses to bring suit as private attorneys general on behalf of the state or the people of the state, including themselves, when authorized to do so by statute. E.g., Adolph v. Uber Technologies, Inc., 532 P.3d 682 (Cal. 2023).

INDEX

References are to Pages
